Global Law in Practice

50th Anniversary
International Bar Association

Global Law in Practice

Editor: J. Ross Harper

KLUWER LAW INTERNATIONAL
and International Bar Association

Published by Kluwer Law International,
P.O. Box 85889, 2508 CN The Hague, The Netherlands.

International Bar Association
271 Regent Street
London W1R 7PA
England.

Sold and distributed in the U.S.A. and Canada
by Kluwer Law International,
675 Massachusetts Avenue, Cambridge, MA 02139, U.S.A.

In all other countries, sold and distributed
by Kluwer Law International,
P.O. Box 85889, 2508 CN The Hague, The Netherlands.

Library of Congress Cataloging-in-Publication Data on File

ISBN 90-411-0460-7

Guest Foreword

Kofi A. Annan
Secretary General of the United Nations

The rule of law is essential to peace, development and the realisation of human rights. The practice of law is a privilege, but a privilege that carries with it a heavy responsibility to ensure respect for the law.

Legal rules are indispensable to human societies. As human relations have become more complex, reaching far beyond national borders, our laws are increasingly global. The United Nations system plays a central role in developing and promoting rules not only to harmonise relations between States and avert possible conflicts, but also to harmonise the laws of different States dealing with shared problems.

Lawyers take part in the work of the United Nations system in a variety of ways. As members of delegations or of expert bodies, they lend their expertise to the multilateral treaty-making process, transforming political goals into viable legal instruments. As legal advisers, they provide opinions and analyses to facilitate policy-making. As jurists and researchers, they promote and disseminate knowledge and understanding of the law. And as officials of international organizations, they contribute to the formation and implementation of the rules agreed upon by States.

In an interdependent world, lawyers must communicate and interact amongst themselves and with others, both at the national and international level. The International Bar Association, as a professional body with a long and distinguished record of achievement, plays an important role in this respect. On the occasion of the Association's 50th anniversary, I am delighted to extend my best wishes to its members and to commend this collection of essays by its eminent practitioners and jurists.

Foreword
Fifty Years in Retrospect

George C. Seward
IBA Honorary Life President
IBA Section on Business Law Honorary President-Founder

The International Bar Association has achieved its current respectable status by a process of trial and error. It was created formally in 1947 following extended planning by the American Bar Association in consultation with bar associations and law societies of other countries. The inaugural meeting in February 1947 was in the house of the Association of the Bar of the City of New York which had been the host for the discussions leading to agreement on a constitution. Thirty five bar associations participated in that initial meeting. Now fifty years later some 173 are members along with 18,000 or so individual lawyers, and the IBA will return to the city of its origin to celebrate its fiftieth anniversary. This volume will commemorate that event.

To those who are familiar with only the current IBA it may be necessary to point out that during the first half of its existence—until 1970—individual lawyers were not officially involved in its structure. They were welcomed as patrons—contributors of funds—but without other status. The original IBA was an association only of bar associations and law societies.

In the years following its creation the IBA found that there were not so many bar association matters of an international nature to discuss as had been anticipated by its founders. The interest of the bar associations waned and activities dwindled to the holding of small biennial conferences. More serious, the combination of dues from bar associations and donations from patrons permitted only extremely frugal existence—with the continuance of that not secure. It was during such state of affairs that the idea of permitting individual business lawyers to set up their own organization within the IBA was proposed. The concept differed radically from that of the IBA founders, but it was accepted after much discussion and introspection. The result was the New IBA, a thriving organization which has a better claim than any other group to world leadership in the legal profession.

It has been an interesting task to fit 18,000 lawyers into a federation of the world's bar associations and law societies; but the partnership has developed better than expected and to the advantage of both sides. It is the foundation for a very strong New IBA which is now beginning to have influence in the world. There is more to do but we have made a good start.

December 1996, New York City

Table of Contents

List of Contributors

Kofi A. Annan
Secretary-General of the United Nations
New York, U.S.A.

George C. Seward
Seward & Kissel
New York, N.Y.
IBA Honorary Life President;
IBA Section on Business Law Honorary President-Founder

Professor M. Cherif Bassiouni
Professor of Law
President, International Human Rights Law Institute
DePaul University College of Law
Chicago, U.S.A.

Ward Bower
Altman Weil Pensa Inc.
Philadelphia, U.S.A.
Chairman, IBA Standing Committee on Multi Disciplinary Partnerships; Council Member, Section on General Practice

Dr. Robert Briner
Lenz & Staehelin
Geneva, Switzerland
Chairman, International Court of Arbitration of the International Chamber of Commerce, Paris; Past IBA Section on Business Law Chairman 1992-94; Past President,

Willem J.L. Calkoen
Nauta Dutilh
Rotterdam, Netherlands
IBA Section on Business Law Chairman 1996-98

Desmond Fernando PC
Colombo, Sri Lanka
IBA President
Vice President, Internatiojnal Commission of Jurists; President, Bar Association of Sri Lanka 1989-91; Distinguished Member, Lawasia Council

Peter Goldsmith QC
London, England
Barrister; Chairman, IBA Standing Committee on Globalisation of Law; Past Chairman, Bar Council of England and Wales 1995

Bernard L. Greer Jr.
Alston Bird
Atlanta, U.S.A.
Chairman, IBA Standing Committee on Foreign Legal Practitioners

Professor J. Ross Harper CBE
Harper Macleod
Glasgow, Scotland
IBA President 1994-96; Founder, IBA Human Rights Institute; Past IBA Section on General Practice Chairman 1990-92

President Nelson Mandela
Pretoria, South Africa
President, Republic of South Africa;
Honorary President, IBA Human Rights Institute

Professor Sheila A. M. McLean
Institute of Law & Ethics & Medicine
Glasgow, Scotland
IBA Chair of Law & Ethics in Medicine at University of Glasgow; Director, Institute of Law and Ethics in Medicine, University of Glasgow; Consultant to World Health Organisation and the Council of Europe

Francis Neate
Slaughter and May
London, England
IBA Treasurer; Past IBA Section on Business Law Chairman 1994-96

Raúl Mantilla Ra66rez
Havana, Cuba
President of the Association of Local Law Firms in Cuba; President of the National Organization of Lawyers' Offices in Cuba

Monty Raphael
Peters & Peters
London, England
Founder and first Chairman, IBA Section on Business Law Committee W (Business Crime)

John Salter
Denton Hall, London, England
Chairman, IBA Standing Committee on United Nations and other Worldwide Organisations (UNWOC);
Past IBA Section on Business Law Chairman 1986-88;
Chairman, Legal Issues Group, ISWA

Jerome J. Shestack
Wolf, Block, Schorr & Solis-Cohen
Philadelphia, U.S.A.
President, American Bar Association, 1997-98;
Past Chairman, IBA Standing Committee on Human Rights and a Just Rule of Law; former U.S. Ambassador to the UN Commission on Human Rights

Professor Shimon Shetreet
Faculty of Law
Hebrew University of Jerusalem, Israel
Former Minister of Economy; Minister of Science; Minister of Religious Affairs, State of Israel

Dr. Richard Susskind FRSE
Centre for Law, Computers and Technology, The University of Strathclyde, Glasgow, Scotland;
Chairman, Society for Computers and Law, 1990-92;
IT Adviser to Lord Woolf, 1994-95

About the IBA

Since its formation in New York in 1947 the IBA has grown in size and stature to become the international legal profession's largest and most active organisation. Membership has reached over 18,000 individual lawyers spanning 183 countries and in addition to this 173 national Bar Associations and Law Societies represent over 2.5 million legal practitioners through their membership and support of the IBA.

The IBA exists to support the rule of law, to defend lawyers' freedom to practise without interference and to provide its members with an international forum for the exchange of information and ideas on developments in the law and its practice worldwide. The breadth of members' interests can be gauged from the 57 specialist Committees which constitute the three Sections of the IBA: Section on Business Law, Section on General Practice, Section on Energy & Natural Resources Law.

The establishment of the IBA Human Rights Institute in December 1995 under the Honorary Presidency of President Nelson Mandela was a major milestone in the history of the IBA. The HRI is committed to the education of the profession worldwide on human rights issues and the improvement of systems of justice where such infringements occur. The Institute reinforces the IBA's stated aim of promoting the independence of the judiciary and the legal profession worldwide. The support of 9,000 individual members, and recognition by Bar Associations through their support of the One Dollar per Lawyer for Human Rights Appeal, demonstrates the value and effectiveness of the Institute's projects.

The authority and expertise of members is acknowledged through the various advisory capacities fulfilled by the Association. The IBA has been granted International NGO status with the UN Department of Public Information, UN consultative status category II (ECOSO) and its subsidiary bodies eg UNCITRAL and the UN division of crime prevention and criminal justice. The IBA is at the heart of the globalisation of law, and performs a vital role with regard to international law making.

Events during this year reflect the latitude of IBA activities. The IBA returns to New York in June to celebrate its 50th Anniversary. Regional Conferences will take place in Argentina, and Slovakia. Specialist Committee meetings will be held on subjects ranging from Practice Management (Amsterdam), International Financial Law (Prague), and Energy Law (Caracas). The year culminates at the Biennial Section on Business Law and Section on General Practice Conference taking place in New Delhi, 2-7 November. IBA members are reflective of the legal profession worldwide, and as such the IBA calendar of events provides opportunities for participation from all fields of practice.

For further information please contact:

International Bar Association
271 Regent Street
London
W1R 7PA
TelL: +44(0) 171 629 1206
Fax: +44 (0) 171 409 0456

Global Practice Now and in the Future

Professor J. Ross Harper CBE

My Two Years in Presidency

It was a privilege beyond belief to be President of the International Bar Association for two years, visiting some forty-four countries, flying many times round the globe and participating in policy-making and policy development.

My first contact with the International Bar Association was accidental. I noticed an advanced and computer technology Seminar being advertised in Amsterdam and enrolled with some misgiving. The Conference was outstandingly well organised under the supervision of current management guru David Andrews and other committed IBA experts. Their enthusiasm not only for the subject but for the organisation was infectious and my interest was aroused when I realised that however successful their management training turned out to be that part of the IBA was but a tiny fraction of the whole.

I have always believed that in unity there is strength and have always taken the view that when lawyers come together they can, by nature of their training, their expertise and social awareness, combine not only in their own interests but also in the interests of the public and society.

The challenge becomes all the greater when society is truly international and the concept of an international association of lawyers, truly worldwide, was exciting and appealing.

THE HISTORICAL PERSPECTIVE

We have now reached our 50th Anniversary year. Just a shade younger than the United Nations, we hold many of its aspirations. Not that the IBA is a perfect instrument of Government. Nor, I suspect, will it ever be.

It started off, perhaps modelled on the United Nations, as a body whose membership was composed of Bar Associations and Law Societies throughout the world. Each and every Law Society and Bar Association has its own problems in its own country—problems ranging from Government recognition, Government interference, through to the allocation of scarce resources. In the last 50 years there have been differing and different rates of development and different establishment of priorities.

Every so often countries produce lawyers of international vision and commitment who lend freely of their services to the many activities which are important in an international legal world.

The International Bar Association, however, some 25 years ago decided, fortunately and properly, to follow the example of one of its founder members, the American Bar Association, and introduce the category of individual membership recognising that the IBA itself could convene meetings and seminars bringing together individual members who might well have had no connection with their own Bar Association or Law Society. These individual members would bring together their own areas of expertise and their own vision and their own idealism.

And, like the American Bar Association, the individual membership rose and rose, and we have produced a system of government which allows the individual members—whose activities generate over 90% of the income of the IBA—a substantial place in the democratic process.

No system of Government in a series of large groupings will ever be perfect. Nevertheless, the goodwill amongst lawyers, their respect for diversity of talent, backed by a sound and committed administration, persuade me to the optimistic view that the International Bar Association will continue from strength to strength towards its centenary and beyond.

The chapters in the book highlight some of our visions in the IBA and some of the problems which we recognise. This 50th Anniversary book does not pretend to be an overview of our activities. Such an overview would merit an encyclopedia.

It rather seeks to highlight in the first instance and analyse in depth in the second problems, pitfalls and opportunities in 1997.

THE LAWYER IN ECONOMIC DEVELOPMENT

We start appropriately enough with, arguably, the greatest lawyer of the 20th century, namely Nelson Mandela. An Honorary President of our Human Rights Institute his biography "A Long Walk to Freedom" is the most compelling story of lawyer, politician, convict and world statesman. An inspiration to us all.

He focuses on the extremely important role of the lawyer in the economic development of a country. This view has been shared and echoed throughout the world. Amos Wako, Attorney General of Kenya and a member of the International Bar Association, when addressing an IBA Conference in Kenya, forcibly expressed the view that if a country could not provide a system of justice and did not recognise the importance of human rights, then it could be denied economic expansion. This view is recognised in Latin America. The connection between the economy and the law is thrust forward in two main areas.

First of all, if a country does not have a legal infrastructure to settle disputes then lawyers will caution against direct investment. There is no point in attempting to run a business in a country where disputes are subject to lengthy, expensive and possibly corrupt legal processes. In some countries, for instance, arbitration disputes must be confirmed by a Court and a licence is given to those who wish to escape obligations by sheltering behind the Courts' backlog. Delayed justice is in itself injustice. As lawyers we must, in every part of the world, contribute to ensuring access to the Courts, justice within a reasonable timescale without fear of bias or corruption. The economy of each and every country does depend on a proper system of law and justice.

The second thrust is a political one. Malcolm Rifkind, the former Foreign Secretary of the United Kingdom, noted when opening the new IBA offices in London in 1996 that the issue of human rights was becoming a major diplomatic factor worldwide. The IBA has used its influence with Governments from developed countries to insist that aid given to a developing country is part of a package which includes a commitment towards the recognition of and observance of fundamental human rights.

GLOBALISATION OF THE LAW

I was extremely happy that Peter Goldsmith took up my suggestion that he should lead a team of IBA experts to further the concept of globalisation of the law.

The idea was not mine. Bob Stein, the energetic Executive Director of the American Bar Association, in a lecture developed his ideas on globalisation, which prompted me to suggest that the International Bar Association should take a major worldwide initiative.

As the world becomes smaller, as cross investment increases, as companies themselves become more international we, as international lawyers, have to provide a more comfortable arena for the law national and international, to operate.

We have two tasks. First in terms of the structure of the law and dispute resolution and secondly with regard to the globalisation of law, either by uniformity or by recognition of decisions and judgements made in foreign jurisdictions.

That is why I was so proud of the Section on Business Law Insolvency Committee's *Cross Border Insolvency Concordat* which is already quoted in case law throughout the world.

As Peter Goldsmith points out within this book, business decisions transcend national boundaries. It is important that international and multi-national companies should not become frustrated by a difference between legal systems and a difference in procedural and substantive law.

Lawyers are responding to the challenge of co-operating on an international basis, providing an international service and helping to fulfill the expectations of the international client. But of course there are problems. There is the understandable problem of the law in one country being separate, historical and at times isolationist.

As Peter Goldsmith notes, we must concentrate on training the world lawyer, the use of new technology and a willingness to marry the strains of law in other countries to our own.

There are many important initiatives in the convergence in laws and we, as lawyers in general and the IBA's Standing Committee on Globalisation of Law in particular, have a duty to identify the problems and harness our resources together.

VIOLATIONS OF INTERNATIONAL HUMANITARIAN LAW

I personally am very pleased that Professor Cherif Bassiouni has contributed a most excellent chapter on Violation of International Humanitarian Law in the former Yugoslavia.

Professor Bassiouni was speaker at an IBA Seminar held jointly with the Arab Lawyers Union in 1996 to examine the implications of the PanAm/Lockerbie bomb tragedy. Professor Bassiouni's work is internationally recognised and admired.

As President I visited the Tribunal which has been set up to try the accused from the territory of former Yugoslavia, noting that the proceedings were televised live throughout the area, offering in itself a cleansing process.

The problems of international crime as a result of war, terrorism, fraud or destruction of the environment are being more clearly recognised. Again as the frontiers of the world shrink so international action is all the more important.

That is why the International Bar Association resolution in Edinburgh in 1995 called for the establishment of an International Criminal Court to be set up by the United Nations. At the moment we have an International Court which deals with civil matters between one nation and the other, a Court which I also visited in my term of office.

But we have, to our discredit, no permanent International Court. Professor Bassiouni is one of many who are lending support to the cause of establishment.

THE ROLE OF THE LAWYER ON HUMAN RIGHTS ISSUES

Jerome Shestack, President of the American Bar Association, has been a formidable friend of, and contributor to, the work of the International Bar Association. His knowledge of human rights is encyclopaedic and we are fortunate to have such a significant chapter in our 50th Anniversary book. As Jerry Shestack properly notes, the International Bar Association is not the only body concerned with human rights. There is plenty to do internationally for all the organisations.

We have been engaged in activities of human rights for many a long year and have had a succession of committed Presidents who have ensured that human rights remained high on the agenda of the International Bar Association.

A letter from the International Bar Association to a national Government normally evokes a response and in many cases it is positive. The presence of an International Bar Association lawyer at a trial is now recognised in many Courts throughout the world and indeed recently in Egypt our observer was asked to give a view to the Judge (which of course he did).

The launch of our Human Rights Institute in 1996 coupled with the acceptance by President Nelson Mandela to become its Honorary President was a significant development. All the more so since each and every individual member from our database of 18,000 members was asked to contribute a sum of money towards funding the Institute.

The membership readily responded and under the joint Chairmanship of Nicholas Cowdery, QC from Australia and Tor Bøhler from Norway, the Institute is quickly identifying tasks to promote human rights throughout the world.

It is noted in the chapter there is a lot of work still requiring to be done as we seek to protect lawyers, secure the independence of the judiciary and promote and maintain the standards set by the United Nations in various declarations and resolutions.

ROLE OF THE LAWYER IN A ONE PARTY STATE

I am grateful to Raoul Ramirez for writing an article from Cuba. Along with Fernando Pelaez-Pier, Chairman of our Latin American Steering Group, I visited Cuba and expect them soon to join the International Bar Association.

Cuba is, of course, a single party state and there is a fundamental perception that because of that it does not address, and indeed cannot address, fundamental human rights.

Raoul Mantila Ramirez demurs from that view and I was taken to various Courts in Cuba including an International Court, and met with lawyers who are licensed to act freely and independently of the state on international matters.

Democracy is, from the ancient Greek, the rule of the people. Nomocracy is the rule of law. Both are important—equally important. If however there is no democracy, as we understand it, it is possible to identify and promote nomocracy.

For that reason I invited Raoul Ramirez to submit a chapter of this book and I am extremely glad that he has responded positively.

JUDICIAL INDEPENDENCE AND FREEDOM OF EXPRESSION

In his chapter, Professor Shimon Shetreet focuses on two important issues for judges as the century draws to a close: the rule of law and the preservation of human rights. As Professor Shetreet says "These two safeguards of democracy are essential foundations for the human well-being of the individual and are vital for orderly conduct and life of organized society as a whole."

Judicial independence is of course the prerequisite of a just society. Judges must, throughout the world, be honoured, respected and properly compensated. The appointment of Judges is clearly critical. Letters of appointment vary from country to country, from an independent Commission in Peru to Government appointment in many other countries. There are career Judges in some countries whereas in other countries Judges are appointed from the ranks of the seniors within a profession.

Countries throughout the world are becoming more and more accustomed to the need for judicial training. As technology becomes more complex, as international law makes more and more inroads into national law, so the urgency and importance of training increases.

If a Judge is good and recognised as good by his peers then he will be honoured and respected. There is still, however, a considerable problem with regard to remuneration of Judges.

A Judge should not require to look over his shoulder at other members of the profession who may be earning more. A Judge's remuneration ought to bear comparison to all but the very top end of the profession.

A Judge must be uninfluenced by those who appoint him or by Governments. His independence is both crucial and critical. And that is why the IBA campaigns continuously for and on behalf of judicial independence.

MULTI DISCIPLINARY PRACTICES—THE FUTURE

We have had the threat (or opportunity depending on one's viewpoint) of Multi Disciplinary Practices (MDPs) for some ten years or more. Some Governments were keen to legislate to allow lawyers to practise with other professionals.

The pace of change was slow until two or three years ago as a result of European threatened regulation and a re-examination of the concept worldwide.

In the two years of my IBA Presidency many colleagues in Latin America and the United States of America were not aware of the growing problem of multi disciplinary practices throughout the rest of the world.

The concept of a multi disciplinary practice is that legislation should allow for different professions—surveyors, architects, lawyers, accountants and the like— to practise together to provide what is quaintly called a one-stop shopping centre. In reality the one profession which is interested in the law is the accountancy profession.

I fear (and this is a personal viewpoint) for the future of the law, should accountants practise law unless there are the most severe, stringent and absolute safeguards. I entered the practice of the law with a fundamental belief in the sanctity of the law and the independence of the lawyer.

As lawyers we have to recognise the other argument—namely that a business client may wish to have his financial affairs and legal affairs ordered under one roof. Suffice it to say lawyers are under attack—from two sources. First of all, regulatory authorities are examining the whole question and the IBA recently sent a delegation to Geneva to speak on the subject with the World Trade Organization (WTO) which is investigating the accountancy profession. The Dutch Bar Association are locked in combat with the Dutch Government in the Courts over the question of MDPs.

The second threat comes from the accountants themselves. While they recognise that in many jurisdictions they are not permitted to share a practice with lawyers, what they are doing is setting up or buying over their "own" legal firm and of course putting in the vast resources which are available to them as international worldwide practitioners.

At the IBA's Berlin Biennial Conference in 1996 I gave an address to the formidable Lex Mundi Association of lawyers pointing out to them the dangers as I saw them of multi disciplinary practices. I was somewhat surprised to be castigated afterwards by a lawyer from Spain who told me that in the following week his practice was being taken over by a firm of accountants.

Foreseeing all the problems which may be caused, and are being caused, I not only alerted the American Bar Association to the MDP problems but set up, under the gifted American management consultant and lawyer Ward Bower, an IBA Multi Disciplinary Practices Committee to represent international lawyers on the global stage. Information is being gathered from all corners of the world and this will be available to individual jurisdictions which are examining the problem, bearing in mind their twin responsibilities to the profession and to the public.

Ward Bower's conclusion that a scenario whereby accounting firms would take over the worldwide provision of international corporate legal services is not implausible in the market place today makes his chapter vital reading for those who have any concern whatsoever for the future.

FOREIGN LEGAL PRACTITIONERS

Hand in hand with the problem of Multi Disciplinary Practices is the problem of how lawyers provide a worldwide service and yet recognise the individual jurisdictions of law and separate qualifications of lawyers.

Ben Greer has been working for the IBA and advising its Council for many a long year.

The IBA has no power whatsoever to insist on a change of rules in a local jurisdiction. Its Council, however, has the authority to issue guidelines and suggestions whereby one foreign legal practitioner can practise law in another jurisdiction.

The practice of law is, of course, divided into the practice of international law, the law of the country, and the law of the foreign legal practitioner and law. For these different types of practice there are different considerations and the IBA endeavours to recognise the interests of the importing lawyer and the exporting lawyer.

Transcending both of these interests, however, is the interest of the client whose needs the lawyer has an overriding duty to meet.

I listened with great interest to the debates which animated the IBA Council over the years. We took into account representations from Japan, the United States, Australia, Europe, indeed each and every country throughout the world. Lawyers must be careful not to be protectionist or to be seen to become protectionist. I visited the annual conference of one jurisdiction which was resisting the import of foreign lawyers stating that local lawyers could meet the needs of all clients including multinational clients. Combined with that assertion I noticed that the regulations governing the conduct of the lawyers did not allow practices of more than one partner.

When addressing the matter publicly I took a simple view. First of all the interests of the client must be met. Secondly, if it appeared that by allowing foreign lawyers to set up large offices in cities thus eroding the potential for local lawyers I expressed the view that the contrary might be the case.

The only way local lawyers will become used to international practice is to work in a successful international practice and what better opportunity if the practice is in the lawyer's home jurisdiction. As young lawyers are trained on working for the international lawyers then they will have the greater opportunities in the future to set up their own practice in their own jurisdiction with the benefit of assistants and partners who have received the best of training.

As lawyers, we have a duty to provide quality of service. I frequently ask colleagues to examine why large international legal practices have not opened up in Australia. The answer to my mind is not difficult in as much as Australian lawyers provide expert services to their clients and they therefore fear no competition from outside.

The International Bar Association is extremely beholdened to Ben Greer for his work over a number of years in examining the problems and concepts of foreign legal practitioners and I commend his chapter in the book.

THE ROLE OF LAWYERS AND THE INFORMATION SOCIETY

Professor Richard Susskind is arguably one of the world's leading experts on information technology and the law. He is a man of high qualification who has a vision that our legal system will be transformed. His predictions for the future make absorbing reading.

The International Bar Association has always been to the forefront of the study and promotion of computer technology. As I remarked earlier, my first experience of the IBA was at a management and computer technology seminar in Amsterdam. In March 1997 I will have revisited the same topic in the same venue.

We are proud that we can lift the practitioner's eyes to the opportunities of the present and vision of the future.

There are some of us in the relative autumn of our life who can perhaps be thankful that we do not require to struggle with the impact of technology in the same way. Those in the spring of their life have been brought up with computers since childhood and I envy them and their ability to word process their own documentation and practice without reliance on secretarial help.

I sympathise with those in the mid summer of their life who did not have the benefit of computer education but have so much of their practice ahead to require them to embark on a steep learning curve.

Richard Susskind's analysis dealing with such issues as the technology lag, digitalisation and legal information services is compulsory reading. The International Bar Association is fortunate to have dedicated management technology and computer Committees to provide advice and share ideas at the highest level.

Whether everyone agrees with Professor Susskind's thoughts that lawyers will provide more of an information than an advisory service in tomorrow's world his reasoning, his thought-provoking and his legal paradigms are both novel and stimulating.

ROLE OF THE LAWYER IN SHAPING THE UNITED NATIONS

When I set up the IBA's United Nations and Other World Organisations Committee under the Chairmanship of John Salter it was suggested to me that this Committee was a Committee specially created for John Salter's knowledge, interest and expertise.

I have long felt that the International Bar Association has a higher and stronger role to play in its dealings with international bodies.

John's first task was to analyse the international links of each and every IBA Committee and we were all surprised to see in one document the strength and breadth of IBA activities at an international level. Our dealings with environmental protection, international trade law, law of the sea, energy, protection of children and the like, demonstrates the breadth and shape of the IBA over the last 50 years.

I always enjoy reading John Salter's work but particularly enjoyed a preview of his chapter in this book. It is good to mark the position as at 1997 in the earnest hope that our contribution to, arising out of our commitment for, work with international bodies will ever increase.

THE ROLE OF THE LAWYERS IN ADR

I must confess I am an ADR fanatic—although I appreciate as Robert Briner points out in his splendid chapter, that there are different meanings to ADR.

Whether it is alternative or appropriate dispute resolution or not, the simple message is clear—we must try and depart from former adversarial positions which are not necessarily in the interests of the client and concentrate on just settlement.

The duty of a lawyer is to provide a just settlement process for his client. The problem in many jurisdictions is that the lawyer is trained from birth to be adversarial. The nickname of Rottweiler for a lawyer is held to be a compliment.

Some ten years ago I foresaw correctly the growth in mediation and warned that if the Courts could not provide speedy justice then clients would go elsewhere.

Initially arbitration got a bad name because it could be even slower than the Courts. The search for speedy justice is the holy grail but it is a search which the IBA pursues with vigour.

Charles Platto is heading a taskforce on civil litigation and we are expecting to see the results shortly. Robert Briner, former Chairman of the Section on Business Law and recently Honorary Life Member of the Association, is Chairman of the International Court of Arbitration at the International Chamber of Commerce and certainly knows, as is evidenced by his chapter in this book, what he is talking about. I particularly like his comment that the skills of the transactional lawyer are needed rather than the adversarial position of the litigation player.

Lawyers must seek to understand the position of the other party and try to accommodate this position without "losing sight of the interests and objectives of his own party". The talents of the negotiator, not the litigator, are part of our legal process for the future and I do hope that Universities at the very earliest level will provide training in negotiation and mediation for the benefit of the client. My own University of Strathclyde is well aware of its responsibilities.

I commend Robert Briner's note that in some jurisdictions the ethical rules require lawyers to draw the attention of a client to other methods to resolve disputes.

It is my view that the IBA ought to take a lead role in persuading all our jurisdictions so to do thus properly exercising our responsibility to society.

THE ROLE OF LAWYERS IN THE FIGHT AGAINST CORRUPTION

Monty Raphael is an extremely influential IBA member with a vast knowledge of the intricacies and problems of business crime.

Corruption is a sinister crime and yet the rules relating to corruption demonstrate vast differences in approach, understanding and tolerance.

What is morally and legally corrupt in one country is a recognised method of trade in another.

An international salesman may well argue that if he is not able to provide a secret commission then he will inevitably lose the contract to another company which permits its employees so to do. Such argument is, of course, the last refuge of the scoundrel but unhappily there are many international scoundrels aided and abetted by their own Governments.

I take my hat off to the Americans in leading the fight against international bribery. Their Lockheed case is well worthy of a detailed study. If we all followed in their footsteps then international corruption would be dealt a mortal blow.

What role have the lawyers? I perceive that the lawyers have every responsibility. If they are party overtly or covertly to any corruption then they must speak out and denounce it or risk being penalised themselves. The Americans have made it a breach of American law for someone to bribe abroad. We should encourage all countries so to do. No lawyer, and I hope no accountant, would ever be party to a breach of law.

The International Bar Association passed a resolution last year on the subject of international corruption and it is important that we follow up this process.

As Monty Raphael so rightly says:

"Lawyers do not create corrupt societies, but they can promote corrupt practices simply by choosing to ignore them. Similarly, lawyers do not start wars, but they do nothing to discourage them by taking part in illicit arms deals, even where they break no domestic law.

"Quite clearly there will be those who read this and say that, provided one is acting lawfully and one is not offending the professional ethics of one's own Bar Association, one should not interfere in other realms. They will say that it is not for the business lawyer to concern himself with the culture, politics or morality of his client, however distasteful any of these may be. And yet, it may equally strongly be argued that without such interference by individual lawyers, or by Bar Associations or, indeed by nations, evils will continue unchecked and the world will become a poorer place."

THE BUSINESS LAWYER AND DEVELOPMENT OF INTERNATIONAL BUSINESS PRACTICE

Francis Neate is of course a great champion of the International Bar Association having successfully served a term of office as the Chairman of the Section on Business Law and now acting as guardian and steward of the finances as IBA Treasurer. As a senior partner in a major London city firm his views command respect.

Francis Neate comments on the profound changes that have taken place in the world of business law and particularly on the dominance of Anglo-American law on international trade. He discounts the suggestion that this rise is due to any inherent superiority of common law over the civil law tradition, ascribing it rather to historical accident; a matter of English being the international business language and the overwhelming importance of American financing worldwide.

Francis Neate goes on to look at the trends that are still developing: the rise of the Asian economies and the liberalisation of the old Communist powers. All these are challenges to be faced and they will no doubt bring with them new pressure for the international business lawyer.

The business lawyer's obligations to the international business community are growing and will continue to grow. Not only must the international business lawyer provide speedy advice 24 hours a day, 7 days a week but must also ensure that the appropriate back-up staff is in place. As work becomes more and more transaction driven then strict time limits are put on the lawyer to complete the transaction.

That having been said, liability falling on the lawyer does not diminish. Rather it increases. As the accountants face multi-billion actions against them we must have concern that actions or threats of actions does not stultify the service leading to the provision of ambiguous or ambivalent advice. The modern client does not appreciate a lawyer who over-emphasises "on the one hand and on the other". An American system or style of damages however could, in my view, clog up the provision of candid legal advice.

While the rewards of the business lawyer may be high the standard of lifestyle is extremely low. I worry, when I hear of assistants and young partners working round the clock—sometimes for two or three days in a row. I worry when I see business lawyers grey with tiredness, with no family life and at the mercy of the current transaction with another one to follow swiftly in its heels.

Did we produce lawyers to become automatons? I must confess I consider myself an extremely hard worker. I am an infant compared to those who work for offices in London and New York. The International Bar Association may well have a role to play in the future to restore some balance and sanity into the practice of law.

VALUE OF THE INTERNATIONAL LAWYER

I commend Willem Calkoen, currently Chairman of the Section on Business Law, for his industry and dedication. This chapter discusses the role of lawyers in international trade, not only in terms of what they actually do but in how they have been perceived over the years. He points out that there is a real need for lawyers, but that this does not make them popular

As Supreme Court Justice Blackmen once said: "You have two types of lawyers: parasites of society and engineers of society." Outsiders view all lawyers as falling into the former category, but Willem Calkoen argues that most, thankfully, fall into the latter; and he gives many examples of lawyers who bring extra benefits to the work that they do.

THE ROLE OF THE LAWYER IN MEDICAL ETHICS

The International Bar Association has played a substantial part in education through a specially created IBA Educational Trust. We also have the advantage of the American based IBA Foundation, Inc.

Some five years ago, the IBA, through the Educational Trust, established a Chair in Medical Ethics at Glasgow University and Professor Sheila McLean was appointed to that Chair. Since that time she has produced many books and articles establishing herself as a world authority on a subject of growing importance.

The law is not only about business or international crime, it is also about the citizen and the impact of law on the citizen's life.

The relationship between law and morality, between law and ethics is assuming a growing significance. Such are the advances in medicine that matters cannot be left to commonsense or Hippocratic oaths.

Sheila McLean identifies the tensions between funding and commitment. Advances in medicine are staggeringly beneficial but frightening in their implications. The lawyer has a major part to play in determining how law should meet modern advances. Is there a right to life? Is there a right to choose when to die? The right to reproduce? The right to choose the sex of an unborn child? The right to clone?

Sheila McLean examines in detail the right of the HIV patient to privacy, examining the conflicting rights—the individual and society.

She examines the protection of individual liberties in the face of increasing claims by the State and suggests that the lawyer must play an increasingly important part not only dealing with guidelines regulating, for instance, abortion. In addition the lawyer and the law can provide the fundamental principles to address the new dilemmas.

She does not suggest that we should hijack medicine or its ethics but rather that we should be there to guide, to contribute—not just to medical ethics—but to patient care in general.

OTHER IBA ACTIVITIES

As I mentioned earlier the chapters on the book provide a snapshot of some of our activities. It is appropriate to mention other activities leading to our 50th Anniversary.

We moved premises to a splendid suite of offices in Oxford Circus allowing more appropriate conditions for our staff.

Paul Hoddinott took over from Madeleine May as Executive Director. Madeleine May had served some 25 years with the IBA and had seen the organisation grow to a size which could not have been contemplated by those in charge some 20 years ago.

The IBA now has a staff of some 40 people, all dedicated to the Law Societies, Bar Associations and individual members who function through our three Sections—Section on Business Law, Section on General Practice and Section on Energy & Natural Resources Law.

I am pleased that my successor Desmond Fernando of Sri Lanka is retaining the impetus on twinning. As the world becomes smaller and countries more accessible it is important that each and every country reaches out one to another. Developing countries have a lot to learn from developed countries and vice versa. I am hoping that over the next two years we shall see great advances made with our twinning programme under the joint Chairmanship of Leslie Wolfson of Scotland, Peter Goldsmith of England and Tom Forbes of Canada.

We have had friendly and productive relationships with the Arab Lawyers Union and I am hopeful that we will see shortly the establishment of an Arab Lawyers Institute.

I set up a Marketing Committee under the Chairmanship of Fred Chilton of Australia and aided by the staff they were able to ensure a record attendance at Berlin.

My first Presidential year was The Year of Africa and the second The Year of Latin America as the IBA searched out to increase its benign influence in all parts of the world.

I have a clear vision that the International Bar Association will grow from strength to strength. More and more lawyers will flock to join, contributing not only in their particular specialist fields but also in pro bono activity, whether that pro bono activity be adopting lawyers from developing countries, twinning with firms less fortunate than their own in different countries throughout the world, contributing to the Human Rights Institute and generally assisting in the pursuit of international justice.

I foresee Bar Associations and Law Societies recognising more and more clearly their international obligations and following in the footsteps of countries and cities such as Norway, Canada and Barcelona who, by their example, have stretched out the hand of fellowship and justice to others less fortunate throughout the world.

As lawyers we have that special knowledge and special training. With that there goes a special responsibility and we shall not shirk from discharging it.

My Presidency has been one of the most rewarding experiences of both my professional and personal lives. In two short years it has enabled me to experience other cultures at first hand. I have been overwhelmed by the warmth and friendship with which I, and the IBA, have been greeted by colleagues from around the world. These are irreplaceable memories which I shall treasure always.

As lawyers we are united in education, training and our love of law. We are bound together by our commitment to the rule of law. We have a duty to society to be at the fulcrum of law reform. Where the law fails society who, above all, must speak out? We, as lawyers.

Yes, we lawyers have an awesome responsibility to society. We have a duty to fellow lawyers in our country and in others. And, we have an overriding duty to our clients. We discharge this duty by our active membership of the International Bar Association and its Human Rights Institute.

My boyhood hero was Clarence Darrow—a noted American attorney who spent his life in the service of others, with financial rewards secondary to the pursuit of justice. Of the practice of law, Darrow once said:

"When I entered the practice of my profession years ago, I determined that there should never be a case, however unpopular or whatever the feeling, that I would refuse to do my duty and defend the case; and I can honestly say that I kept that faith; I have never turned my back on any defendant, no matter what the charge; when the cry is the loudest the defendant needs the lawyer most; when every man has turned against him, the law provides that he should have a lawyer."

Our client is justice—international justice—and we shall not turn our back on that client because we are privileged to be the proud servants of the law.

The Future of the IBA

Desmond Fernando PC

INTRODUCTION

1947 was an important year in the history of the legal profession. For it was in 1947 that the founding fathers of the IBA met and decided to set up an international organisation for the legal profession.

Article 1 of the IBA sets out its aims as follows:

- To establish and maintain relations and exchanges between Bar Associations and Law Societies and their members throughout the world.
- To assist such Associations and Societies and members of the legal profession throughout the world to develop and improve the profession's organisation and status.
- To assist members of the legal profession throughout the world, whether in the field of legal education or otherwise, to develop and improve their legal services to the public.
- To advance the science of jurisprudence in all its phases.
- By common study of practical problems to promote uniformity and definition in appropriate fields of law.
- To promote the administration of justice under the rule of law among the peoples of the world.

- To promote in the execution of these objects the principles and aims of the United Nations in their legal aspects and to co-operate with and promote co-ordination among, international juridical organisations having similar purposes.

In these 50 years we have made great progress. The IBA is today the voice of the legal profession. Almost every Bar Association in the world is a member.

What is more, it is effective. This is largely because at a crucial stage in its history it decided in 1970 to admit individual members. For this initiative we are grateful to George Seward, IBA Honorary Life President and Section on Business Law Honorary President-Founder. Another significant milestone was the setting up, in 1995, of the Human Rights Institute, an initiative of immediate IBA past President, Professor J Ross Harper CBE. Today the Institute plays an important role in the protection and promotion of Human Rights.

THE FUTURE

Human Rights and the Rule of Law

The IBA's Human Rights Institute is well on the way to being an extremely powerful force for the promotion and protection of the Rule of Law. Its special focus is the independence of the judiciary, the independence of the legal profession and the securing for every one of the right to a fair trial. (This is the right set out in Article 14 of the International Covenant on Civil and Political Rights.)

In the years to come the major and most significant contribution of the legal profession will be through the IBA's Human Rights Institute.

Those in positions of power will always be tempted to abuse the rights of others: we must not be so optimistic as to believe that in the future, human nature, and the effect of power on human nature, will change. But we will not be too optimistic if we believe that the IBA's

Human Rights Institute will grow to be a powerful countervailing force, effectively protecting and promoting Human Rights.

The United Nations has set International Human Rights standards. This it has done in several important instruments such as the Universal Declaration of Human Rights, the International Covenant on Civil and Political Rights and the International Covenant on Economic, Social and Cultural Rights. These International Human Rights standards reflect values which are shared by all human beings. These Human Rights standards will be promoted by the Institute.

THE CORE: THE COUNCIL OF THE IBA

The last two decades have witnessed tremendous growth, dynamism and vitality at the periphery of the IBA: the Committees of the various Sections, the General Professional Programme Committee and the Standing Committees have been extremely active. Ad hoc Committees have dealt effectively with problems that have come up from time to time. Yet what of the core – the Council of the IBA? The Council is the central decision making body of the IBA.

It has dealt competently with organisational matters. However, much of its time has been spent on house-keeping matters. During the Presidency of Ross Harper, the Council began to take a leadership role in the legal profession. It began to address itself to matters which have an impact on society. Two such examples were the Resolutions that dealt with Money Laundering and the setting up of an International Criminal Court.

Members of the Council are leaders of the legal profession in their own countries. The Council has an immense wealth of legal talent. Many Councillors attend meetings during their tenure of office as Bar Presidents. Until recent times many were somewhat bewildered at their first meeting and could not participate fully.

The Councillors and their Member Organisations will be briefed well in time so that Councillors can participate fully. The Council will in the future become the most important forum of the legal profession. There is no limit to what the leaders of the legal profession, drawn from every country in the world, can achieve. The Council will become the conscience and voice of the legal profession. It will become a new power in the world.

INTERNATIONAL CO-OPERATION

The future will see greater co-operation within the legal profession. This co-operation will be two-fold. First there will be greater consolidation of the great initiatives of the International Bar Association. Let me give some examples:

- The twinning programme, where the Bar of a developing country is twinned with a Bar from a developed country, will empower the legal profession of third world countries to be a great force for the Rule of Law.
- The Arab Legal Institute will give the necessary training for judges and lawyers in the region who share our values.

Secondly, there will be greater co-operation and collaboration between the International Bar Association and regional legal organisations such as Lawasia. Organisations such as Lawasia have specialised knowledge and a long history of service in the Asia Pacific region. Likewise the Inter Pacific Bar Association. The International Bar Association will work together with the regional and international legal organisations such as AIJA.

CONCLUSION

In the years to come the legal profession must be conscious of its heavy responsibilities. Not only individual lawyers, but more important Bar Associations, and most important of all, the International Bar Associations.

The profession must continue to provide legal services of the highest quality, to promote and protect the Rule of Law and Human Rights and to provide the legal skills which are necessary for economic development.

The IBA has the experience, expertise and the organisational capacity: we face the future with confidence.

Role of the Lawyer in Human Rights Issues

*Jerome J. Shestack**

To discuss the role of lawyers in human rights issues is to embrace the entire field—from the start of human rights in religious and moral philosophy to the current fervent advocacy of human rights by lawyers on a multitude of fronts. That is not surprising. The lawyer's ministry is justice—and human rights, while anchored in moral philosophy, are driven by justice. Indeed, it would be strange if lawyers were not at the helm of the human rights vessel. What is strange is that it has taken so long and that there are so few.

THE DEVELOPMENT OF THE LAW OF INTERNATIONAL HUMAN RIGHTS

Modern human rights are rooted in legal and moral philosophy. The goal of human rights advocates is to establish human rights as a world rule of law, fully implemented in customary practice. In that

* The writer expresses appreciation to his colleague, Elizabeth Vrato, for her research assistance.

ongoing endeavour, many lawyers have had, and do have, a prominent role.

There are, to be sure, glimmerings of human rights in Sophocles and Aristotle, in the Old and New Testaments, and in the writings of medieval theologians, such as Thomas Aquinas. But the genesis of the modern secular theory of human rights must be attributed to Hugo Grotius, a lawyer, whose development of natural law qualifies him as the father of modern international law. Grotius defined natural law as a "dictate of right reason, that is, an act that has in it a quality of moral necessity or moral baseness, depending on whether it is in conformity with rational nature." Grotius saw the law of nature as embodying both laws which have as their source the will of man, and laws derived from the principles of the law of nature. Whatever confirmed the nature of men and women as rational social beings was right and just; whatever opposed it by disturbing the social harmony was wrong and unjust. This theory, of course, has immense importance for the status and legitimacy of human rights as part of a system of universal international law.

John Locke, although not a lawyer, built on Grotius' theory and utilised legal principles to conceive a "social contract" by which individuals entered the body politic but retained their natural rights of life, liberty and property. Government was obliged to protect the natural rights of its subjects, and if government failed this obligation it would forfeit its validity and office.

Thus, the emphasis in human rights was on *rights*—namely fundamental, inalienable legal obligations to maintain the natural worth and autonomy of the individual. This, indeed, was the rationale for the United States Declaration of Independence, the French Declaration of the Rights of Man and the constitutions of numerous later states, particularly those created upon liberation from colonialism.

During the 19th and 20th centuries, there was a regression from natural rights theory to positivist theory. Positivism was also based on legal principles; but in positivism, the source of all rights was found in the enactments of the sovereign state. In this jurisprudence, rights could not transcend the empirical realities of existing legal systems.

Law can be just and uplifting, and law can be draconian and degrading. By divorcing legal systems from ethical and moral consideration (the "ought" in law), positivism encouraged the belief that the law must be obeyed, no matter how immoral.

Thus, the legal philosophy of Grotius and the enlightenment philosophers was submerged and overridden by 19th and 20th century positivist doctrine which sacrificed human rights to the altar of the state—a philosophy which served totalitarian regimes such as Nazi Germany, in which the establishment of concentration camps and the abhorrent mass murder in the Nazi crematories all took place under domestic German law.

As World War II came to a close, there was increasingly revealed the horror that could result from a positivist system such as Germany, in which individual rights counted for nothing. It is not surprising that there should emerge a renewed search for immutable principles to protect humanity against such brutality. Many lawyers took the lead in this endeavour.

What developed and became embodied in the United Nations Charter was a qualified natural law approach, marked by an attempt to identify values which have an eternal aspect. The upshot of the new rights doctrine is a focus on the autonomy of the individual in choosing his or her ends. Put another way, the new theories were based on concepts of natural necessity, that is, prescribing a minimum of what it means to be human in society. Whatever the refinements of this philosophy, it meant a crucial break with the dominant tradition of national sovereignty over individual human rights. This renaissance of rights theory had a seminal influence on international human rights norms.

Those who gathered in San Francisco in 1945 to establish the United Nations and draft its charter were determined to protect the rights of the individual, which had been so brutalised in the war. The preamble to the U.N. Charter grounded such an international protection by affirming the dignity and worth of each person and the equal rights of men and women. The United Nations Charter thus broke with the tradition of national sovereignty holding dominion over human rights. Most importantly, it provided a strong foundation for a series of building blocks that cumulatively built the international human rights legal structure.

After the Charter, the Universal Declaration of Human Rights commenced in 1946 and was adopted in 1948. Rene Cassin, a prominent French lawyer, and Eleanor Roosevelt were the principal actors in framing the Universal Declaration. The Universal Declaration is a legal document—a Bill of Rights for the world. Twenty articles deal with freedom of speech, religion and assembly, freedom from torture, freedom of movement, right to a fair trial—an array of civil and political rights. Ten articles were new in the rights vocabulary and deal with social, economic and cultural rights, such as the rights to health care, to an adequate standard of living, education and other elements of distributive justice.

The Universal Declaration only started the process of building the edifice of human rights. What followed was the creation of the substantive law of international human rights. The Universal Declaration was fleshed out by years of comprehensive law making, with specific human rights treaties covering Genocide, Civil and Political rights, Economic, Social and Cultural rights, Slavery and Forced Labor, Racial Discrimination, Rights of Refugees, Rights of Women, Torture and Rights of Children. By now, we have a full, comprehensive and impressive body of substantive international law to protect the rights of the individual. On regional levels, the European Commission of Human Rights and the European Court of Human Rights, the American Commission on Human Rights and the Inter-American Court of Human Rights have established not only standards, but judicial bodies to effectuate the standards.

It bears emphasis that in creating these human rights standards, mechanisms and entities, the architects, for the most part, were lawyers—initiating drafts, laboring in working committees, and building the consensus necessary for a vision to translate into concrete treaties and to find solid rooting in international law.

THE IMPLEMENTATION OF HUMAN RIGHTS - THE NGOs

The establishment of international human rights legal principles is, of course, a necessity if human rights are to prevail. But equally important is the implementation of human rights. For many years after the Universal Declaration and the covenants that followed, implementation of human rights law lay dormant. At the United Nations, in particular, complaints of abuse multiplied and went unaddressed. Resolutions of condemnation were largely limited to South Africa, the territories occupied by Israel and Chile. There were few human rights organisations and redress of human rights abuses was virtually non-existent.

Law without remedies, or at least without advocates of remedy, is barren. Implementation of human rights became an extremely aggravating and unaddressed issue as abuses multiplied in the world of the 1950s and 1960s. The earliest responses came from non-governmental human rights organisations. While these were not lawyers' organisations as such, they were substantially lawyer organised and directed. Three early ones deserve particular mention.

The International League for Human Rights is the first of the international human rights organisations centred in the United States. Founded in 1942 by Roger Baldwin, it included a heavy mix of lawyers in its subsequent leadership, including John Carey, Leo Nevas, Roger Clark, Father Robert Drinan, Sidney Liskofsky and the writer. The League developed human rights affiliates around the world and has undertaken many missions to investigate, report and publicise human rights abuses and to advocate human rights at the United Nations.

The International Commission of Jurists (ICJ), founded in 1952, is the first human rights NGO to organise a highly select group of lawyers and judges with a mission to develop the rule of law in the human rights area. Together with the International League, the ICJ played a seminal early role in persuading governments to include human rights objectives in their foreign policy. Principal activities have been to protect the independence of lawyers and judges and to advocate social and economic rights. Its leadership includes prominent human rights advocates: Michael D. Kirby of Australia, Desmond Fernando of Sri Lanka (now president of the IBA), Theo van Boven of the Netherlands, Claire l'Heureux-Dubé of Canada, Antonio Cassese of Italy, Arthur Chakalson of South Africa, Soli Sorabjee and Fali S. Nairiman of India and Dato'Param Cumaraswamy of Malaysia are some of the advocates that come readily to mind.

Amnesty International began in 1961 and eventually became the world's pre-eminent human rights organisation. While its original focus was on political prisoners, it soon broadened its scope to encompass all aspects of human rights violations. Its leadership too has been heavily supplied by lawyers, and its already high reputation was enhanced when it won the Nobel Peace Prize in 1977.

There were precious few other human rights organisations as late as 20 years ago. Of some four to five thousand international organisations then listed in the International Yearbook, less than two-tenths of one percent were exclusively in the human rights field. Indeed, as late as the mid 1970s, human rights activity in general was still sparse.[1] While lawyers were prominent in standard building at the U.N., few lawyers were active in implementation. In academia, barely a handful of law professors wrote on human rights subjects and human rights was rarely taught. However, at the midpoint of the 1970s, there was a sea change.

One critical advance was the Helsinki Final Act in 1975, by which the countries of Europe, the United States and Canada agreed to measures of cooperation and security, including a pledge to further human rights covenants and declarations. The Helsinki Accords made untenable the argument that human rights were only a matter of domestic concern and brought human rights into the calculus of international negotiation and agreement.

---

1 See Shestack, J., *Sisyphus Endures*, 24 New York Law School Law Review 89 (1978).

The second major development was US President Jimmy Carter's advocacy of human rights beginning in 1976. Until then, the human rights cause lacked a champion in the family of states, particularly one that was a superpower. Carter saw to it that, at the least, attention was paid to human rights. And Carter's concern was promoted by global communications advances that enabled human rights standards and goals to be disseminated throughout the world, touching the aspirations and yearnings of repressed peoples. Human rights raced to a position high on the global agenda.

By the mid 1980s, a new mosaic emerged. Hundreds upon hundreds of new human rights NGOs were actively engaged in the human rights movement, including the outstanding New York based Watch Committees. Academic legal journals became filled with human rights articles. Human rights missions were abundant. Dissenters found new hope and encouragement. Human rights, long a sleeping force, had awakened. In all of these efforts, the roster of human rights activists sparkled with lawyers.

THE ORGANIZED BAR AND HUMAN RIGHTS

While individual lawyers were early leaders in human rights endeavours, the organised bar, not to its credit, was a late starter.

The *International Bar Association* (IBA), formed in 1947, is the world's largest international organisation of law societies, bar associations and lawyers, now celebrating its 50th anniversary. Although the IBA had a long expressed concern with human rights abuses, particularly of lawyers and judges, it was not until the beginning of the 1990s that human rights became a significant element in IBA activities. In 1991, the IBA, under the leadership of President Giuseppe Bisconti, convened a conference of world bar leaders in Montreal to consider an IBA Human Rights Action Plan, which I had drafted. Its purpose was to marshal the IBA's constituent bar organisations around the world on behalf of human rights advocacy, including the establishment of a trial lawyer observer corps to monitor trials with international human rights implications. (More of this shortly.) The IBA adopted this plan. Then in 1995, IBA President Ross Harper launched the IBA Human Rights Institute. The institute has liaison with more than 100 national bar associations and is immersed in protesting human rights abuses and in a variety of other human rights initiatives.

The *American Bar Association* (ABA) actively entered the field in 1969. At that time, as chairman of the ABA's Section of Individual Rights and Responsibilities, I established the ABA's first Committee on International Human Rights to press for ABA endorsement of human rights treaties. Subsequently, the ABA's International Law and Practice Section took a significant role in human rights endeavours. By the mid 1970s, the ABA had urged ratification of the major human rights treaties and frequently endorsed human rights initiatives. The ABA has established rule of law protest letters, signed by the president of the ABA, to heads of states that engage in gross human rights violations. ABA activity in the human rights area now includes many of its sections and committees. The ABA's Section of International Law and Practice is rendering particular service in support of an international criminal court and training of counsel for war crimes tribunals.

The *Lawyers' Committee for Human Rights* has become the leading lawyers' organisation in this field as a subsidiary of the International League for Human Rights. In 1977, I founded the committee and served as its first chairman. The independent Lawyers' Committee now conducts fact-finding missions to investigate abuses, publishes comprehensive reports of its findings on significant human rights issues, and is a strong advocate for indigent refugees and asylum seekers. The committee also has a lawyer to lawyer network which marshals lawyers on behalf of colleagues who face official reprisals because of their professional activities in the human rights area. Under the leadership of its executive director, Michael Posner, the committee has involved hundreds of volunteer lawyers and many firms in human rights activities.

This enumeration is not exhaustive. The *Union Internationale des Advocats* has engaged in notable human rights endeavours. In the

United States, England and Western Europe, in particular, human rights activities have been undertaken by national and local bar associations and societies and by specialty bars, enlisting lawyers in missions, reports, public meetings and other human rights action and excellent legal papers have been delivered on frontier issues in human rights. That the number of such organisations is now so large as to preclude listing here is, indeed, a heartwarming advance.

LAWYERS AS VICTIMS

This account of the lawyers' role in human rights issues has been largely the story of lawyers in democratic nations committed to human rights and devoting time and talent to advancing its causes.

There are also many highly courageous lawyers who have fought for human rights within repressive regimes, whose defense of human rights has placed them at considerable risk to themselves and their families. So too, many judges seeking to maintain their independence and follow a just rule of law have found their independence and themselves in serious jeopardy.

Thus, around the world, judges who sought to maintain unbiased and independent judgment and lawyers defending human rights have been subject to assassination, death threats, dismissal, and more subtle pressures such as stripped jurisdiction and denial of resources. Lawyers engaged in human rights counselling and advocacy have been harassed, detained without charge or trial, suspended from practice, disbarred, sentenced to prison, forced into exile, tortured and murdered.

The reason for the attack on judges and lawyers by repressive regimes is that lawyers and judges turn human rights into reality. If they themselves become victims and are thus immobilized, a repressive rule it becomes easier to sustain. In some cases, the lawyers are activists in their own right, and this too fuels their prosecution.

As a result, in many repressive states, it has become extremely difficult and sometimes impossible for human rights activists and "political prisoners," or "prisoners of conscience"—to receive a fair trial or to secure the services of an experienced defense lawyer. Generally, the targeted lawyers represent unpopular clients such as human rights activists, trade unions, peasant or minority groups, university faculties, and various political opponents of the regime.[2]

Examples over the years abound. In Columbia, Guatemala and Peru, judges have often been threatened and sometimes assassinated because they sought to administer the law impartially. In Argentina, in 1970, the military regime stripped all members of the judiciary of their tenure. Even in 1993, when the Junta no longer ruled, every single member of the Buenos Aires provincial judiciary received death threats. In 1981, nine of Pakistan's highest judges were dismissed because they were not sufficiently pliant to General Zia's wishes. Even now, judges still are subject to serious government interference with their autonomy. In Sudan, Malaysia, China, Indonesia, Pakistan and Kenya, the independence of judges has been regularly violated. There are many other examples.

Lawyers have suffered far more. In Argentina, during the despotic rule of the Junta, more than a score of lawyers were assassinated and over 100 lawyers disappeared. Lawyers disappeared in Guatemala and many were imprisoned in Chile, Brazil, Uruguay and Paraguay during repressive regimes. Lawyers engaged in human rights activity have been disbarred, suspended or harassed in most Eastern European states, in the Philippines, South Korea, Syria, and in many other countries during repressive periods.

In Northern Ireland, there has been a steady pattern of harassment of lawyers representing defendants in political violence cases. Solicitors in such cases often receive anonymous death threats. The ICJ report for 1992–93 found that 39 lawyers in Northern Ireland had been subjected to abuse or threats from police officers. The situation has eased as peace talks have continued but is still tension-laden.

---

2 See *Attacks on Justice, The Harassment and Persecution of Judges and Lawyers* issued by the Center for Independence of Judges and Lawyers (1995).

One of the major abusers of lawyers has been Turkey. In 1955, the ICJL reported 113 attacks on lawyers, with 74 detained and 32 tortured. Most of the lawyers defended Kurdish clients.

Today, human rights defense lawyers are threatened and harassed in China, Indonesia, Myanmar, East Timor, Malaysia, Pakistan, Kenya and in other states. This troubled saga continues.

Bar associations, too, have often been under attack. In 1980, President Assad of Syria dissolved the Syrian Bar Association because of its one-day protest over a state of emergency. Iraq, Iran Cuba, Libya, Saudi Arabia, and the Sudan are notable examples of nations where no independent legal profession functions. Guatemala and the Philippines are other states which have interfered with the independence of bar associations. Turkey has egregiously harassed and punished officials of its bar association. Kenya is another current example of government harassment of Kenyan bar leaders.

During the past six years alone, reports by human rights organisations and bar associations have documented nearly 500 cases per year of lawyers, judges, law students and professors who suffered harassment threats, confinement, reprisals, torture and even death in the representation of unpopular clients and the advocacy of human rights.[3]

Lawyers in democratic nations have a particular obligation to address these abuses. Many have done so as discussed above in noting the work of the IBA, the ABA, the ICJ and the Lawyers' Committee for Human Rights. A relevant question is how effective have such activities been on behalf of harassed and abused lawyers?

Causation is hard to determine in evaluating the effectiveness of human rights interventions. But it is a fact that many of the lawyers on whose behalf the Western on bar associations have written or cabled have been released from detention in countries including Argentina, Cuba, Kenya, Paraguay, Pakistan, the Philippines and

3 For about a decade, the Lawyers Committee for Human Rights and the Center for the Independence of Lawyers and Judges have chronicled hundreds of cases in which individual judges and lawyers, as well as bar associations and advocacy groups, have been victims of human rights abuse.

South Africa. Other progress also has been achieved. For example, death sentences were commuted in Malawi; lawyers were allowed to return to Chile after involuntary exile; banning orders were lifted against South African attorneys even during apartheid. Sending observers to trials of human rights advocates as the IBA, ABA and Lawyers' Committee have done, often provides a salutary benefit to the fairness of the trial, even if it is not officially acknowledged. Comprehensive reports of abuses by missions of lawyers often result in easing of restrictions or release of political prisoners.

In short, timely and informed interventions and exposure of governmental abuses of human rights, through what has been described as the "mobilisation of shame" and the use of "discrete indignation," can produce positive, individual outcomes. Human rights groups can all point to successes, although never as many as they hope for. Still, in this area every rescue is a victory for human worth.

To sum up, experience teaches us that individual lawyers, bar associations and human rights organisations can make a difference by assisting individual victims of human rights violations, as well as by challenging broader patterns of abuse. It is a challenge that lawyers should eagerly accept.

SECURING THE INDEPENDENCE OF JUDGES AND LAWYERS

The harassment of lawyers and judges often represents attacks by the regime against human rights standards. But underlying the attacks is resistance to a just rule of law secured by an independent judiciary and protected by an independent bar committed to the rule of law.

The struggle to maintain the independence of judges and lawyers has been a long one, and it is still raging. Unfortunately, international law was quite late in addressing the issue of independence of lawyers and judges. The Universal Declaration of Human Rights introduced the basic principle that human rights should be protected by the rule of law. From the start, it should have been self-evident that an independent judiciary is a *sine qua non* of a just rule of law. And, a corollary of an independent judiciary is an independent legal profession. Yet, paradoxically, the self-evident is sometimes hard to delineate. Year after year went by with numerous highly touted conferences trying to delineate standards for independence, selection, training and status of judges and lawyers. In these efforts, there was much duplication and wheel spinning.[4]

Finally, in 1985, Basic Principles on the Independence of the Judiciary were adopted by the United Nations Congress on the Prevention of Crime and the Treatment of Offenders. The General Assembly of the United Nations has endorsed these principles, but, unfortunately, in many nations they have yet to be implemented.

Five years later, in response to the gross violations against human rights defenders, the Congress adopted Basic Principles on the Role of Lawyers. Basic Principle #1 states:

> "All persons are entitled to call upon the assistance of a lawyer of their choice to protect and establish their rights and to defend them in all stages of criminal proceedings."

Basic Principle #2 provides:

> "Governments shall ensure that efficient procedures and responsive mechanisms for effective and equal access to lawyers are provided for all persons within their territory and subject to their jurisdiction, without distinction of any kind, such as discrimination based on race, color, ethnic origin, sex, language, religion, political or other opinion, national or social origin, property, birth, economic or other status."

And Basic Principle #4 states:

> "Governments and professional associations of lawyers shall promote programmes to inform the public about their rights and

---

4 The long road to standard setting is set forth in CIJL Bulletin No. 25-26 *Independence of Judges and Lawyers: A Compilation of International Standards*@ (April-October 1990).

> duties under the law and the important role of lawyers in protecting their fundamental freedoms. Special attention should be given to assisting the poor and other disadvantaged persons so as to enable them to assert their rights and where necessary, call upon the assistance of lawyers."

Other basic principles cover safeguards for the individual in criminal justice matters, the necessary qualifications and training of lawyers, the duties and responsibilities of lawyers in loyally respecting the interests of their clients, and the safeguarding of lawyers when their security is threatened as a result of discharging their functions.

The UN has asked Member States to inform the Secretary-General every five years of the progress achieved in the implementation of these basic principles, "including their dissemination, their incorporation into domestic legislation, practice, procedures and policies, the problems faced in their implementation at the national level and assistance that might be needed from the international community ... "[5]

The UN's endorsement of the basic principles is commendable. As the crystallisation of efforts made by human rights lawyers in years past, it is a victory for human rights advocates and a high point in the ongoing fight for human rights. Proper implementation of these principles throughout the countries of the world will be as much of a challenge as many other battles taken on by human rights lawyers.

Lawyers, both individually and in the organised bar, have accomplished much for human rights. Yet, critical issues remain: how to

---

5 In addition, the UN has established a Special Rapporteur on Independence of Lawyers and Judges. Dató Param Curaswamy, the current reporter, is a courageous outstanding lawyer who has headed the Malaysian Bar and the Asian-Pacific Bar.

increase ratification of human rights covenants; how to firm up human rights standards as customary law binding on all nations; how to hear and decide individual complaints of human rights violations; how to protect human rights advocates and the independence of judges; how to ensure access and safety for trial observers; how to deal with a government's excuse of an "emergency" as a reason for suspending rights; how to finally bring about an international criminal court; how to bring about human rights implementation in countries still repressive and resistant to a just rule of law; how to deal with cultural relativists who seek to diminish human rights standards under the charade of cultural differences; how to undertake judicial implementation of human rights at the United Nations; and more.

The list of unresolved questions and of unmet needs and challenges is long and pressing. Lawyers must persevere in addressing these issues. Lawyers have the science and skill to do so. More compelling, their calling as lawyers obligates them to the pursuit of justice.

Judicial Independence and Freedom of Expression

Professor Shimon Shetreet

INTRODUCTION

Two of the most significant legal foundations of democracy, the rule of law and human rights, are the principles of judicial independence and the right of freedom of expression. These two safeguards of democracy are essential foundations for the human well being of the private individual and are vital for orderly conduct and life of the organized society as a whole.

In this paper on these two important issues, in the 50th anniversary volume of the IBA, I shall attempt to chart the past course and the blueprints of the future on a number of central issues related to judicial independence and the administration of justice and to freedom of expression.

The first section analyzes the concept of judicial independence in the general context of the values underlying the administration of justice. The IBA played a very important role in developing the contemporary standards of judicial independence by adopting the IBA International Code of Minimum Standards of Judicial Independence in New Delhi in 1982.[1] The paper will analyze and comment

---

1 For the text of the IBA Code of Minimum Standards of Judicial Independence, see Shetreet and Deschenes (eds.), Judicial Independence - The Contemporary Debate, 1985, Martinus Nijhoff Publishers, ch. 31; for the Montreal Declaration see ibid, ch. 39. The volume contains national reports and analysis of the topic from various aspects.

on the IBA code and its contribution to the development of transnational jurisprudence on judicial independence.

The safeguard of judicial independence is of even greater importance in light of the increasing judicial role in society involving the courts in judicial review of legislative and executive actions, and in politically charged cases. The second section also analyzes the judicial role in society in recent times.

The challenge of freedom of expression has been aggravated by borderline cases where courts and society have to make a distinction between different scopes of protection for different categories of speech. The third section will examine the right of freedom of expression. One of the most challenging aspects of the protection of speech is the demarcation of the limits of free speech on the grounds of national security and on the grounds that the speech incites violence or hatred. These two issues will be examined in greater detail.

JUDICIAL INDEPENDENCE: THEORY AND TRANSNATIONAL JURISPRUDENCE

1. *The Contemporary Concept of Judicial Independence*

The judiciary has developed from a mere dispute-resolution mechanism, to a significant social institution exercising a broader constitutional role and participating along with other institutions in shaping the life of its community. Social, political and economic changes, in recent times, in most countries, have confronted the courts and judges with new challenges and new problems.

The centralization of the responsibility and supervision of court administration and judicial administration has raised the issue of the relationship between the judiciary and the executive, and made it necessary to redefine and delineate the boundaries of the scope of executive control on judges, courts and judicial administration, and court financing. It was also necessary to shape the rules, traditions, and practices governing the conduct of judges off the bench, in the various areas of activities.

A modern conception of judicial independence cannot be confined to the individual judge and to his substantive and personal independence, but must include collective independence of the judiciary as a whole. The concept of collective judicial independence requires a greater measure of judicial participation in the central administration of the courts including the preparation of budgets for the courts or court personnel. Depending on one's view of the nature of judicial independence, the extent of judicial participation may range from consultation, joint responsibility with the executive, or exclusive judicial responsibility.

Examination of the law and practice of various countries, concerning issues which have a bearing on judges and judicial independence, reveals differences and even conflicts. These differences sometimes result from differences in conceptions and perceptions, and sometimes stem from historical reasons or diversity of circumstances, including a lack of initiative to review old practices and introduce reform.

In recent times, the issue of judicial independence has been highlighted by numerous incidents of violation of judicial independence in many parts of the world. These violations of judicial independence took different forms, and occurred in countries with different systems of government. This includes interference with personal independence such as unjustified removal, suspension or transfer, interference with salaries and budgets, closing down courts, preemption or frustration of judicial decisions, and attempts to influence legal proceedings[2].

---

2 See Shetreet, Judicial Independence: New Conceptual Dimensions and Contemporary Challenges in Shetreet and Deschenes, *id.*, 590 at 606-620.

2. The IBA Project of Judicial Independence and the Montreal Declaration

These events, the apparent diversities and conflicts between different countries on the law and practice, concerning judges and judicial independence, and generally the developments in modern society, in political and social conditions, called for the review of conceptions, traditions and principles bearing on judicial independence. Moreover, the concepts on the nature of judicial office and on the role of the individual judge and the judicial branch have undergone changes. The time was ripe for a crystallization of these changing concepts in a set of International Minimum Standards of Judicial Independence.

These were the main reasons behind the decision of the International Bar Association in August 1980 to embark upon a project for the development of an international comprehensive code of minimum standards of judicial independence. In 1982, after over two years of intensive work since the initiation of the project, it was possible to develop an international code of judicial independence based on the General Report, on 29 National Reports, and 15 topical reports. The National Reports followed the guidelines laid down by the General Rapporteur, detailing the specific questions which the National Rapporteurs were requested to address.

It was in 1980 at the 18th Biennial Convention in Berlin that the International Bar Association embarked upon the project for the development of an international comprehensive code of minimum standards of judicial independence. The Project was the responsibility of the Committee on Administration of Justice in the Section of General Practice. Justice D.K. Haese of Australia, the Chairman of the Committee acted as the Project Coordinator, and this author served as General Rapporteur of the Project. Justice Haese succeeded Chief Justice L. King, also of Australia, in the office of Project Coordinator, in the beginning of 1982.

National rapporteurs and topical rapporteurs of the highest academic and professional standing from over 30 countries took part in the Project. The participating countries were geographically representative of the world, and fairly represent the major legal families of judicial systems, as well as the major systems of government. After debates and deliberations in Lisbon in 1981 and in Jerusalem in early 1982, the final text of the IBA Code of Minimum Standards was approved in New Delhi in October of 1982.

In addition to the IBA project, other important international projects took place. These include the Montreal Universal Declaration on the Independence of Justice, the Syracuse Principles, the Tokyo Law Asia Principles, and the United Nations Basic Principles on Judicial Independence.[3] In June 1983 the First World Conference on the Independence of Justice was held in Montreal under the leadership of Chief Justice Jules Deschenes. Justice Deschenes succeeded in the difficult task of gathering under one roof about 130 distinguished jurists representing some 20 international organizations, in order to approve a Universal Declaration on the Independence of Justice.

The Montreal Declaration dealt with five topics and approved Five Chapters of the Declaration: The International Judges, The National Judges, The Lawyers, The Jury and The Assessors.

The Declaration was conveyed to the United Nations' Human Rights Subcommittee which is engaged in the study of the independence of judges, lawyers and juries. It was submitted by the General Rapporteur of the Montreal Conference, Dr. Singhvi, who acted as a Special Rapporteur of the UN study.

This author and others who were involved in the IBA Project were very pleased to note the high involvement of the IBA delegates in the Montreal Conference. With all due modesty, it is to be noted that the IBA Code of Minimum Standards of Judicial Independence has had a significant impact on the text of the Declaration in several main areas: a) The recognition of the concept of collective independence; b) the emphasis on the vital importance of the administrative independence of the judiciary; c) the recognition of the concept of internal judicial independence, i.e., the judges independence vis-a-vis his fellow and superior judges; d) the restriction of

---

3 See Shetreet and Deschenes, *id.*, at pp. 381-501.

executive power over the judiciary; e) the encouragement of the idea that the judiciary should fairly reflect society.

An important international statement on judicial independence was the United Nations Basic Principles on the Independence of the Judiciary which were approved at the Seventh United Nations Congress on the Prevention of Crime and the Treatment of Offenders which was held in Milan in Summer 1985. The Principles were formulated as guideline following the Sixth U.N. Congress on the Prevention of Crime and the Treatment of Offenders, which had called on the Committee on Crime Prevention and Control to formulate guidelines on the independence of the judiciary. The Committee's guidelines were formulated at its eighth session, and at the UN Inter-Regional Preparatory Meeting for the Seventh Congress, held at Varenna, Italy in September 1984.

The UN General Assembly welcomed the Basic Principles in December 1985. It was decided that UN Member States were to report to the Secretary-General every five years on their progress in implementing the Principles.

The final version of the basic Principles owes much to the International Bar Association Code of Minimum Standards and to the Montreal Universal Declaration of the Independence of Justice. Highly active in preparing the Basic Principles was Dr. Singhvi, who was entrusted in 1980 by the Economic and Social Council's Sub-Commission on Prevention of Discrimination and Protection of Minorities with the task of preparing a report on the independence and impartiality of the judiciary, jurors and assessors and on the independence of lawyers. Dr. Singhvi played an active role in bringing about the adoption of the Basic Principles.

3. Toward an International Code

The development of an international code of judicial independence is highly important. Numerous incidents of violation of judicial independence have been recorded in recent years. These violations have many faces and many colors, and may be direct or indirect, covert and overt. The country studies contain numerous illustrations of violations of judicial independence, such as suspension of the operation of the courts, transfer tantamount to de facto removal, withholding of increases in judicial salaries, withholding sufficient resources and judicial personnel from the courts, the use of pre-emptive and retroactive legislation to prevent recourse to the courts or to reverse retroactively specific judicial decisions.[4]

Against such a background the development of international standards of judicial independence with the support of prestigious professional organizations had a most important, dynamic effect on the enhancement of judicial independence.

The aim of the IBA Project was to develop international, minimum standards of judicial independence. The aim was not necessarily to photograph or reflect the prevailing practice in the world. Rather our aim was to formulate such standards that the nations of the world should strive to comply with. True minimum standards are not the ideal, most desirable standards, and they must not exceed the boundaries of feasibility and reasonableness. We certainly were aware of this, but we made an honest effort to turn the International Minimum Standards of Judicial Independence into a dynamic catalyst for the introduction of the necessary reforms, to assure compliance with the Standards. We felt that we proceeded in this important project upon the premise that it was our duty to assume a responsibility of leadership, not merely a static reflection of the reality. Throughout my involvement in the IBA Project and in the Montreal Declaration, I was convinced that this was the course which would lead to the promotion of judicial independence in our communities around the world.

The IBA Standards approved in Jerusalem and confirmed in New Delhi were based on this underlying conception which was shared by the participants in the Lisbon Conference, in the Planning Conference in Jerusalem, and in the IBA Convention in New Delhi. Among many other things, the IBA Standards stress the importance of the collective independence of the judiciary vis-a-vis

---

4 Id. at 606-620.

the Executive and the Legislature, and the need for judicial autonomy in matters of judicial administration and court budgets. They recommend selection committees for judicial appointments, and they stress the idea that judges are independent statutory officers of the state and not civil servants of the executive government. The Standards call for the security of terms of judicial office, the safeguard of adequate judicial salaries, and regular pay increases according to economic changes by constitutionally protected procedure. The Montreal Declaration generally followed the IBA lines of thinking.

It is important to emphasize the interdependence between the protection of human rights and the Independence of Justice. In the last 50 years, the international community has made a giant step towards the crystallization of substantive human rights. Beginning with the Universal Declaration of Human Rights in 1948, human rights were embodied in international treaties, global and regional, general and specialized.

Substantive human rights are worthless without an effective mechanism for their enforcement. The enforcement of rights is assured by an independent and impartial tribunal. The establishment of clearly stated standards on the meaning of independence will have no doubt enhanced the promotion of human rights around the world.

4. The Elements of Judicial Independence

a) Personal and substantive independence

The conception of independence of the judiciary carries two meanings: the independence of the individual judges, and the independence of the judiciary as a body. The independence of the individual judge is comprised of two essential elements; the substantive independence and the personal independence. Substantive independence means that in the making of judicial decision and exercising other official duties, individual judges are subject to no other authority but the law.

Personal independence means that the judicial terms of office and tenure are adequately secured. Personal independence is secured by judicial appointment during good behavior terminated at retirement age, and by safeguarding judicial remuneration. Thus, executive control over terms of service of the judges, such as remuneration, pensions, or travel allowances, is inconsistent with the concept of judicial independence. Still much less acceptable is any executive control over case assignment, court scheduling, or moving judges from one court to another or from one locality to another.

b) Judicial conduct

Independence of the judiciary implies not only that a judge should be free from executive or legislative encroachment and from political pressures and entanglements, but also that he should be removed from financial or business entanglement likely to affect, or rather to seem to affect, him in the exercise of his judicial functions. The Standards are aimed at removing judges from political and business entanglements and from controversies or improprieties. As to judges and the Press, IBA Standards 33-35 allow for interviews to the Press, subject to the duty to preserve judicial dignity. Similar rules have been laid down by the Montreal Universal Declaration of Independence (art. 2.09-2.10, and 2.26-2.31.)

c) Collective independence

A modern conception of judicial independence cannot be confined to the individual judge and to his substantive and personal independence, but must include collective independence of the judiciary as a whole. This is now widely recognized as in Standard 2 and 9 of the IBA Code and Article 2 of the Montreal Declaration. The concept of collective judicial independence requires a greater measure of judicial participation in the central administration of the courts, including the preparation of budgets for the courts. IBA Standard 9 calls for exclusive judicial responsibility for judicial administration on the central level, or at least joint responsibility with the Executive. The Montreal Declaration provides that the main responsibility for court administration shall vest in the judiciary (Art. 2.40).

The concepts of personal independence and substantive independence of the individual judges are long-standing and universally recognized by law and by legal writers. The concept of collective independence of the judiciary which this writer has advocated in recent years[5] is now also widely accepted and is gaining further recognition.

The significance of the IBA Standards, and following them, the Montreal Declaration, was the recognition of the concept of collective independence of the judiciary, which calls for greater administrative independence of the judiciary in matters of central court administration including the participation in the formulation of the courts' budgets.[6] One of the important achievements of the IBA Standards and the Montreal Declaration was the emphasis on this most significant conceptual aspect of the principle of judicial independence in modern society.

d) Internal independence

Another aspect of judicial independence which in the past has not attracted sufficient attention is the internal independence of the judiciary. That is the independence of a judge from his judicial superiors and colleagues. This also transcends both the substantive and personal independence of the judge vis-a-vis his colleagues and superiors. IBA Standard 46 stresses this point; and, in the commentary for this IBA Standard, we recommended that separate and dissenting opinions be permissible in order to encourage internal judicial independence.[7] In this context it should be noted that IBA

---

5 See e.g. Shetreet, "The Administration of Justice: Practical Problems, Value Conflicts and Changing Concepts," 13 UBC L. Rev. 52 at 57-62 (1979); Shetreet, S., *Justice in Israel: A Study of the Israeli Judiciary*, ch. 15 (Martinus Nijhoff, 1994).

6 IBA Standards 10, 13. The Montreal Declaration Art. 2.41.

7 Cf. the Montreal Declaration Art. 2.03.

Standard 11 calls for a division of work among judges according to a predetermined plan, to be conducted by the head of the Court according to clearly defined rules. This Standard generally accepts the civil law concept of natural judge or Gesetzlicher Richter in German terminology.[8]

e) Judges and the executive

The protection of judicial terms of service from Executive interference is attained by the Standards in many ways. Executive participation in disciplinary procedures for judges is limited to referring or initiating complaints. The Executive is excluded from adjudication of such complaints. (Standard 4). The IBA Standards call for judicial removal by a judicial tribunal or by the Legislature upon a recommendation of a judicial tribunal.[9]

As to judicial appointments, IBA Standard 3 calls for appointment by a predominantly judicial body, but allows the continuation of judicial appointment by non-judicial bodies, in countries, where by long historic tradition, such a practice operates satisfactorily.[10]

The IBA Standards exclude the Executive from involvement in judicial matters and matters concerning judges (Standard 5), and vest the judiciary with the responsibility for such matters (Standard 8).[11] Thus the power to transfer a judge should be vested in a judicial authority (Standard 12),[12] and the execution process is put under judicial supervision (Standard 7).[13]

The Standards call for security of judicial remuneration and provision of adequate judicial salaries by regular and timely pay

---

8 Shetreet, S., *Justice in Israel: A Study of the Israeli Judiciary*, 518 (Martinus Nijhoff, 1994)

9 Cf. the Montreal Declaration Art. 2.33.

10 For the Montreal Declaration see Art. 2.14 which stresses professional participation in less specific terms.

11 The Montreal Declaration Art. 2.05, 2.07.

12 *Id.* Art. 2.18.

13 *Id.* Art. 2.47.

increases (Standard 14).[14] They prohibit a decrease of judicial salaries which is not part of an overall economic measure (Standard 15).[15] One of the most pressing problems of the Court system in recent times is the limited resources. Standard 13 responds to this issue and imposes on the relevant government a duty, to adequately finance the Court Services.[16]

The Standards impose on ministers a duty to refrain from adverse statements on judges (Standard 16), and call for cautious exercise of the power of pardon (Standard 17).[17]

Against the background of incidents of closing down courts, and frustrating of judicial decisions by Executive action, Standard 18 prohibits Executive pre-emption or frustration of judicial resolution of cases,[18] and provides that the Executive shall not have the power to close down or suspend the operation of the court system at any level.[19]

f) Security of judicial tenure

Probationary appointments are considered inconsistent with judicial independence, except for legal systems where judges are appointed without prior practical experience (Standard 23). Temporary appointments of judges are also rejected by the Standards, except where they exist by long historic, democratic tradition.[20] Part time judges can only be appointed, subject to proper safeguards.

Detailed principles are set down in Standards 27-32 concerning the procedure and the grounds for judicial discipline and removal.[21] The Standards call for a judicial procedure and a judicial tribunal

---

14 *Id.* Art. 2.21.

15 *Id.* Art. 2.21(c).

16 *Id.* Art. 2.41.

17 See generally the Montreal Declaration Art. 2.07.

18 Cf. Art. 2.07(d).

19 Cf. Art. 2.07(c).

20 *Id.* Art. 2.20.

21 Cf. generally *Id.* Art. 2.32-2.38.

for removal or discipline of judges. In cases of Legislative removal, the Standards call for a recommendation by a judicial tribunal.

g) The legislature and judges

The Standards recognize the problems emanating from adverse Legislative interference with judicial terms of office and judicial adjudication. Standard 19 prohibits retroactive legislative reversal of specific decisions.[22] Standard 20 qualifies the application of legislation, changing terms of judicial office or abolishing courts to future holders of office,[23] and not to present judges serving at the time of the passage of the legislation.[24]

h) Standards of judicial selection

Standard 26 provides that selection of judges should be based on merit. The commentary on this standard emphasizes that the selection process of judges should take into account the fair reflection on the bench of the various social classes, ethnic groups, geographical regions and ideological inclinations, so as to insure equality of access to judicial office, and a broad spectrum of community attitudes and feelings among the persons holding judicial office. This principle is expressly provided in the Montreal Declaration which requires that "the process and standards of judicial selection shall give due consideration to ensuring a fair reflection by the judiciary of the society in all its aspects" (Art. 2.13).

In conclusion, it is important to stress that the confirmation of the Jerusalem Approved Standards in New Delhi by the IBA Convention was a significant step in the improvement of the administration of justice and the better protection of human rights in our world, as were the confirmation of the Universal Declaration of the Independence of Justice and the UN Basic Principles of Judicial Independence.

---

22 *Id.* Art. 2.08.

23 *Id.* Art. 2.22.

24 *Id.* Art. 2.39.

5. The Principle of Judicial Independence in the Broader Conceptual Context

Judicial independence is one of the most significant principles which lies at the foundation of the court system. However, we should keep in mind that it stands together with other values and should be examined and analyzed in that broader context.

In order for the court to be able to resolve disputes impartially and to pass judgment which will be accepted by the rival parties, particularly when one of them is the government or one of its agencies, the court must be independent and must be free from any external pressure of influence. The protection of the courts from interference with the judicial process is secured by a number of principles.

In addition to the principle of judicial independence, which is at the center of our attention, there are other mechanisms and doctrines which assure the objectivity and impartiality of the judicial process, and which render the judge immune to external pressures and influence: the universal principle that a judge may not sit on trial in a case of bias; the doctrine of judicial immunity; the doctrine of *sub judice* excluding comment on pending trial which exist in some legal systems; parliamentary procedural rules have been established to govern the method and manner which the disputes are resolved by the courts. An elaborate and complex body of laws and rules govern court procedure and regulate the method of evaluating and weighing the facts and evidence submitted to the courts. In particular, these rules are concerned with safeguarding the rights of persons charged with violating the law. The purpose of these rules and laws is to attain justice and assure a fair trial by subjecting the conflicting claims to a vigorous and thorough investigation so as to ascertain the truth.

In spite of the differences between different judicial systems, there are a number of central values and fundamental principles that are shared by a majority of legal systems. The following principles and values lie at the foundation of the administration of justice: independence of the judiciary; high quality of the adjudicative process, assuring justice in the individual case and developing and maintaining sound rules of law in the legal system; maintaining public confidence; efficiency of the judicial process and efficiency of judicial administration; accessibility of the judicial system—providing judicial services to the public at a reasonable cost, providing means to go to court (legal aid) for those who are unable to afford it, and increasing the awareness of the people that they can go to court to defend their rights and to obtain redress for wrongs and providing geographical accessibility by establishing courts in remote areas as well.

An important value of the administration of justice is constitutional protection of judicial independence and other values so as to avoid violation by simple parliamentary majority or by executive legislation or actions. The value of constitutionality is not secured in many countries because the provision relating to courts, judges and administration of justice are not included in the constitution but only in ordinary legislation. The constitutional protection should include a prohibition against *ad hoc* or special tribunal, assurance of proper execution of court decisions, maintaining strict separation between the judiciary and the public service, a prohibition on detrimental changes of terms of office of judges, and a predetermined case assignment plan or the natural judge principle. All these principles should be part of the constitutional provision on judicial independence.[24a]

Here we focus on the central principle underlying the administration of justice, the independence of the judiciary. The meaning and content of this principle vary somewhat from one country to another depending on the system of government, local traditions and climate of political opinion. Indeed, even in the same country the concept of judicial independence carried different meanings in different periods. One need not go to the historical analysis of the 18th and the 19th century to show this point. This can clearly be illustrated by the American experience regarding executive control

---

24a Shetreet, supra note 8, at 515-519.

over court administration. Until 1939 the central responsibility for court administration at the Federal level in the US lay with the Attorney General. In that year this responsibility was vested in the hands of the US judiciary.[24b]

JUDICIAL INDEPENDENCE IN THE CHANGING JUDICIAL ROLE IN SOCIETY

1. The Judicial Function

The judiciary and the courts in any society are in a continuous process of change and transition. At one time the courts were viewed as an institution for dispute resolution entrusted with the task of "declaring" the law. Today, it is widely acknowledged that the judiciary performs the function of lawmaking; and that it is a branch of the government, playing a constitutional role of no less significance than other political branches of the government. In this context, social, political and economic changes in the recent times in most countries have confronted the courts and judges with new challenges and new problems.

The primary function of courts within any society is the resolution of disputes. At the heart of the judicial system lies the premise that self help by force is unacceptable so that parties who are unable to solve their dispute amicably may bring it before the court for an impartial settlement. This basic scheme of dispute resolution mechanism promotes good government and an orderly society, and ultimately, by resolving disputes and redressing violation of rights, the courts serve to develop new law and enforce existing laws.

In addition to the resolution of disputes, the courts also help to shape the society by pronouncing innovative and creative judg-

---

[24b] See Shetreet, *supra* note 8, at ch. 2.

ments. The courts perform an important function of educating and reprimanding the parties before the court, and on occasions, the general public and the social and political institutions. The impact on the system of court extends beyond the immediate parties to the cases. The very knowledge of the existence of the judicial system influences the conduct of the members of the society in business as well as personal relationships. This impact of the law has been referred to as the "shadow of the law". Judicial decisions are thus able to shape societal ideas and mores, to create laws, as well as to resolve specific disputes.

The courts resolve many types of disputes. In civil cases, the court has to determine the rights and duties of citizens.[25] Civil law governs the relations between private citizens and private corporations and defines their legal rights.[26] In contrast, in constitutional cases, the courts determine the rights and duties of individual citizens, and the duties, powers and immunities of the government or branches of the government, as set forth in the laws and the constitution of the land.[27] Constitutional law defines the state's political organization and powers, imposing substantive and procedural limitations on the state's exercise of its governing power. The resolution of a constitutional dispute may have a very broad impact on society. In criminal matters, the courts are asked to pass judgment on disputes when society's organized machinery of sanction is set in action against law violators.

2. *System Factors in Judicial Role*

The role of courts in society is shaped by the nature of disputes brought to the courts for resolution. It is also dependent on a host of

---

25 Shetreet, S., The Administration of Justice: Problems, Value Conflicts and Changing Concepts, 13 U.Brit.Colum. L.Re. 52, at 56 (1979); see also, Shetreet, *supra* note 8, at ch. 12.

26 Abraham, H.J., The Judicial Process: an Introductory Analysis of the Courts of the United States, England and France (1975).

27 Shetreet, (UBCL Rev.) *supra* note 25, at 56.

other factors. The individual inclinations of judges and the collective traditions significantly influence the role of courts in society. The role of courts in different societies depends also on the system factors prevailing in each society. The system factors include the nature of the constitutional system of that society and other circumstances prevailing at the time. In a society such as that of the United States, the judges are vested with broad powers as arbiters and interpreters of a set of values which are encompassed in the written constitution, the provisions of which are stated in general terms. In such a system, the scope of the judicial function is wider than in other societies which do not bestow upon the courts the function of constitutional arbitration. As Justice Cardozo states, "a constitution states, or ought to state, not rules for the passing hour, but principles for the expanding future".[28] Hence, in such a system, there is more room left for judicial innovation and creativity.

Depending on a society's system factors, the scope of the judicial role may range between two ends of the spectrum far apart: on the one end, judicial self restraint and excessive judicial deference to executive policy, and on the other, judicial activism and a wide scope of the judicial role, such as setting standards for prison administration, determining voting regions, administering school bussing plans, administering estates, and overseeing the reorganization of business.[29]

The role of the courts in a society may be shaped by legislative action or inaction. Where the legislature is diligent and expeditious in adopting the law to changing economic and social conditions, the role of the judiciary will be more limited. The courts will not be faced with new problems or major policy issues unforeseen by the existing law and requiring innovative judicial decision-making.

Generally, legislatures are slow to introduce law reforms to ensure that the law adapts to changing times and changing social and moral norms. This may be due to the preoccupation of the leg-

---

[28] Cardozo, The Nature of the Judicial Process, at 83.

[29] Mckay, Civil Litigation and the Public Interest, 31 U.Kan L.Rev. 355, at 359-360 (1983).

islature with political problems and a lack of interest in legislative reform in areas where no political pressure can be exerted. It may also be due to reluctance of the legislature to resolve political questions and its avoidance of being held politically responsible for their resolution.

Courts may have to deal with problems involving political and social issues where the political institutions have failed to resolve those problems in the ordinary political process. The legislature or the executive may shirk its political responsibilities by passing on such questions to the courts. As Sir Ninian Stephen put it, "elective bodies have much to fear if they have to decide such issues for themselves; wise politicians may well prefer to avoid the issue for fear of political backlash".[30]

Public expectations of the judicial role in society may influence the judges' perception of their role and may consequently influence their actual role in society. Public debate on judicial role and judges may help judges in understanding the public expectations of them.

3. The Changing Judicial Role

The recent decades have witnessed a constant trend of the expansion of the judicial role in society. The increasing judicialization has been the result of a number of factors and processes. Among these, one is the expansion of the welfare states. Primary and secondary legislation have been enacted to regulate the rights and duties of citizens and government authorities. This legislation has led to a corresponding expansion in litigation against government agencies, as well as the development of social rights, a typical by-product of the welfare state. The increased judicialization of society has also been brought about by the use of collective procedures (such as the class action). These procedures contributed to the

---

30 Stephen, Sir Ninian, Judicial Independence—A Fragile Bastion in S. Shetreet, (ed.), *Judicial Independence: The Contemporary Debate*, 529, at 543 (1985).

"massification" of the law and the legal process. In addition, industrialization has also increased the judicialization of society.[31]

Not only has there been a substantial increase in the judicialization of society, but there have also been changes in the functions of the courts. The traditional function of the court is dispute resolution, described as a "bipolar" contest between two interests to be resolved on a "winner-takes-all" basis.[32] The right and remedy are integrally related, with the compensation being derived from the harm caused by the wrong which gave rise to the cause of action. The traditional model of litigation is that of "a self-contained episode"[33] with the impact of the judgment limited to the parties before the court.

This traditional function has somewhat changed; courts have begun to take a more active role in policy-making at many levels.[34] The expanded judicial role has entrusted the courts with what has been termed "structural reform,"[35]where in place of individual plaintiffs and defendants, the whole political and social institutions come before the court.

The increase of concern in consumer issues, environmentalism and civil rights has led to an increase in legislation, a rise in the

---

31 Shetreet, S., Judicial Independence: Conceptual Dimensions and Contemporary Challenges in S. Shetreet, *supra* note 30, 590 at 593. M. Cappelletti, "Who Watches the Watchman? A Contemporary Study on Judicial Responsibility", 31 Am. J. Comp. L.1, (1983). For further discussion on the increased judicial role in society see Vescovi, E. La Independencia de la Magistratura en la Evolucion Actual del Derecho, in Habscheid W. (ed.) *Effectiveness of Judicial Protection and Constitutional Order*, 161, at 159-172 (1983). For an explanation of the "massification" of the judicial system in criminal cases, see Whitbread, II, D.H. (ed.), *Mass Production Justice and the Constitutional Ideal* (1970); Shetreet, *supra* note 8, ch. 22.

32 Chayes, The role of the Judge in Public Law Litigation, 89 Harv. L. Rev. at 1281 (1976).

33 Ibid, at 1283.

34 Fiss, E.G., The Supreme Court 1978 Term—Foreward: The forms of Justice, 93 Harv. L. Rev. 1 at 17 (1979); Mckay, *supra* note 29, at 364; Resnick, Managerial Judges, 96 Harv. L. Rev. 374 at 391 (1982).

35 Fiss, Ibid at 2 and 18-29.

number of administrative agencies and the volume of regulations, and consequently, in the number of conflicts which must be settled.[36] There is also a torrent of litigation raising issues of public concern, known as extended impact cases, or structural litigation. These cases are characterized by lengthy trials, resulting in remedies requiring protracted judicial supervision and affecting large numbers of people. Frequently, there are determinations on public law issues.

The trend of shifting policy and administrative decisions in environmental and other areas from the executive to the courts is not confined to common law systems with a written constitution, such as of the United States. As Professor Arens has reported[37] the same trend prevails in the Federal Republic of Germany's civil law system. Likewise, as has been noted by Justice Aharon Barak[38] and by this author[39] the same is true with regard to Israel, a jurisdiction without a written constitution.

The use of tribunals of inquiry and commissions or committees chaired by judges to inquire into political controversies and industrial disputes in England, Canada, Australia, India and Israel, is another illustration of the judicialization of politics, which in turn brings about, to a certain degree, the politicization of the judiciary.[40]

---

36 437 U.S. 153 (1978). For example, in the United States, there have been a number of cases in the environmental area where the courts have had to decide on difficult issues. In the case of *Tennessee Valley Authority* v. *Hill*, the Tellico Dam was closed down on the grounds that its operation might endanger a certain rare, endangered fish.

37 Arens, P., Recent Trends in German Jurisdiction: The Transfer of Political and Administrative Duties to the Courts, in S. Shetreet (ed.), *The Role of Courts in Society*, 97 at 98.

38 Barak, A., Constitutional Law Without a Constitution: The Role of the Judiciary, in S. Shetreet (ed.), Ibid. at 448.

39 Shetreet, S., Reflections on the Contemporary Trends of Judicial Role in Israeli Society, in S. Shetreet (ed.) Ibid, at 158; Shetreet, *supra* note 8, at ch. 22, ch. 23.

40 Shetreet, S., Judicial Independence and Accountability in Israel, 33 Int. & Comp. L.Q. 979, at 983-988 (1984); A. Segal, Judges as Chairmen of

The greater judicialization of society and the increasing number of cases coming before the courts have led to a search for ways to expedite judicial procedures, without sacrificing justice in the individual case. In the struggle for greater efficiency, the judge's role has become that of a manager heading a team of law clerks and secretaries, with his responsibilities shifting to a certain extent from the adjudicatory to the supervisory.[41] Greater attention is being paid to judicial mediation, to alternative dispute resolution methods and to introducing measures of making the adjudicative process more efficient and less costly.

An examination of the law and practice of various countries concerning issues which have a bearing on judges and judicial independence, reveals differences and even conflicts. These differences sometimes result from differences in concepts and perceptions, and sometimes stem from historical reasons or diversity of circumstances, including a lack of initiative to review old practices and introduce reform.

4. *Adjudication of Politically-charged Cases*

In many countries there has lately been a tendency towards referring heavy political issues to the courts for determination. In Israel, for example, the courts have had to deal with issues such as the failure to call Yeshiva students for compulsory army service; the introduction of summer daylight savings time; the validity of division of television time between political parties in an election campaign; the rights of a one-man faction in the Knesset; the time to put a no-confidence motion to the vote; the allocation of funds to Yeshiva institutions.[42] The Supreme Court of

---

Commissions of Inquiry, S. Shetreet (ed.) Ibid. See also Purvis, Extra-Judicial Activities: The Canadian Experience, S. Shetreet, (ed.), Ibid, at 356; Shetreet, *supra* note 8, at ch. 23

41 See generally S. Shetreet, Limits of Expeditious Justice in *Expeditious Justice* (1979), Canadian Institute of the Administration of Justice, 1 et seq: Cappelletti, *supra*, note 25, at 7-9.

42 See Shetreet, S. Ibid. See also Barak, *supra* note 38; Shetreet, *supra* note 8, at ch. 22.

Israel had to resolve the issue of the validity of a pardon granted to the heads of the Israeli security service (the Shin Bet) in the midst of heated public debate[43] and to adjudicate the dispute over the power of the Minister of Justice to refuse to surrender a criminal fugitive declared extraditable by the Courts.[44] In Germany, the administrative courts constantly adjudicate cases concerned with issues such as the licensing of large scale technical projects, including airports and atomic energy plants.[45]

In a democratic society, the greater recourse to the courts to solve political questions reveals a number of paradoxes. People turn to the judiciary because it is independent of politics, and in so doing, inevitably immerse it in politics.[46] The adjudicative function of the judge is to be insulated from societal pressures and realities of day-to-day politics, but his very function forces him to deal with such realities since the cases involve live persons, real life facts and actual problems of life.[47]

5. *Judicial Review of Legislation*

Judicial review of legislation is a phenomenon which has grown rapidly in Europe and elsewhere, particularly since the Second World War.[48] Its growth has been seen in many countries at the national level. It has also grown on the transnational level, with review of national legislation and its conformity with European Law being undertaken in many states of the European Union, and on the international level within the framework of the European Human Rights Convention.[49]

---

43 *Barsilay v. The Minister of Justice* 40 (3) P.D. 505 (1986).

44 *Aloni and Adler v. Minister of Justice* 42 (2) P.D. 1 (1987).

45 Arens P., *supra* note 37.

46 Cappelletti, M. The Expanding Role of Judicial Review in Modern Societies, in S. Shetreet (ed.), *supra* note 37, at 79.

47 Ibid at 92.

48 Ibid at 90-91.

49 See Cappelletti, *supra* note 37, at 51, for explanation of the growth of judicial review.

The problem that is raised by judicial review is the question of its legitimacy. As Professor Cappelletti has put it, the concern is not merely a problem of the procedural legitimacy of review as a process of controlling the conformity of one legal norm with another, but it is rather a problem of the compatibility of such a process and its lawmaking results with democratic values. The question touches upon the democratic legitimacy of judicial review and not its formal procedural legitimacy.[50]

Review of legislation is undoubtedly needed in order to ensure the effectiveness of a constitution and make it binding on the political branches. In order for the review power to be effective it can only be entrusted to those who are unaccountable for their substantive decision making to political power, that is the judges. Some have advocated caution in the approach to judicial review. It is recognized, even by its advocates, that it leads to the inevitable politicization of the judicial branch.[51] But, in spite of this paradox, as long as there are constitutional judges to act in order to enforce fundamental freedoms, one cannot deny the democratic legitimacy of judicial review.

I support the less restrictive approach on this issue of judicial review of legislation. It seems that societies all over the world have come to recognize the advantages of adjudicative determinations. They recognized the shortcomings of entrusting an appointed, seemingly non-democratic institution, with the resolution of politically charged issues and the making of policy choices, but at the same time they realize that the alternative is to leave the field open for majoritarian tyranny, or to political convenience-decisions by the political branches, unlimited by effectively enforceable shields and boundaries.

In this respect it is important to emphasize the view expressed by Norman Redlich. He submits that the legitimacy of judicial review can be defended not only by the classical arguments set forth in defense of judicial review of statutes, but rather by an argument

---

50 Ibid at 92.

51 Ibid.

based on a different assumption. All the traditional arguments in defense of the legitimacy of the exercise of judicial authority in a democratic society accept the premise "that judges really are not instruments of popular will, and that legislatures and elected executives are".[52] Redlich questions this assumption and suggests that "in the contest for legitimacy, the legislative and executive branches have no claim to sole ownership of the democratic mantel".[53] He reasons that it is illusory to think that laws of legislatures or executive decisions always represent the popular will. Moreover, he dismisses the assumption that an independent judiciary has no links to the people. Rather, judges are instruments of democracy[54] when they are appointed by a democratic system.

There are interrelations between the judiciary and the legislature. When a problem remains unresolved by legislative enactment, the courts have to fill the vacuum. On many occasions, the legislature is unwilling to deal with particular issues, and it is left to the courts to deal with these matters. To illustrate legislative inaction it is possible to mention the question of legal aid for defendants in criminal proceedings. In England, the Legal Aid Act of 1949, extending earlier legislation, provided legal aid for defendants, and the legal aid scheme was extended to cover wide areas, including office consultation. In the United States, on the other hand, the legislature did not act to resolve this question and it was left to the courts to establish the constitutional right to counsel in criminal proceedings.

Members of a legislature may wish, for political or moral reasons, to avoid voting on a question which is morally or politically controversial. In a coalition government, as in Israel, the political factions may not agree on how to resolve a particular question, and

---

52 Redlich, Norman, Judges as Instruments of Democracy, S. Shetreet (ed.) *supra* note 37, at 152.

53 Ibid at 153.

54 Ibid at 155-157.

so, by default of the political parties, the question will be shifted to the courts, hence turning it into a legal issue.[55]

In West Germany, the courts have been seized with quasi-legislative questions in cases where the legislature is hesitant in passing laws concerning controversial matters. This is particularly so in the area of labor law, which is mainly judge-made.[56]

6. Judicial Selection and the Principle of Fair Reflection

The importance of the high personal and professional standards of the people selected to sit on the bench has always been recognized as a prerequisite for the proper administration of justice and for maintenance of the rule of law. Jewish law places the emphasis on ethical standards rather than on intellectual qualifications. As Professor Shilo points out, Maimonides, the leading Jewish law scholar, enumerated seven qualities which a judge must have: wisdom, fear of God, disdain of money, love of truth, love of his fellow man and a good reputation.[57] It is beyond dispute that judges must comply with high standards, both at the ethical and the intellectual levels. The controversy seems to lie on the legitimacy of taking into account the ideological inclinations of the judges, their ethnic background or their geographical origin in a federal state.

In the American context, it is recognized, as Professor Mckay points out, that the President is fully entitled to nominate to the bench and to other federal offices, "individuals whose general political philosophy is compatible with that of the President".[58] There is also a strong opinion[59] that the Senate has equal power to screen the President's nominees not only on the grounds of their personal

---

55 See Shetreet, *supra* note 39.

56 Arens, P., *supra* note 37, at 104.

57 See Shilo, Shmuel, The Role of Judges in Jewish Law, S. Shetreet (ed.), *supra* note 37, also reference with approval, Mckay, Robert, Appointments and Disappointment Judicial Selection in the Federal Courts, S. Shetreet (ed.), Ibid, at 212.

58 Ibid at 213.

59 Ibid at 213-214, and Redlich, *supra* note 52, at 155-56

and professional qualifications, but also on the grounds of their ideological inclinations. Professor Mckay forcefully argues this view: "The Constitution gives the President the authority to nominate and the Senate the authority to confirm. Unless either partner in the process is less equal than the other, for which there is no constitutional basis, the Senate is equally entitled with the President to assert its views about matters of judicial philosophy."[60]

The approach is imperative because, as Professor Redlich rightly put it, "judges are part of the dialogue". They "are partners in the common endeavors of representative government".[61] As such they must not be removed from the community and must not espouse to a narrow ideological philosophy of one part of the community, but should reflect a broad cross-section of society.

The United States is not unique in its concern for a fairly reflective judiciary, and particularly in its Supreme Court. As Professor Habscheid outlines,[62] this concern is shared by the Federal Republic of Germany where the Federal Constitutional Court is elected in a process which maintains a careful ideological balance in its composition.

Professor Mckay and Professor Redlich speak of the use of ideological consideration as a qualifying mechanism, to check Presidential avowedly ideological nominations. For a number of years I have advanced the thesis of the principle of fair reflection,[63] that is, the judiciary must be fairly reflective of the society it judges in terms of ideological inclinations, geographical distribution, cultural traditions and ethnic composition. I preferred the term "reflective" to the term "representative", since judges, unlike legislators or elected executives, do not "represent". Likewise, the

---

60 Mckay, Ibid at 214.

61 Redlich, *supra* note 59, at 156.

62 Habscheid, W., The Selection of Judges to the German Federal Constitutional Court and to the Supreme Federal Courts in Germany, in S. Shetreet (ed.), *supra* note 37, at 232-233.

63 Shetreet, S., Who Will Judge? Reflections on the Process and Standards of Judicial Selection, *61 Australian Law Journal* 766-778 (1987); Shetreet, S., Justice in Israel (1994)

courts should not be numerically representative; "reflective", therefore, is a more appropriate term to indicate this idea.

The principle of fair reflection is both positive and negative in nature. It imposes on those participating in the selection of judges a duty to ensure that the judiciary is reflective, and must avoid a situation of a narrow composition of the judiciary. The approach advanced by Professor Mckay and Professor Redlich, on the other hand, is of a negative nature only. The Senate may legitimately reject the President's nominees if they belong to the narrow ideological philosophy shared by the President. Since I first advanced this thesis of the principle of fair reflection[64] its validity has been further strengthened. It was strengthened by the contemporary controversy instigated by the rigorous appointment policy of President Reagan, consciously selecting believers in the narrow constitutional interpretation ("original intention" doctrine). This debate clearly supported the negative part of the principle of fair reflection that the judiciary must not reflect one ideological inclination. The positive part of the principle is equally important and is the other side of the same doctrinal coin. The detailed analysis of Justice Barak[65] of the process of judicial reasoning clarified the importance of fair reflection of the judiciary. As Justice Barak explains, judges decide cases upon background understandings and assumptions based on fundamental values of the system. Those understandings are judge-made and are based on the interpretation of the judge. If the judiciary is not reflective of society as a whole, the adjudication may be based on background understandings strongly colored by a narrower set of values. The profound examination of the constitutional adjudication offered by Professor Neuborne provides further clarification of the sophisticated nature of the judicial process and

---

64 Shetreet, S., Judicial Independence, Background Paper for the International Bar Association Conference, Lisbon, May 11-15, 1981, Lisbon, Portugal at p. 8 (unpublished). See also Shetreet, *supra* note 31, at 633-635.

65 Supra, note 38.

the importance of the public official—the judge—who is charged with the function of decision making.[66]

7. *Fair and Expeditious Justice*

The courts are under a duty to provide fair and expeditious justice. The values of fairness and efficiency are sometimes in conflict and care has to be exercised to resolve properly this conflict.[67] The increasing workload of the courts raises the issue of the proper approaches to writing of judicial opinions as well as the policies concerning the publication of judicial opinions. It must be admitted that the existing practice of writing and reporting judicial opinions calls for careful revision.[68]

Another aspect of the administration of justice which deserves careful attention and critical examination is the use of law clerks at appellate courts. The practice raises the serious issue of the appropriate boundaries of the delegation of judicial power to non-judicial staff, whose input into adjudication is internal and not subject to comments by the parties to the case.[69] A number of suggestions have been advanced, such as opening the work of the appellate staff attorneys to public view and allowing the parties to comment on the work of the appellate staff.[70]

Judges and the public in general must be aware and take care of the doctrinal and ethical problems involved in the present practice.

In their pursuit of fair and expeditious justice, those in charge of judicial administration have not placed sufficient emphasis on judicial mediation.[71] Modern computer technology can offer remedies

---

66 Neuborne, The Origin of Rights: Constitutionalism, the State and the Democratic Process, in S. Shetreet (ed.), *supra* note 37, at 187.

67 Shetreet, *supra*, note 25.

68 Schuchman, The Writing and Reporting of Judicial Opinions, in S. Shetreet (ed.), Ibid, at 319.

69 Thompson, E. and T., Research Staff at Appellate Courts, Function, Personalities and Ethical Restraints, S. Shetreet (ed.) Ibid at 244.

70 Ibid, at 260.

71 Galanter, M., A Settlement Judge, Not a Trial Judge—Judicial Mediation in the United States, in S. Shetreet (ed.), Ibid, at 295.

to the long standing problem of disparity of sentences, which introduces both unfairness and inefficiency to the administration of criminal justice.

FREEDOM OF EXPRESSION

1. Free Speech and Democracy

A democratic system of government is largely dependent upon the protection of the freedom of expression. Free speech is the safeguard for the transparency of government, for public accountability of public officials, higher and lower, and for the competition of ideas in the free market of ideas.

The social significance of freedom of expression is not confined to the political level, for the protection of political and public speech. Freedom of expression is equally important for the commercial and economic sphere. Commercial speech is very important for the effective operation of a market economy and business life.

Freedom of expression is essential for governmental accountability but is also very significant for corporate and professional accountability. Our life is not only governed by government officials. It is also dominantly influenced by corporations which sometimes control important aspects of our lives, and professionals who equally perform important social functions. The ability of society and its institutions to supervise misconduct of corporate officials or professionals is an important mechanism for the exercise of social controls over economic and professional spheres. This includes supervision of corporate practices regarding safety of products, insider trading, environmental quality and golden parachute contracts for senior officials of corporations. This also includes control of professions such as the medical or legal professions, which affect the life and health of the citizens.

2. *Balancing of Interests*

The main thrust of the protection of free speech lies in the striking of the proper balance between the value of assuring freedom of expression and other competing values, which are no less important for society. The competing values include the right for a good reputation and against unjustified libel, national security, the prevention of incitement to violence, the assurance of morality and of minors, and the assurance of a fair trial.

The trend worldwide in recent times has been to extend the scope of protection of free speech at the expense of the competing values. Thus the concept of a public figure laid down in *Sullivan* v. *New York Times*[72] has carved an exception for greater freedom of speech regarding public officials. This concept has been accepted in other jurisdictions.

3. *National Security and Free Speech*

Freedom of expression has always faced the challenge of national security. The trend has been toward the expansion of the scope of protection of free speech even in the face of security decisions and considerations. The British have been less than successful in curbing the publication of a book written by former secret agent (*Spycatcher*).[73] The Israelis have been equally unsuccessful in preventing publication of a book by a former Mossad agent (Victor Ostrovsky).

The prevention of the media from full coverage of wars was sharply criticized. The British were criticized for their restriction of the press in the Falklands War[74] and the United States' restrictions on the press were also sharply attacked for their withholding of

---

72 376 U.S. 254.

73 Peter Wright, Spycatcher: The Candid Autobiography of A Senior Intelligence Officer (1987); Lord Oliver of Aylmerton, Spycatcher: Confidence, Copyright and Contempt, in S. Shetreet, Free Speech and National Security, 23 (Martinus Nijhoff, 1991); Fysh (ed.), *The Spycatcher Cases* (1989).

74 Y. Cohen, Information Policy and the Falklands Conflict, in Shetreet, *Id.*, at 143.

information in the Grenada Operation.[75] The Gulf War (1991) coverage was almost a live war as were many other wars.

The jurisprudential developments on the scope of judicial review of security decisions, including censorship decisions, are very significant indeed. In the past courts have interfered in security decisions only when the court found that the authority exceeded its jurisdiction, or breached the duty to act in good faith.[76] In recent times the courts have been willing to review security decisions on a much broader scope. In some jurisdictions the courts have ruled that the causes and scope of judicial review of security decisions is equal to the review of other decisions, and security decisions should not be accorded special protection.[77]

4. *Controlling Excessive Centralization of Media*

The importance of the media in society has resulted in the application of monopoly rules on the media industry. In many jurisdictions there is a limit on the extent of centralization of control by one corporation over newspapers and radio and television stations. The limits on cross ownership of radio, television and newspapers is aimed at the prevention of centralization of media power in the hands of few, too few. Such centralized control is not only detrimental from the economic point of view, but it is also warranted from a democratic viewpoint.

The increasing power of media, and the owners of the media has introduced new legal dimensions to the concepts of the regulation of the press. There have been suggestions that the press should be subjected to some public law norms, and not only to private law

---

75 Redlich, Can a "Free" Press Cover War?, in Shetreet, *supra* note 73, at 155; Diane Zimmerman, "Private" War: The Problem of Access, in Shetreet, *id.*, at 181.

76 Shetreet, S., The Scope of Judicial Review of National Security Considerations in Free Speech and Other Areas: Israeli Perspectives, in Shetreet, *supra* note 73, at 41.

77 Schnitzer, V., Chief Military Censor (1988) 42 (ii) P.D. 617. See Z. Segal, Security Censorship: Prior Restraint (Schnitzer Case) in Shetreet, *supra* note 73, at 207.

norms. This has also been implemented regarding radio and television by the concept of access of opposing views to these electronic media.[77a] But the emerging idea is that the press should be subject to other public law norms in terms of fairness, prohibition of misuse of economic power, against or by the press, such as by an advertisement boycott.

An essential element of freedom of expression is access to information. Dramatic developments took place in a number of jurisdictions, providing what is normally termed freedom of information, i.e. access to governmental data and information bases. This right of access is part and parcel of the broader concept of freedom of expression.[78]

5. *Free Speech and Incitement against Democracy*

A major challenge that is facing society is the incitement to hatred and violence, and particularly religious speech inciting to violence. Israeli society, which has experienced a major crisis following the assassination of the late Prime Minister, Yitzhak Rabin, and societies which experience similar crisis, have to approach the issue of the limits of free speech and incitement against democracy in different ways than other societies that have not experienced such a traumatic social and political event. It is my view that in the same society, in different times that are not colored by such traumatic events, the analysis of the issue, legally and socially and politically, may and should be different. This is because the law is a social mechanism employed by society and its institutions to regulate behavior, to keep the fabric and the structure of the system of government, and the well-being of the members of society.

77a *Red Lion Broadcasting Co.* v. *Federal Communications Commission*, 395 U.S.367 (1973).

78 See eg. 5 U.S.C. 552 (Freedom of Information Act) 50 U.S.C. 421-26 (Intelligence Identities Act); See P.G. Chevigny, "Information, the Executive and the Politics of Information", in Shetreet (ed.), *supra* note 73, at 130.

Writers have analyzed the response of German society and its legal institutions in the post Second World War and Nazi Era. Israel had to also face the challenge of confronting racist and anti-democratic actions, and delegitimatization of the State of Israel.

During the late 70's and the early 80's, the Israeli political and legal system did well in defending itself from extreme parties such as *Kach*, Rabbi Meir Kahana's movement. After the first attempt to disallow the *Kach* party from running in the elections failed, as the Court reversed the Election Committee's decision[79], the Knesset quickly acted by amending Art. 7(a) of the *Basic Law: The Knesset* to disqualify from running a racist party, as well as parties denying the Jewish character of the State of Israel, and required all parties running for election to abide by the standards of Art. 7(a) through a similar amendment to Art. 63 of the *Elections Act*. In the meanwhile, MP Meir Kahana continued his sedition against the Arabs. Attempts to deny him entering racist motions or extrapolating his racist and seditious views on the Knesset's podium or on national television were also denied by the Court.[80]

Again, the Legislature responded, by amending its regulations in order to include Reg. 134(c) which allowed the Speaker of the Knesset to disallow motions which did not conform to the regulation whose content is the same as that of Art 7(a). The first success of these actions was when Kahana's attempt to get the regulation annulled failed, as the Court upheld it.[81] The second success was not late in following, as the Court denied Kahana's party, *Kach*, from participating in the 1988 elections.[82] It is worthwhile noting that an appeal to disallow the *Hadash* party from running the same elections

---

79 See E.A 2,3/84 *Neiman v. The Chairman of the Election Committee for the Eleventh Knesset* **PD 39(2) 225**.

80 H.C.J 742/84 *Kahana v. Speaker of the Knesset* **PD 39(4) 85**; H.C.J 306/85 *Kahana v. Speaker of the Knesset* **PD 39(4) 485** and H.C.J 399/85 *Kahana v. The Executive Board of the Broadcasting Authority* **PD 41(3) 255**.

81 H.C.J 669/85 *Kahana v. The Speaker of the Knesset* **PD 40(4) 393**.

82 E.A. 1/88 *Neiman v. The Chairman of the Election Committee for the Twelfth Knesset* **PD 42(4) 177**.

was denied.[83] This sequence of events came as a continuation of the *El Ard* decision, which applied the theory of the "defensive democracy" that had previously been employed in Germany. The Israeli society relied not only on the political process in order to institutionally face off extremism, but employed legal tools in order to protect democracy.

While it can be said that the socio-political Israeli system created effective institutional protection against anti-democratic or racist parties, one cannot say that the Israeli system of government rose to the challenge of the extreme anti-democratic extra-parliamentary general. In this matter it can be said, and I was personally a part of the system of government which was supposed to face up to the extra-parliamentary extremism, that the institutional machinery of government failed in providing a sensible solution to the extra-parliamentary extremism.

The ineffectiveness of the machinery of justice vis-a-vis the extra-parliamentary extremism, which was supported by the parliamentary leadership (the billboard depicting Rabin as an SS officer occurred in a rally which included the top leaders of the *Likud* party). A week before the assassination, the late Prime Minister Yitzchak Rabin asked the Legal Advisor to the Government how it was possible that a man who had broken off his car's symbol had been released from custody (Itamar Ben-Gvir), and received only evasive answers, despite the fact that Israeli law and practice allows keeping suspects in custody for longer periods.

Before the assassination, not only was the penal code not enforced, or at least put to judicial test, thus giving the courts the opportunity to set the limits, but even the disciplinary rules pertaining to office holders were not enforced against those who broke them, according to the explicit interpretation of the Legal Advisor to the Government. Dayanim and Rabbis on the governmental payroll signed petitions of *Pikuach Nefesh*; other Rabbis discussed the applicability of *Din Rodef* on the Prime Minister, yet no one in the

---

83 E.A 2/88 *Ben-Shalom v. The Chairman of the Election Committee for the Twelfth Knesset* **PD 43(4) 221**.

law enforcement system protested or tried to stop them, and the situation did not change even after the tragic assassination.

6. Political Speech, Commercial Speech and Religious Speech

Political speech is considered by many jurisdictions as deserving wider protection than commercial speech. This approach has been advanced in the United States in several cases.[84] The same approach has been adopted in other jurisdictions.[85] It is also generally accepted that academic speech is accorded wide protection, and so is artistic speech.

The issue of incitement against democracy in the Israeli context is very much associated with religious speech, that is, expression of opinion about the halachic law by religious leaders such as Rabbis, and dayanim—judges of state religious courts. In recent years they have often expressed halachic opinions on issues such as killing of a gentile (*Eido Elba* case),[86] the validity of withdrawal from territory in peace agreements (*Pikuach Nefesh*) and the expression of opinion whether the late PM Rabin was a "rodef", that is—someone who pursued another in order to harm him, and therefore, by halacha, it is permissible to use force, including even causing his death, in order to prevent him from causing danger to others.

---

84 Most notably: *Virginia State Board of Pharmacy et al* **425 U.S 748**; see also: *Ohralik v. Ohio State Bar Association* **436 U.S.447**; *Metromedia Inc. v. San Diego* **453 U.S. 490**: and by some scholars—Shiffrin S., "*The First Amendment and Economic Regulation; Away from the General Theory of the First Amendment*" **78 Northwestern U.L.R (1983), 1212**; Neuborne B., "*The First Amendment and Government Regulation of Capital Markets*" **55 Brooklyn L.R (1989) 5**.

85 See e.g. Israeli jurisprudence: *Kidum* case, H.C.J. 606/93 *Kidum Entrepreneurship and Publishing (1981) Inc. v. The Broadcasting Authority* **PD 48(2) 1**; and the case of *Maio Simun*—H.C.J. 5118/95 *Maio Simun Marketing Advertisement and Public Relations Inc. v. The Second Authority For Radio and Television* [not yet published].

86 In Criminal Appeal 2831/95 *Eido Elba v. State of Israel* (not yet published), a rabbi was convicted of racism for the publication of an article arguing that Jewish law allows killing a gentile.

On first glance, religious speech should be accorded similar protection to that given to academic speech. But there is one difference in terms of content, which distinguishes between religious speech and academic speech. Academic speech is an expression of opinion by an academic person that has no binding power in the eyes of his audience or readers. He enjoys personal prestige and professional status, but his speech has merely convincing power, morally or academically. Religious speech, on the other hand, has binding power in the eyes of the followers of the religious leader. The examination of the probability of the religious expression of incitement against democracy causing action (consequentiality) is legally and conceptually relevant according to the established principles of the unprotected speech. I refer to the test of clear and present danger[87] or the near certainty test in the *Schnitzer* case.[88]

Presumably one could say that there is a need to give greater protection to weak minorities and disabled persons, as they lack power, while publicly elected officials should not receive such greater protection. Yet, in my opinion, in certain situations even heads of state and CEOs of corporations, and even public figures, become vulnerable due to their position. It is of interest to note, that although the American First Amendment and the German Criminal Code seem as polar as one could imagine, they eventually reach the same conclusion, by use of the same general logic—the more the target of a defamatory statement is acting in public, the higher the thresholds for a criminal conviction of a person attacking such a public figure in his or her capacity, because a person must accept more interferences with his honor while he is trying to create public opinion.[89] Different approaches taken by legal systems are a direct consequence of their past, and coupled with the knowledge that each country is unique, it is easy to realize that today, the Israeli legal system must find a new balance point, for the price of prevention is

---

87 *Kol Ha'am v. Minister of Interior* **7 P.D. 871 (1953).**

88 Schnitzer, see *supra* note 77.

89 Art. 5 of the German Basic Law; *New York Times v. Sullivan* 376 U.S. 254.

always smaller than the price of rebuilding and healing the scars, and so I believe that incitement against heads of state should be limited in order to preserve democracy. One might ask where is it better to err—in more protection of democracy or less protection of it.

CONCLUSION

The examination here of the principle of judicial independence and the right of freedom of expression illustrates that these two issues pose a challenge to society, to its political leadership, to its judicial institutions, and to the legal and academic professions. They all have to join in an intensive effort to develop new concepts that adopt the principles to changing times and changing circumstances so that law can go hand in hand with society and provide adequate responses to society's needs.

The Role of the Lawyer in Medical Ethics

Sheila A.M. McLean

The ancient jurisprudential debate about the relationship between law and morality or ethics has seldom been more relevant than it now is. Increasingly, law is expected, invited, even required to enter arenas which were previously regarded as the exclusive territory of other disciplines. The tradition of leaving professional ethics solely to the professional group involved has modified with the changing face of medical practice and the increased intervention of government in health care. Society and individuals have moved away from a willing subordination to any one professional group to a more challenging and demanding position. As is generally the case, the struggle to be heard, to vindicate rights and interests is successful only to the extent that the individual, or group, can gain access to and utilise appropriate mechanisms—most notably legal ones. Ultimately, no matter the conflict, it is to the law that we look for resolution.

Thus, although professionals such as doctors continue to shape and substantially control their own professional practice, it is no longer the case that they do so without the light of legal scrutiny being shone on them. Most publicly, this has resulted in an increase in litigation in many countries, but it has also led to a subtle but powerful intervention into the profession's own ethical standards. For many years, doctors sought answers to ethical dilemmas by reference to the Hippocratic Oath. Nowadays, the wisdom of reliance on this ancient oath is challenged by legal and social reform and physicians cannot ignore the impact that legal development or law reform has on their professional practice. The modern statement of medical ethics, taken from the work of Beauchamp and Childress,[1] provides a framework, based on concepts such as beneficence, non-maleficence, autonomy and justice, which shares and overlaps with the aspirations of the law.

In addition, no matter how health care systems are funded, the issue of resources is increasingly influenced by the legal structure by which medicine and its practice are controlled. To an extent, of course, this last is a matter of politics and pragmatics but it is also a matter of ethics. The drive to function in a certain way or within externally imposed constraints affects the underlying tone of medical practice and may, for some at least, provoke the kind of tensions in practice which amount to a direct challenge to previously held ethical commitments. The patient population is, for example, changing; more people are living longer and suffering the concomitant problems of old age. This group is increasingly demanding of resources, but how is the doctor to judge who should receive therapy when increasing demands are not met by increased resources? Advances in medicine make the decision whether or not to offer treatment one of the most difficult, and one which is increasingly being debated in courts. Decisions which were previously taken in relative privacy and guided by the individual ethics of the physician are now the subject of legal analysis—not infrequently at the instigation of the doctor.

Moreover, the capacity to sustain life which would otherwise have been lost has generated a whole new set of dilemmas. Reference to ancient oaths, developed when such dilemmas were unthought of and unthinkable, is now widely recognised as

---

1 Beauchamp, T.L. ad Childress, J.S., *Principles of Biomedical Ethics*, (4th Ed.), OUP, 1994.

essentially unhelpful.[2] The modern patient or clinician will rather now turn to the law to provide the framework within which decisions are appropriately made—effectively, our law is now performing a role beyond describing what is good or bad, culpable or innocent; it is, like it or not, shaping standards which can broadly be described as ethical and which doctors are expected to follow in preference to their own internal etiquette or ethics.

In this chapter I will use some examples to show two things: first that legal analysis has a role to play in shaping ethical practice, and second that this role can truly be described as essential and valuable (assuming that it is adequately played) since it is to the law that we look for the kind of disinterested decision-making which is needed if complex and sensitive dilemmas are to be resolved in a principled or ethical manner. This is not to commend an overly intrusive legal response but rather is to set the matter in context. In essence, the law straddles two distinct but related sets of interests—those of the individual and those of the state—and must on occasion adjudicate within them as well as between them. This is particularly relevant to medical ethics, since codes of medical ethics from Hippocrates to current international agreements have tended to emphasise the individual over the community to which he/she belongs.

Concepts such as autonomy, self-determination and privacy dominate the discussion of the relationship between health care providers and their clients. Increasingly, also, health care systems are focused on individualised matters such as patient choice. Indeed, in the Twentieth Century many political and social manifestos have opted for the individualising model as the best and most effective way to press their claims. Perhaps most notably, this was the case with the women's movement. However, a more recent trend has been to recognise the inherent flaws in the complete atomisation of the individual from the society of which they are a part and to revise previously firmly held commitments to the individual as supreme.

---

2 For further discussion, see Rachels, J., *At the End of Life: Euthanasia and Morality*, OUP, 1986; McLean, S.A.M. and Britton, A., *The Case for Physician Assisted Suicide*, London, Pandora Press, 1997.

Nonetheless, this limited ideological shift of emphasis has not moved the individual from centre stage. For example, the Council of Europe's Convention on Human Rights and Biomedicine[3] begins in traditional style with a reaffirmation of the supremacy of individual rights. Article 1 says 'Parties to this Convention shall protect the dignity and identity of all human beings and guarantee everyone, without discrimination, respect for their integrity and other rights and fundamental freedoms with regard to the application of biology and medicine.', and Article 2 confirms that 'The interests and welfare of the human being shall prevail over the sole interest of society and science.' Thus, whilst recognising that the individual and the state may come into conflict, it is the intention that the individual remains the central focus, whatever the changing face of medicine, health care provision and disease.

This domination of the individual over the State has its roots in experiences and events far removed from the merely clinical setting. History shows that States and other organisations can, if sufficiently powerful, abuse the individual, and for this reason the language of human rights has become the 20th Century's most powerful political tool.[4] Advances in medicine have added to deontological discourse—the right to life, the 'right' to choose when to die, the 'right' to reproduce, and so on. However dubious their status as rights, patients and potential patients have come to address their clinical care as a matter of individual rights and interests. And, drawing its roots from the Hippocratic Oath, a kind of privacy or confidentiality right is widely accepted as being the cornerstone of the doctor/patient relationship.

---

3 Convention for the Protection of Human Rights and Dignity of the Human Being with regard to the Application of Biology and Medicine, DIR/JUR (96)14, Strasbourg, November 1996; for a discussion of the Draft Convention, see McLean, S.A.M. and Elliston, S., 'Bioethics, the Council of Europe and the Draft Convention', *European J. Health Law,* 2: 5, 1995.

4 For discussion, see for example, Campbell, et al (eds), *Human Rights: From Rhetoric to Reality,* Oxford, Basil Blackwell, 1986.

In part, it is the contention of this chapter that rights discourse is increasingly under threat—albeit a subtle one—in contemporary health care. The identification of new diseases and the technological advances made by medicine have significance well beyond the individual patient, and may affect the rights and interests of others, leading to the possibility of the development of plausible arguments which would favour the rights of States or communities over those of individuals. In examining the role of the law in medical ethics this conclusion is highly significant. The mere fact that such tensions are possible provides one major reason why the law should be involved at all in contributing to the shape of health care and its provision. Not only can legal analysis provide an additional form of enquiry, but it comes to the problem both deeply rooted in respect for persons and vastly experienced in resolving disputes between different interests.

In order to demonstrate this potential tension, two examples—HIV/AIDS and the 'new' genetics—will be explored briefly. Although at first sight these are significantly different, it will be argued here that they point up similar potentialities for conflict between individual and the community whose resolution needs to be in the hands of a wider set of ethics than the merely clinical. This is so because the issues involved, and the consequences which flow from them are directly congruent with basic legal principles, such as privacy and respect for persons. Both knowledge of HIV status and information about genetic status have direct and profound effects on the individual. Each could represent a death sentence, or at least predict the demands which the individual may or will place of health care resources. The person who is HIV positive will certainly die if this develops into full-blown AIDS and just as certainly will require access to expensive medical care, for however long. The individual who carries a gene which will result in the development of a condition such as Huntington's Disease will also predictably require care from the community at some stage in their lives.

From the perspective of the individual, of course, it is probably most desirable that their condition is maintained in secrecy. For the person who is HIV positive, this is largely because of the stigma and possible discrimination which flow from this tragic diagnosis. But from the perspective of the State, it may be thought that there are compelling reasons for disclosure. These reasons might include the potential harm to other individuals if the person affected continues with a lifestyle which creates the risk of the condition spreading. Estimates about the number of people currently affected with HIV and those who are likely to become infected clearly make HIV/AIDS a public health threat on a large scale and states may argue that their obligation to all members of the community can or should outweigh their obligation to protect the privacy of the individual.

Indeed, to an extent, this attitude is already prevalent in some countries. The mandatory testing of immigrants for HIV status is described by those states which endorse it as a public health strategy. The mandatory testing of Russians who have been out of that country for three months is endorsed in new legislation—again on public health justifications. Leaving aside whether or not such measures could ever achieve this purported aim, their value has been endorsed by a number of countries with different ideological traditions, for example Australia.

Still other countries have opted for a more individual centred approach, although the extent to which this stance will be maintained should the threat become greater is unclear. In the United Kingdom, for example, AIDS has not yet been made a notifiable disease. Doctors are not, therefore, required to inform a central bureaucracy when a diagnosis is made. The ostensible reason for this is that, even if that information could be maintained in strict secrecy (in itself a doubtful proposition), disclosure of HIV status as a routine would have a profound impact on those who fear that they may be infected. Such people, it is said, would be reluctant to come forward for testing and for counselling if they knew that their status would be reported on. For the moment, then, the care offered directly to the individual takes precedence over any perceived benefit to other individuals or the community as a whole.

Equally, in the case of *X v. Y*,[5] an English Court issued an order preventing the publication in a newspaper of the names of two doctors who were HIV positive and continuing to practice medicine. Although the judgement was not entirely dependent on matters of privacy, the court nonetheless was unwilling to use public interest arguments as a rationale for disclosure. The newspaper argued that HIV, especially if a health care provider was infected, represented a significant problem. It was, they said, in the public interest that such information should be made available. However, the court drew a sharp distinction between what the public wanted to know and what was in the public interest, thus requiring that confidentiality be maintained, at least to the extent that the doctors in question could not be identified in the press.

This position seems to be in line with the Council of Europe's Convention, which states in Article 10: 'Everyone has the right to respect for private life in relation to information about his or her health.' and provides that restrictions on this may occur only in exceptional cases and in the interests of the patient.

Equally important considerations are raised by rapid advances in genetic knowledge and the progress of the Human Genome Project.[6] It is estimated that by early next Century (probably within 10 years from now) the entire genetic map will have been drawn. Each individual's unique make-up will be readable as easily as taking a sample of saliva and analysing it in a laboratory. The potential benefits of this are manifest, as—unfortunately—are the possible problems.[7] Few societies manage successfully to give equal status to those who are disabled or different in any way. Discrimination can only increase unless principles are elucidated now which render it unlikely. But also, other interests come into play which force, as in

---

5 [1988] 2 All E.R. 648.

6 For discussion of this project, see Wilkie, T., *Perilous Knowledge: The Human Genome Project and its Implications*, London, Faber and Faber, 1993.

7 C.f. McLean, S.a.m. and Giesen, D, 'Ethical and Legal Implications of the Human Genome Project', *Med. Law International*, 1994, Vol. 1, 159.

the case of HIV/AIDS, the individual into a potential conflict with the community of which he/she is a part.

Article 12 of the Convention on Bioethics seeks to place tight controls on the use to which predictive genetic information can be put, but there will undoubtedly be—if there are not already—strong moral and political arguments which run counter to the absolute protection of the privacy of the affected individual. Morally, it might be said, the person who knows him or herself to carry the gene which will result in a statistically significant risk of developing a particular condition might be thought to have an obligation to share that information with those who share the genetic pool from which he/she derives.[8] In other words, what might otherwise have been intensely private information might be re-evaluated as information which a child or a sibling has a right to.

If this is so it will radically alter the relationship between family members, may significantly affect reproductive choices and could create a legal equivalent of the 'rescue principle'. Expecting such information to be shared will—unusually—impose an obligation of altruism. And, although the law may never be used to enforce such a moral obligation, it will nonetheless be engaged in it. For example, it will be necessary for the law to consider what sanctions, if any, are to be imposed on a physician who believes that the public interest is served by disclosure of his/her patient's genetic standing. In addition, the law will need to address the legal nexus between the doctor, the individual and other patients of that same doctor who may be related to the first individual and to whom a duty of care is owed on an individual basis.

Further problems will be generated by the role of other interested parties. Employers, social services, educators and insurance

---

8 For discussion see, for example, Suter, S.M., 'Whose Genes are these Anyway?: Familial Conflict over Access to Genetic Information', *Michigan Law Review*, Vol. 9, Jume 1993, 1854; Whittaker, L.A., 'The Implications of the Human Genome Project for Family Practice', *Journal of Family Practice*, Vol. 35, No.3, 294; McLean, S.a.m., Mapping the Human Genome—Friend or Foe? *Soc.Sci.Med.* Vol. 39, No. 9, 1221 (1994).

companies are among the groups who might claim a legitimate interest in this private information.[9] In a world in which insurance, for example, is no longer the mere cushion of the rich but is rather an almost essential part of daily life, the interest of the individual in not making disclosure will doubtless be balanced against the survival of the industry itself and will be shaped by the nature of the contract which is one of uberrimae fidei.

From the State's perspective, knowledge of the possibility of degenerative or other disease developing could be argued to be a major consideration in the provision and allocation of health care funding and services. A rational provision of health care might be said to be one which is based on the needs which the system can identify as being likely to occur. Genetic information could provide one of the few scientifically accurate ways of making informed determination of future needs, and of forming the basis for allocation decisions.

For the medical ethicist, therefore, the traditional precepts of beneficence, non-maleficence, autonomy and justice may require to be reconsidered in a world where interdependence is increasingly significant. Some may even be tempted to redefine these concepts away from their concentration on the individual and towards a community-based ethic, a move which would radically reform the existing expectations and experiences of both patients and doctors.

The second strand to this chapter concerns the system as opposed to the individual, and the conclusion will seek to marry these two sets of issues together. It is trite, but necessary, to remind ourselves that it is not only the one-on-one doctor patient relationship which affects individual rights. The mechanisms for delivery of health care also impact on integrity, privacy and health status. Indeed, ultimately, the extensive accessing of medical and quasi-medical services, whilst of immediate and direct concern only to the patient and his/her physician, is of necessity also a political matter.

---

9 Brahams, D., 'Human genetic information: the legal implications', in *Human Genetic Information: Science, Law and Ethics*, Ciba Foundation Symposium 149, Chichester, John Wiley & Sons, 1990, 111.

In the United Kingdom, for example, it was estimated that 'On an average working day, about 3/4 million people see their family doctor and about the same number get medicines on prescription from their local pharmacist. About 300,000 go to the dentist. At least 100,000 are visited by nurses or other health professionals working in the community. Around 70,000 attend community health clinics and 40,000 have their sight tested. Over £5,000 million a year is spent on primary care.'[10] In the United States, Schwartz notes that the US spends about 14% of its gross domestic product on health care[11] making it a major drain on national resources.

The massive—and growing—level of contact between the individual and health care provision clearly demands that an adequate system is in place if the goals of health care and the rights of the individual are to be respected. On the other hand, it is well known that the amount of money available to health care is limited in all jurisdictions, no matter how the health care system is funded. Health care provision has been high on the political agenda recently in the United Kingdom, but perhaps most publicly in the United States. The Clinton health care reform proposals reflected much more than a mere political gesture. Rather, whatever one's views as to their content, they reflected a rights-based attempt to create universal access to health care—a goal central to the National Health Service in the UK.

In fact, the UK experience offers a good and long-standing example of how health care systems and their related ideologies can impact on individual rights. It is, of course, well known that the NHS was created not just as a health care system but rather as a part of a package of social reforms which—taken together—were to improve the health of the nation and guarantee no discrimination took place based on economic or social standing. Unfortunately, the first political consideration which must be mentioned briefly and

---

10 *Promoting Better Health*, Cm 249/1987, p. 1, para. 1.2.

11 Schwartz, R.L., 'Life style, health status, and distributive justice', in Grubb, A. and Mehlman, M.J. (eds), *Justice and Health Care: Comparative Perspectives*, Chichester John Wiley & Sons, 1995, 225, at pp.225–226.

which doomed the NHS from the outset was that no matter how well the NHS did its own work, the failure to offer the other services necessary for the vision which underlay it defeated the goal. This clearly affected in an immediate and direct way the rights of the individual. As has been said, 'The NHS arose out of the optimism of post-Second World War Britain and its founder saw it as part of a movement of social change that would include full-employment policies, the provision of decent housing, social insurance and better education. it was the whole prescription and not a single pill that would effect the cure.'[12]

More recently, ideological considerations have been used by the UK Government which also affect patients' rights. An ideology based on choice and financial incentives is central to the strategy of the current UK Government. Choice, financial considerations and value for money were major considerations guiding recent NHS reforms. They affect both the macro and the micro allocation of resources and have had a profound impact on the delivery of health care and on the rights of individuals. As Small has said:

'Since the Second World Was health policy has occupied a central position in the public world of policy making, just as health care has in the private world of personal experience. Further, it has provided a location for the construction of ideological paradigms about the relationship between the state and the individual and the nature of a caring society. Both the structure of health care delivery and the ideological assumptions that exist alongside it have been subject to considerable scrutiny in recent years. This scrutiny has generated some hope and a lot of fear.'[13]

The law is both implicated in and separate from the generation of this fear. It is, nonetheless, the sole mechanism which can shape a better or more appropriate response. Certainly, the ethics of medicine alone are insufficiently weighty to optimise health care—at least if they stand alone. In any event, the ethics of health care

---

12 Small, N., *Politics and Planning in the National Health Service*, Milton Keynes, Open University Press, 1989, at p. 175.

13 Op.cit., Preface, at p. ix.

practice are in flux, facing new challenges, both practically and theoretically, which will profoundly affect health care and its providers for many years.

It has, as was argued above, traditionally been a feature of much of health care ethics that the significant player is the individual. Concentration on the private interaction between health care worker and patient has shaped the nature of the relationship and provided the paradigm within which expectations are raised and practices are judged. It is not intended here to suggest that this is inappropriate, but rather that it is likely to be re-evaluated in the light of a number of superimposed factors. If we are to maintain our commitment to the vindication of individual rights in the face of competing (and powerful) State interests, it will be insufficient in the contemporary world, simply to depend on the tenets of medical ethics or the rhetoric of rights. Arguments, sturdy and logical, need to be developed to enhance intuitive commitments, especially when these become more and more difficult to meet in practical terms, and where they are increasingly under attack from consequentialist theories.

The threat to individual privacy rights mentioned at the beginning of this chapter is capable of being neutralised only if the individual is appropriately allocated a place in a community. Equally, this applies to the second strand of this argument. In a health care system based in reality and not Utopian fantasy, apparently excessive concentration on the individual at the expense of other interests could become increasingly counterproductive unless the argument contains within it a level of sophistication which arguably has been lacking to date. Whilst the focus on the individual is perhaps the paramount way of protecting certain rights, we should not continue to be lulled into the false sense of security which suggests that this rhetoric will inevitably result in the conclusion we desire, or that it may not prove to be defeasible in the face of other arguments which wield more political power.

Protection of individual liberties in the face of increasing claims by the State disguised as rational planning or legitimate interests has seldom been more important. Whether the interests to be protected are the individual privacy of the AIDS patient or the right to receive health care independently of discrimination and judgementalism, critical evaluation of matters which transcend the clinical relationship, which until relatively recently has dominated ethical consideration of health care, is required. This is not to say that this relationship is unimportant. The individuality of the relationship still plays a key role in either enhancing or reducing individual liberties, but the danger is that medical ethics as an individual-centred discipline is no longer adequate by itself to protect the interests of those involved. Systems too play a role, as do third party interests, and cognisance must be taken of this. It is too easy to accept the claims of the State, dressed up as they generally are in plausible arguments about efficiency and choice, strategy and planning. Certainly planning is necessary and has the capacity to enhance individual freedoms, but, as Small says: 'Planning is often seen as a mechanism used by the state as a device to further its legitimation needs ... it may be that the very language used includes distortions and repressions and so planning as a communicative process may have been distorted by political ideology and may run the risk of being neither comprehensible nor sincere.'[14]

CONCLUSIONS

Health and health care have taken on an enhanced significance both for individuals and states—indeed, for the international community. Technological advance, the political significance of health status and the social prominence of the role of the clinician combine to require careful examination of the possible tensions between individual rights and interests and the welfare of the community or state. Examples of atomisation abound, with medicine having the potential both to neutralise prejudice and to set up previously unthought of conflicts. The claim here is that it is short-sighted to

---

14 *Op.cit., at p. 126.*

develop individual claims in a vacuum which does not identify and analyse the impact of systems on rights and interests. This has profound implications for the generation of a relevant system of ethics in contemporary medicine. A new health care ethic may be needed—one which sites the individual and his/her community firmly in the role of partners and not competitors and which positions health care ethics in a socially and politically relevant relationship with other ethical perspectives which also have the capacity to affect individual rights. Real rights are seldom generated or enhanced by a narrow focus. Nor are they necessarily ideally derivative from overly individualised or overly societalised perspectives. The medical ethics of the future must accord appropriate importance to the individual and his/her community if the rights of all are to be respected.

It is here that the role of the law, and of the lawyer, is at its most significant. Guidelines which regulate abortion, which deal with issues at the end of life and which control the rapid expansion of knowledge in molecular biology form one part of this. But the additional benefits derived from a rapprochement between law and medical ethics are also important. The law—and the lawyer—can offer two additional things. First, the fundamental principles on which the law is based provide an ideal basis from which to address the new and puzzling dilemmas confronted by medicine, leading, as they do, logically to the conclusion that the individual is to be protected from unwanted intervention no matter how beneficently intended. The template for individual protection is already there and well developed. Second, as an over-arching structure, the law can assist by decontextualising issues of human rights. In a very real sense human rights are essentially the same no matter whether one claims them as a patient or a purchaser. As the only mechanism which has a total view of these issues, divorced from professional practice and in line with underlying principles, the law—and those who interpret and use it—inevitably contribute to the shaping and refinement of ethical standards.

However, it should be noted that what has gone before does not postulate or commend the hijacking of medicine or its ethics by the law. It suggests, however, that rather than apparently being left behind by the rapid and ethically challenging advances in medicine and science, law should have both a reflective and a proactive contribution to make, in a way which is neither rigid nor antagonistic. The increasing interest which physicians show in both the form and the content of the law is to be admired as their recognition of the law's potential influence. The frequency with which doctors turn to the law for guidance is to be welcomed, especially when driven by a genuine desire for ethical and legal guidance. The lawyer, then, by effective communication and by the utilisation of the intellectual skills which form the basis of legal analysis can contribute significantly to the preservation and development of the medical ethic in a way which is relevant to contemporary concerns. In this way, a contribution is made not just to medical ethics but also to patient care in general.

In Search of Justice

The Work of the Commission of Experts Established Pursuant to Security Council Resolution 780 (1992) to Investigate Violations of International Humanitarian Law in the Former Yugoslavia: 1992 - 1994

*M. Cherif Bassiouni**

1. BACKGROUND

The break-up of the Former Yugoslavia and the resulting armed conflict, although occurring in several stages, is a single conflict which has evolved in fits and bursts.[1] At various times, it has involved fighting between and within the former "republics" of that federated State, the Social Federal Republic of Yugoslavia (SFRY). The fighting has been in connection with, or has occurred after, a republic's secession and declaration of independence from the SFRY.

The armed conflict that ensued from the political fragmentation of the SFRY occurred along ethnic and religious lines, with external

---

* The views expressed herein are solely the author's.

1 *See* M. Cherif Bassiouni (with the collaboration of Peter Manikas), *The Law of the International Criminal Tribunal for the Former Yugoslavia (1996).*

support from one or another of the republics involved.[2] This armed conflict, *largo sensu*, developed in three stages.

The first stage began as a result of the secession of Slovenia and took place between 27 June and 7 July 1991. This stage involved an armed conflict between Slovenians and the Yugoslav National Army (JNA), which acted for and on behalf of the SFRY. Fortunately, this conflict was of a short duration and produced few casualties on both sides.

Almost as soon as that conflict ended, the next one followed. It developed after Croatia's secession and declaration of independence in May 1992. It opposed Croatians to the JNA. That conflict, which started on 22 July 1992, and ended with a cease-fire on 3 January 1993, erupted again briefly in 1995 in the Krajina when the Croatian Army (HV) captured that territory from the self-declared Serbian Republic of Krajina, which then ceased to exist. The armed conflict in Croatia was violent and bitter, and left much destruction in its wake.

The third stage erupted in Bosnia on 6 April 1992 after that republic declared its independence and it lasted until 1995. Of all the conflicts, this was the bloodiest and most destructive.

The establishment of break-away "republics" within the newly independent Former Yugoslav republics of Bosnia and Croatia further complicated the situation. In Bosnia, these self-proclaimed republics included the Serbian Republic of Bosnia (Republica Serpska) and the Croatian Republic of Herceg-Bosna, which subsequently became part of the US-brokered Bosnian-Croat Federation of Bosnia-Herzegovina.[3] In Croatia, ethnic Serbs formed the Serbian Republic of Krajina. The break-away Serb republics received

---

2 For an extensive analysis of the "triadic relationships" of national minorities, nationalizing states and external national homelands see Roger Brubaker, *National Minorities, Nationalising States, and External Homelands in the New Europe. What Future for the State?* 124 Daedalus 107 (1995).

3 The Bosnian-Croat Federation was established in March 1994. The Dayton Accords of 1995 established a framework for a federal republic in Bosnia-Herzegovina and added the so-called "Republica Serpska" to the previously established federation.

arms, military equipment and logistical support from their supporters in the new Republic of Yugoslavia (Serbia and Montenegro) and the Republic of Herceg-Bosna received similar support from the Republic of Croatia. Throughout these conflicts, the regular armies of the Republic of Yugoslavia and the Republic of Croatia also intervened directly in support of their satellite breakaway republics.

The conflict, at times, has been fought by and among six warring factions[4] and has seen the widespread participation of civilians as part of 83 identified paramilitary groups, auxiliary to police forces and as part of the local militia forces. These warring factions frequently shifted alliances, fighting against one side or the other. For a long period of time, it was a confused and confusing military situation. Yet, notwithstanding this apparent confusion, the political leaders on all sides have, nonetheless, demonstrated a capacity to control military events, policies, and practices.

It became evident during the course of the conflict that even though military and political leaders were at times unable to exercise effective day-to-day control of all activities in the field, they were in overall control. In fact, the military confusion that existed in 1992-1993 was exploited by the respective leaderships for political purposes and for deniability of responsibility.

The political goal of many Serbs in the Former Yugoslavia was to create a "Greater Serbia," linking regions of Bosnia and Croatia with Serbia proper. Their claim to a national entity representing their ethnicity was based on self-determination. However, the population in Bosnia-Herzegovina was multi-ethnic, and its distribution throughout the territory was as mixed as it

---

4 The warring factions include the Yugoslav National Army, the Croatian army, the Bosnian Government Army (Muslim), the Bosnian Serb Army, the Krajina Serb army (Serb minority in Croatia), and the HVO Army (Bosnian-Croat). At times, the warring factions have established varying alliances. The HVO and the Croats have fought against and alongside the Bosnian Government. The Bosnian Serbs have fought with the Krajina Serbs but have also failed to come to their aid in times of great need. See Final Report of the Commission of Experts Established Pursuant to Security Council Resolution 780 (1992), U.N. SCOR, Annex III.

was diverse. There were also no clear linkages between territory and identifiable ethnic groupings. Furthermore, the diversity of ethnic groups throughout that territory was such that it could not be divided along an ethnic territorial linkage basis. As a result, the Serbs developed a policy of "ethnic cleansing" which involved terror-violence practices in order to forcefully remove the non-Serb population from the areas they had identified and more particularly for obvious strategic purposes along the Drina and Sava rivers. The Serbs' goal was to control the Bosnian territories which were contiguous to Serbia and which would also link Serbia to Serb-held territories in Croatia. This policy and the practices that ensued, shocked the world.

The Croats had entertained the goal of having a Croatian State inhabited primarily by Croats. But there were historic Serb-inhabited areas in Croatia, such as in Krajina and Slavonia that did not lend themselves to the establishment of an ethnically exclusive state. To achieve that goal the Croats forcefully removed the indigenous Serb population from the Krajina in 1995 and from other parts of Croatia as well during the second half of 1991.

Media-disseminated information regarding the extent of the tragedy that occurred, and the atrocious crimes committed mostly against helpless civilians between 1991-1992, stirred world public opinion and compelled the need for an international response. But, in 1991, the centrifugal and irredentist forces that split, and subsequently reconfigured, the territories and peoples of the Former Yugoslavia appeared to catch the world community by surprise even though it was a highly predictable crisis which had been widely forecast since 1989.[5] The world's major powers, however, concentrated their attention on other issues. The United States was still focused on the aftermath of the Gulf War and entering an election year; Germany was absorbed in its reunification; Eastern Europe and the

---

5 No one should have been surprised; least of all politicians who had teams of analysts and mountains of information all pointing towards conflagration in the Former Yugoslavia.

former Soviet Union were emerging from socialism; and France, Germany and the United Kingdom were concentrating on the Maastricht Treaty leading to the European Union. The world, for a moment, seemed gripped by geo-political myopia; not a time for the West, in particular, to pay too much attention to the disintegration of the Former Yugoslavia.

When hostilities erupted in June of 1991, the United States, following the United Kingdom's lead, characterized the conflict as internal, and passively asserted a policy aimed at maintaining the territorial integrity of the Former Yugoslavia while deferring diplomatic initiatives to the Europeans. The new European Union, anxious to present a unified voice, was, however, already confronting dissonance among its members.

The world community seemed unable, although in reality unwilling, to militarily intervene to stop the war. Western Europe and the United States expressed their intentions not to militarily intervene and instead looked for a diplomatic solution. The efforts to mediate a political settlement at a time when different sides were still attempting to achieve territorial gains by use of force, was an impossible task. The United Nations and European Community mediators had neither a stick nor a carrot of sufficient inducement power to achieve their goal, but they persevered against great odds. Meanwhile, news of terrible atrocities flooded world public opinion and caused a wave of outrage; that this was happening in a Europe that believed it would never again see images reminiscent of World War II. Something had to be done.

At the height of the conflict in October 1992, and in the midst of an international climate of great uncertainty, the Security Council established a Commission of Experts to investigate violations of international humanitarian law in the Former Yugoslavia. It was the world's first effort since Nuremberg to establish the beginning of an effective international criminal justice system. The Commission's mandate was broad and comprehensive. If carried out, it could establish not only the individual criminal responsibility of perpetrators, but also the command responsibility of military and political leaders. However, those were precisely the persons with whom the

European Community and United Nations mediators needed to negotiate with in order to achieve a political settlement. If the investigatory process proceeded effectively, this would necessarily impact on the willingness of the warring factions' political and military leaders to negotiate a political settlement. The incongruence between the goals of justice and political settlement was obvious. However, it was necessary for the Security Council to respond to the pressures and indignation of world public opinion in order to show that something was being done to discover the violators of international humanitarian law and, thereafter, to prosecute them. The fact that the United States was the principal promoter of the pursuit of justice was a critical factor.

2. MANDATE

On 6 October 1992, the United Nations Security Council adopted resolution 780 establishing a Commission of Experts to investigate and collect evidence of grave breaches of the Geneva Conventions and other violations of international humanitarian law committed during the conflict in the Former Yugoslavia.[6] This was a historical decision, as its mandate was the broadest of its kind since the International Military Tribunal at Nuremberg. The Resolution's mandate was:

> ... to examine and analyse the information submitted pursuant to resolution 771 (1992) and the present resolution, together with such further information as the Commission of Experts may obtain through its own investigations or efforts, of other persons or bodies pursuant to resolution 771 (1992), with a view to providing the Secretary-General with its conclusions on the evidence of grave breaches of the Geneva Conventions and other violations of

6 M. Cherif Bassiouni, *The United Nations Commission of Experts Established Pursuant to Security Council Resolution 780 (1992)*, 88 Am. J. Int'l L. 784-805 (1992); M. Cherif Bassiouni, *Former Yugoslavia: Investigating Violations of International Humanitarian Law and Establishing an International Criminal Tribunal*, 25 Security Dialogue 409 (1994); M. Cherif

international law committed in the territory of the former Yugoslavia.[7]

Because the Commission was established by the Security Council, it was a subsidiary organ thereof. It consisted of five members appointed in their personal capacity by the Secretary-General. The independent Commission reported to the Security Council through the Secretary-General.

3. FUNDING[8]

Notwithstanding the Commission's broad mandate, the United Nations did not provide any funds for the Commission's field investigation, database and analysis of the facts. At the request of the Commission, the Secretary-General established, on 26 March 1993, a Voluntary Trust Fund to which 17 countries contributed over a period of 16 months, the modest sum of US $1.3 million. The Commission did not, however, have access to these funds until July 1993.

The United Nations had no space available, nor any personnel or equipment, to carry out even the most elementary task of gathering the evidence provided by governments and NGOs in order to analyse it. The Special Rapporteur on the Gathering and Analysis

---

Bassiouni, *The Commission of Experts Established Pursuant to Security Council Resolution 780: Investigation of Violations of International Humanitarian Law in the Former Yugoslavia*, 5 Crim. L.F. 279-340 (1994); and M. Cherif Bassiouni, *The Commission of Experts Established Pursuant to Security Council Resolution 780 (1992): Investigating Violations of International Humanitarian Law in the Former Yugoslavia* (Occasional Paper #2, 1996, International Human Rights Law Institute, DePaul University).

7 S.C. Res. 780, U.N. SCOR, 47th Sess., U.N. Doc. S/RES/780 (6 Oct. 1992).

8 *See* Final Report of the Commission of Experts, U.N. Doc. S/1994/674 (27 May 1994).

of the Facts, and later the Chairman of the Commission, had to establish a database and documentation centre at the International Human Rights Law Institute (IHRLI) at DePaul University, Chicago. IHRLI received infrastructure support from DePaul University and funding from private foundations. The cost of the database project from December 1992 to December 1994 exceeded US $1.4 million. Thus, the private funds sources exceeded the funds contributed by Member States. To overcome its financial constraints, the Commission relied on seconded personnel from various governments, as well as on professional volunteers, to assist it in its work. These contributions in kind, particularly from the governments of Canada and the Netherlands were invaluable to the work of the Commission.

4. METHODS

The Commission of Experts relied on three methods to fulfil its mandate: (1) the collection and analysis of data sent to, or requested by, the Commission from governments, inter-governmental organizations, and non-governmental organizations; (2) on-site investigative missions in the Former Yugoslavia and in other countries to interview witnesses, collect additional information, and verify facts; and (3) the collection of information and evidence by governments on behalf of the Commission.

Based on its investigative work, 35 field missions, and the database reports, the Commission prepared for the Security Council two interim reports[9] and a final report completed in May 1994.[10] In May 1995, the Final Report was followed by 23 Annexes totalling some 3,300 pages. These Annexes contain the substantive support for the findings stated in the Commission's Final Report.[11] They

9 U.N. Doc. S/25274 (1993) and U.N. Doc S/26545 (1993).

10 U.N. Doc. S/1994/674 (1994).

11 U.N. Doc. S/1994/674/Add.2 (Vol. I-V).

were based on 65,000 pages of documents and over 300 hours of video-taped material assembled by the Commission and by the database established by IHRLI which supported the Commission's work. Almost all the substantive work done had to rely on resources external to the United Nations, and that work relied heavily on personnel contributed by governments and professional volunteers.

5. THE INVESTIGATIVE AND RESEARCH WORK

The IHRLI documentation centre and database project facilitated the organization, retrieval, and analysis of the information submitted to the Commission by governments, inter-governmental organizations, non-governmental organizations, human rights groups, and individuals, as well as the Commission's area field investigation. The documentation centre processed 65,000 pages of material throughout the duration of the project. Based on the reports received, over 6,000 cases were opened relating to thousands of victims of crimes committed during the conflict. The IHRLI staff, which was comprised over a two-year period of an average of 40 attorneys and law students working under the direction of the Rapporteur on the Gathering and Analysis of the Facts, also prepared periodic reports on the database findings.. These reports were then used by the Commission to help determine future investigations and created a basis for its reports to the Secretary-General for transmission to the Security Council.

Given the large amount of available information and its limited resources, the Commission conducted on-site investigations on a selective basis. Nevertheless, because of contributed and volunteer personnel, the Commission was able to conduct the extraordinary number of 35 field missions from July 1993 to March 1994. The most extensive of these were the following:

1. A partial mass grave exhumation in Ovčara near Vukovar, Croatia. The grave allegedly contained over two hundred bodies of wounded and sick Croats who were in the Vukovar

hospital when the Yugoslav National Army (JNA) and Krajina Serb militias took over the city in November 1991. The exhumation team, which consisted of 65 officers and soldiers from a Dutch engineering unit and 18 forensic scientists from eight countries who were organised by Physicians for Human Rights (a non-profit organisation from the United States), found several bodies and other traces indicating the likelihood that a mass killing had taken place.

2. A mass grave exhumation in Pakracka Poljana, Croatia (UNPA, Sector West). The mass grave allegedly contained 1,700 bodies of Serbs missing from the area. After 71 digs, however, the Commission team discovered only 19 bodies, which were exhumed and subsequently properly reinterred.
3. A rape and sexual assault investigation. The Commission conducted an unprecedented in-depth investigation of rape and sexual assault in order to supplement the findings contained in the database. A team of some 40 female attorneys, female mental health specialists (and two male mental health specialists), and female interpreters, most of whom were volunteers, interviewed 226 refugees from Bosnia-Herzegovina and Croatia in Croatia, Slovenia, and Austria. The results of the interviews, in addition to the cases reported in documents received by the Commission, indicated five identifiable patterns of rape.[12]
4. A radiological investigation in the Krajina region of Croatia. Based upon reports submitted by Krajina Serbs alleging that Croatia was dumping nuclear waste in UNPA Sector West, the Commission deployed a team of two specialists from the Royal Netherlands Army Nuclear, Biological, and Chemical School. The team took several soil samples from locations throughout the area, analysis of which indicated normal levels of radioactivity.

---

12 M. Cherif Bassiouni and Marcia McCormick, *Sexual Violence: An Invisible Weapon of War in the Former Yugoslavia* (Occasional Paper #1, 1996, International Human Rights Law Institute, DePaul University).

5. A study of the battle of Dubrovnik and the destruction of cultural property in that historic city. A team of military lawyers from Canada and Norway and a French art historian investigated the destruction of cultural property and attacks against civilians in Dubrovnik.
6. An investigation of the ethnic cleansing of *opština* Prijedor, Bosnia-Herzegovina. Commissioner Greve conducted an investigation into ethnic cleansing and the attack against non-Serbs in *opština* Prijedor in April 1992. She collected over 400 interviews as well as reports from the Serb-controlled media. Based on this data, she prepared an extensive report describing the violations of international humanitarian law and the high level of victimisation that occurred throughout the *opština*. The Commission found that the practice of ethnic cleansing, particularly in Prijedor, could legally constitute crimes against humanity and possibly genocide.
7. An investigation of the Medak Pocket in southwest Croatia. Prior to relinquishing control of a group of villages to Serb forces, Croatian forces injured and killed civilians, burned or blew up all of the houses, killed or stole the livestock, and looted personal property. The Commission deployed a team of investigators to the area to interview witnesses and obtain UNPROFOR reports of the incident.
8. A study of the warring factions' military structures, order of battle, and para-military groups which revealed the manner in which the armed conflict developed and explained some of the reasons for the high level of victimisation.
9. A study of the battle and siege of Sarajevo which revealed the intentional shelling of protected civilian targets, and the killing of civilians.

6. FINDINGS

The Commission found that the scale of victimization throughout the territory of the Former Yugoslavia between October 1992 and April 1994 was significantly high and particularly violent. The Commission found that there were an estimated 200,000 civilian and military casualties among the warring factions; 187 reported mass graves each containing between three and 5,000 bodies, which tend to corroborate the high number of reported casualties; 960 reported prison camps and short-term detention facilities, where an estimated 500,000 persons were detained and where crimes such as rape, killing, and torture were reported to have occurred (most of the mass graves are located around the major camps); an estimated 50,000 persons may well have been tortured; 1,400 rape and sexual violence cases were reported, which referred to another 4,500 cases, and this leads to the estimate of 20,000 cases of rape and sexual violence; 83 paramilitary groups which operated during the conflict and committed some of the worst atrocities against persons and the massive destruction of private and public property, particularly the systematic destruction of cultural property and national and religious heritage were identified; extensive looting and pillage of personal property took place throughout all areas of the conflict.

Some of the Annexes to the Commission's Final Report are particularly revealing. Annex III, a report on the military structure of the warring factions, describes the structure, strategy, and tactics of the military forces in the conflict. It also provides a history of the military and the territorial defense forces of the Former Yugoslavia dating back to World War II. This study shows how the policy of "ethnic cleansing" was conducted in concert between the Army, the paramilitary groups, and the police and its auxiliaries, under the overall command of the senior military and political leadership. The more focused Prijedor study, mentioned above, clearly shows how this policy of "ethnic cleansing" was carried out in the Prijedor district. Annex VI, a 1,300 page chronology of the battle and siege of Sarajevo, documents the number of shells falling on the city each day, specific targets that were hit, known damage to targets, sniping activity, and the total number of casualties reported on a daily basis. The Annex also shows the correlation between the shelling and sniping on the one hand and international political activity, such as peace negotiations, on the other. The purpose of the chronology is: (1) to record the events and effects of the battle and siege; (2) to evaluate the patterns of violations; (3) to determine command responsibility; and (4) to reveal the correlation between political events and unlawful military targeting of civilian and protected targets.

The macro-analytical conclusions reached by the Commission revealed the complexity of the military structures, as well as the strategies and tactics of the warring factions. The linkages between regular army units, paramilitary units, armed civilians and local police—all of which were engaged in the armed conflict—pointed to a state policy of "ethnic cleansing"[13] linking political and military leaders who were part of the chain of command to violations of international humanitarian law in pursuit of that policy. The result of this revelation[14] had a chilling effect on political negotiations. The incongruence, therefore, of pursuing negotiations with the very leaders who were the architects of these policies and practices became ever-more evident, but did not prevent the completion of the 1995 Dayton Accords. Subsequently, however, it became apparent that the responsible leaders who were indicted by the ICTFY would not be apprehended by IFOR and that the major powers and the Security Council would do nothing to support the apprehension of indicted criminals until such time as the peace has not taken hold in the territories formerly at war with one another.

---

13 Systematic rape and the destruction of cultural property were integral parts of that policy.

14 The Commission's revelations have been supported by CIA photographs showing the destruction and ethnic cleansing of approximately 3,000 villages in Bosnia.

7. ESTABLISHMENT OF THE ICTFY[15]

The Commission's First Interim report concluded that the establishment of an international criminal tribunal to prosecute war criminals would be consistent with its work. Based in part on the Commission's initial findings, the Security Council decided to establish such a tribunal in resolution 808 (1993) and requested that the Secretary-General prepare a statute. The Commission provided its expert advise on the preparation of the ICTFY's statute and this writer contributed to the definition of the crimes which were included in the ICTFY's Statute, Articles 2 to 5.

8. PREMATURE TERMINATION OF THE COMMISSION

Trials can always occur at a different time and place; however, without evidence a trial is impossible. So too does the absence of evidence prevent future trials. This is why the Security Council saw the need for the Commission to continue its work until the ICTFY's Prosecutor was in place to take over.

Despite the Security Council's resolution 827 quoted above, the United Nations Office of Legal Affairs in December 1993 unexpectedly terminated the Commission administratively effective as of 30 April 1994, even though at the time there was no Prosecutor. The Security Council requested the Commission to continue its work until the appointment of a Prosecutor. Yet the Prosecutor did not take office until August 1994—four months after the termination of the Commission. The Security Council, which created the Commission, never made a decision to terminate the Commission. No explanation for this administrative action has been given. One possible explanation is that timely investigations can lead to politically undesirable results.

---

15 *See, supra* note 1.

Because of its premature termination, the Commission had to curtail several investigations in course, even though there were enough funds remaining in the Voluntary Trust Fund to allow it to complete its work. In fact, over $250,000 was left in the Voluntary Trust Fund as of 3 April 1994, and the monthly costs of the Commission were approximately $60,000. Thus, the Commission could have functioned with its existing resources for four additional months until the Prosecutor took office.

Despite the termination of the Commission, the Chairman continued to work on a volunteer basis from May 1994 to December 1994 with a small staff at IHRLI to complete the 3,300 pages of Annexes to the Commission's Final Report which were transmitted to the Security Council in December 1994, but not published by the United Nations until July 1995. The cost of publication did not come out of United Nations resources but out of the Commission's remaining funds (some $250,000). No final accounting was given by the United Nations of the remaining funds.

Between May and December 1994, the Chairman undertook the transfer of all the material available to the Prosecutor and assisted him and his staff during the early critical stages of the office's work.

With the premature termination of the Commission, as stated by this writer in another forum:

> There is no one to complete the historical record that the commission began. The Office of the Prosecutor will collect such information as is needed to prepare cases for prosecution. With limited resources, however, that office cannot conduct the type of broad-based investigation and analysis that the commission did. As a result, many voices will go unheard and many stories will go unrecorded. That applies in particular to violations of international humanitarian law in the fighting that has taken place since 30 April 1994. The absence of an authoritative and objective body capable of conducting investigations to document those events is a tragedy that could have been avoided.[16]

---

16 *Transition*, Vol. 1, No. 20, 3 November 1995.

9. OUTCOMES

The Commission accomplished a great deal under difficult, and sometimes almost impossible circumstances. These accomplishments provided the basis upon which the Prosecutor of the ICTFY began his work. The Commission transferred the contents of the database and all its documents to the Office of the Prosecutor at The Hague. Two days after the Prosecutor took office on 15 August 1994, the Commission Chairman and members of the IHRLI staff gave briefings in the Hague to the Prosecutor's staff on the Commission's work and findings. An excellent working relationship developed between the Prosecutor and the Commission Chairman, and their respective staffs worked closely on the transition and with respect to the publication of the Annexes in order to avoid the release of information prejudicial to prosecutions.

Despite the difficulties surveyed in this article, the Commission produced extraordinary results. Without the foundation laid by the Commission, the Prosecutor would have had nothing to start with in the pursuit of his prosecutorial endeavors, even though many specific investigations needed to be conducted by that office to convert the Commission's findings into evidence useable in specific cases. Quite clearly, the fact that the first indictments concerned events in Prijedor on which the Commission produced an impressive report, indicate how useful the Commission's work had been at the early stages of the ICTFY.

The high visibility of the Commission and its work gave it credibility, which in turn gave the United Nations credibility. It also gave impetus to the Tribunal. Above all, the Commission established a significant public record of violations that no one can ignore. The Secretary-General acknowledged that fact in a letter to the Chairman where he stated:

> I take this opportunity to reiterate my gratitude and appreciation for the work done by the Commission of Experts, as well as the

skill, time and effort invested in the preparation of its Final Report and voluminous Annexes. I wish, in this connection, to single out the International Human Rights Law Institute...which, under your direction, established the database as the core project of the Commission.

The material and information collected and recorded in the database, now transferred to the Tribunal, will not only assist in the prosecution of persons responsible for serious violations of international humanitarian law, but will constitute a permanent documentary record of the crimes committed in the former Yugoslavia, and thus remain the memorial for the hundreds of thousands of its innocent victims.[17]

The Tribunal's first annual report also acknowledged the Commission's work:

157. Not long after the establishment of the Tribunal, the judges had the opportunity of meeting with Mr. Cherif Bassiouni, Chairman of the Commission of Experts established pursuant to security Council Resolution 780 (1992). On 25 February 1994, the Acting Deputy Prosecutor and other staff members of the Tribunal met at the Hague with Mr. Bassiouni and other members of the Commission. The work and findings of the Commission were discussed at length and certain materials were handed over to the Office of the prosecutor. Subsequently, the Acting Deputy Prosecutor visited the Commission's premises in Geneva. A staff member also visited Chicago to inspect and be instructed in relation to the Commission's computer database. The Acting Deputy Prosecutor also had meetings with most of the Commission's commissioners and staff members.

158. During April 1994, the office of the Prosecutor obtained a copy of the Commission's database. Subsequently, in May 1994, all of the documents from Chicago, which form the basis of the information in the database, were received by the Tribunal. By the end of May 1994, action had commenced to scan those documents

---

17 Letter from Boutros Boutros-Ghali, Secretary-General of the United Nations to M. Cherif Bassiouni, President, International Human Rights Law Institute, DePaul University, 4 January 1995.

onto the Prosecutor's own computer system. This process involved some technical difficulties initially but eventually the system of integrating the Chicago database into the Prosecutor's system was achieved. The Office of the Prosecutor has enjoyed a close working relationship with the Commission of Experts.[18]

10. CONCLUSION

The Commission's *Final Report* concluded:

It is particularly striking to note the victims' high expectations that this Commission will establish the truth and that the International Tribunal will provide justice. All sides expect this. Thus, the conclusion is inescapable that peace in the future requires justice, and that justice starts with establishing the truth. The Commission would be remiss if it did not emphasise the high expectation of justice conveyed by the parties to the conflict as well as by victims, intergovernmental organisations, non-governmental organisations, the media and world public opinion. Consequently, the International Tribunal must be given the necessary resources and support to meet these expectations and accomplish its task. Furthermore, popular expectations of a new world order based on the international rule of law require no less than effective and permanent institutions of international justice. The International Tribunal for the Prosecutions of Persons Responsible for Serious Violations of International Humanitarian Law Committed in the Territory of the Former Yugoslavia since 1991 must, therefore, be given the opportunity to produce the momentum for this further evolution.[19]

---

18 *Annual Report of the International Tribunal for the Prosecution of Persons Responsible for Serious Violations of International Humanitarian Law Committed in the Territory of the Former Yugoslavia Since 1991*, ¶¶ 157-58, U.N. SCOR, 49th Year, Agenda Item 152, U.N. Doc. S/1994/1007 (29 Aug. 1994).

19 *Final Report of the Commission of Experts Established Pursuant to Security Council Resolution 780 (1992), "the Commission's Establishment,"* ¶ 320 (citation omitted).

The record of the ICTFY is yet to be established, but no matter what that record may be, the ICTFY's very establishment is a historic achievement. The dedication of its judges, prosecutorial staff and other staff can only be applauded. Whether their efforts will produce the results expected depends on the political will of the major powers.

For a view exists among some of the major powers that peace is more important than justice, and if the latter has to be abandoned in favor of the former, so be it.

In the end, however, there can be no peace without justice, and justice begins with establishment of the truth. The Commission was able to establish this only in part for the period from 1992 to 1994, but since then there has been no body in place to achieve this important task. The Tribunal must necessarily focus on specific cases. So far it has tried one person and indicted 75 others, and it has seven persons in its custody. But major indicted offenders are still free, and there appears to be no will to apprehend them.

The problems which face the prosecution are still quite significant. The Republic of Yugoslavia and the so-called Republica Serpska refuse to recognize the Tribunal's competence, and will not surrender anyone accused by it. IFOR will not seek out anyone for arrest in the areas it patrols. The major powers' political will to make justice work is lacking. Yet, world public opinion opposes compromise in the form of amnesty or *de facto* impunity, at least for the more serious violators of international humanitarian law. The prognosis will remain grim until the major powers come to grips with the fact that justice is an indispensable component of peace, and cannot be sacrificed in the name of *realpolitik*.

As Pope John Paul VI said in 1972, "If you want peace, work for justice."

The Rule of Law – Cornerstone of Economic Progress

An address to the International Bar Association's South African conference, 9 November 1995, read by the Honourable Minister of Justice, Advocate Omar, on behalf of the President of the Republic of South Africa, Mr. Nelson Mandela

As a I am a lawyer myself I have over the years followed with profound and keen interest the activities of the International Bar Association through reports of the many events which it has convened or participated in. Its important mouthpiece and monthly magazine, the *International Business Lawyer*, has been particularly useful in this regard. Its success in capturing the interchange of information and views on laws, practices and procedures affecting business, finance and commercial activities throughout the world has not only been spectacular but has proved to be an invaluable resource not only for scholars and practitioners, but also for policy makers and government officials.

It is therefore greatly comforting to witness the addition today to this impressive list of achievements of yet another milestone in the form of this meeting's theme, which is indeed an important one to everyone in South Africa, namely a discourse on the rule of law and economic prosperity.

That this conference should focus on it during this period of the celebration of the 50th anniversary of the UN Charter and of the United Nations itself, is singularly appropriate. For as we all know the dual concepts of human rights and rule of law or due process, as it is very often referred to by members of the legal fraternity, gained a unique dimension and momentum with the emergence of the UN system. It is mainly due to that system that important milestones in the fields of the promotion/and protection of human rights have occurred. Not only have we seen many conferences, seminars and discussions on these concepts, but we have also been witnesses to notable results in the form of covenants, treaties, regional charters, commissions, as well as national statutes, national bills of rights and constitutional guarantees of human rights. Indeed even national, as well as international and regional courts and tribunals have been set up for the sole goal of ensuring that human beings can be protected in their dignity, persons and property.

SOUTH AFRICA

But to return to the situation in South Africa, it is good to reflect again that we all prayed and made sacrifices to bring about a South Africa that we could hold out as a true example of the democracy, equality and justice for all which the apartheid system was constructed and intended to deny. Today we can rejoice, for we have in fact managed to establish the impossible—the rebirth of a nation and a country.

The vision you all shared with us was one of a nation and a country in which we would use the resources of our country to create a society in which all our people would be emancipated from the scourges of poverty, disease, ignorance and backwardness. We are progressing well in this regard.

We, however, also want to create a South Africa that is a good neighbour to and an equal partner with all the countries of our own and other continents, one which will use its abilities and potentials to help advance the common struggle to secure South Africa's rightful place within the economic and political systems of the world.

In order to succeed in these goals we have fortunately as a nation laid a solid foundation with the acceptance of those values and principles that will guarantee rule of law, in our interim constitution.

ECONOMIC GROWTH

We are all agreed that sustained economic growth is a necessity for achieving our goals. In turn, growth requires more trade, and more investment, from domestic sources and from outside. The South African government's determination to lead the country along a path of sustained growth has therefore led it to establish an economic task force which is charged with devising a process to strategically focus the countries energies along a path of growth.

Simultaneously we are addressing urgent challenges such as bringing crime and corruption under control; enhancing the effectiveness with which programmes for social upliftment are implemented; and rising to the economic opportunities offered by reconstruction and development and our acceptance in the global market and village.

RULE OF LAW

What should be emphasised, however, is throughout all our endeavours we have been guided and will continue to be guided by a set of norms universally accepted as constituting rule of law. The historic elections held during April 1994 presented South Africa with a unique opportunity to redress the imbalances of the past through transformation to a just and democratic order; to a legal order that makes the constitution and its chapter on fundamental rights the highest law of the land, binding all legislative, executive and judicial organs of state at all levels of government. A legal order committed to the creation of an open and democratic society based on freedom and equality.

This supremacy entrenches rule of law and brings to an end an era in our history in which the law and the rights of our people were subjected to the legal doctrine of parliamentary sovereignty, which, *inter alia*, meant that the validity of laws made by parliament could not be disputed. The task of the courts was to enforce laws made by parliament(in our country a whites only parliament), no matter how unjust such laws might be.

Our country suffered under a grossly distorted form of parliamentary supremacy - not only did an abuse of rights take place, but our economy suffered greatly. That time is over. Now it is the responsibility of the judiciary to uphold and protect the rights of our people as entrenched in the constitution.

But of course constitutions and bills of rights are fragile things. In the words of a distinguished American constitutional lawyer:

> "It is worth pausing to recall that courts have no power to enforce their decrees against the executive. They possess neither the purse nor the sword. Constitutionalism as a constraint upon government depends, in the first instance upon the habit of voluntary compliance and, in the last resort, upon a people's realisation that their freedom depends upon observance of the rule of law. The realisation must be strong enough for the community to rise up and overwhelm, morally and politically, any notable offender."

But what is "rule of law" and what are the characteristics desired in this regard?

DEFINITIONS

The question of the precise meaning of the rule of law has been much debated. At its most basic, the rule of law has been held to mean simply that the government is required to act in accordance with valid law. While this is undoubtedly desirable, it is not an exhaustive description of the characteristics of a system which meets the criteria of the rule of law. Various other wider definitions have been proposed. These have included the requirement of procedural justice; something which is now generally recognised as part of the rule of law. Others have gone further and argued that material or substantive justice in all its forms is part of the concept of the rule of law.

Material or substantive justice is a praise worthy goal, but the late Professor A. S. Mathews, one of the leading writers on the subject of the rule of law in South Africa, warned that the concept of the rule of law should not be defined so widely that it has no meaning. On the other hand, Mathews recognised that procedural justice is impossible unless certain basic rights are recognised. Accordingly he defined the rule of law as follows:

(a) Government according to the rule of law means that with a view to the preservation of the basic rights enumerated in (b) below, the relevant laws shall take the form of pre-announced, general, durable and reasonable precise rules administered by regular courts or similar independent tribunals according to fair procedures.

(b) The basic freedom of person, conscience, speech, information, movement, meeting and association shall be equally guaranteed by the law to all citizens of the society.

(c) Any limitations on the civil rights of freedoms enumerated in (b) shall be in the form of rules conforming to the requirements of legality expressed in (a). Furthermore, restrictions on the basic freedoms shall be limited in scope and, except in times of genuine crises or emergency, shall not encroach upon essential content of such freedoms.

Legal change since Professor Mathews wrote these words in 1986 have brought the national legal position much closer to the ideal which he formulated. The constitution of the Republic contains specifically a chapter of fundamental rights which guarantees both the procedural aspects of the rule of law and those basic rights which are necessary to make procedural justice possible. South Africa therefore now has a basic legal framework which makes it possible for it to co-operate with other states who respect the principles of the rule of law as they have been developed by the international community. It also now has a framework within which the search for economic progress can take place.

Not only does rule of law form the cornerstone of economic progress world-wide, in South Africa we had to first establish rule of law anew in its full connotation so as to address violence and serious crime, create and establish accountability for human conduct and behaviour and to ensure that a new culture based on respect for human rights is promoted within all justice and administrative structures and society in general. It also had to form the basis for our process of nation building and economic development.

All of us recognise that peace and stability are crucial for economic growth and development. I wish to re-iterate that the South African Government of National Unity is determined to ensure that all South Africans, including those who fear democracy, can rest assured in the knowledge that change is in their interest too. We face a long and hard road to ensure social justice stability and the building of a people-centred and caring society.

JOINT EFFORT

Fortunately what brought our nation together is an over-riding commitment to a joint national effort to reconcile our nation and improve its well-being. The unique product of our negotiations - the interim constitution and charter of fundamental rights, coupled to the reconstruction and development programme - constitute a firm foundation to meet our challenges.

Democracy has taken root in our country and in our region, and with it has come stability. But all this will be little more than the shifting sands of illusion, if we do not take decisive measures to strengthen the moral fibre of our nation.

CRIME AND CORRUPTION

In taking concrete steps against crime and corruption we have linked hands with the community, with the business section and have simultaneously started with socio-economic programmes which are already seen as highly successful.

We have also started with the transformation of the police into an effective and legitimate service, freed from the legacy of its past role and based on community policing. They have under adverse conditions started to successfully implement new anti-crime programmes. The national community safety plan has also registered considerable success in bringing down the levels of violent crime.

The justice system has similarly been subjected to a process of transformation so as to restructure it and its institutions so that they would be truly democratic, accessible, representative transparent and accountable.

I believe that our integrated strategies will assist in the war against crime and ensure a secure and safe future for all its citizens.

The government has also been actively co-operating with other countries and agencies on a bilateral regional and intentional basis - not only to help ensure rule of law and stability, but also to stimulate economic progress.

TRUTH AND RECONCILIATION COMMISSION

In the process of nation building and helping to establish a culture of human rights we have also embarked on the road of reconciliation with the past. The issue of truth and reconciliation commission has generated much public interest and debate. In a nutshell what is required is a means of dealing with the past that contains gross violations of human rights.

There are a number of functions envisaged for the truth and reconciliation commission.

F1rst there is the constitutional requirement that we should provide for amnesty and more particularly for mechanisms, criteria and procedures including tribunals, if any, through which such, amnesty shall be dealt with.

This constitutional requirement is dealt with specifically in the National Unity and Reconciliation Act and specifies that:

(a) A Committee headed by a judge shall deal with all applications for amnesty. This is the only body in the country with the power to grant amnesty. Neither the president nor the executive is granted such a power.

(b) There is no general amnesty. Each and every person desiring amnesty must make an application. The Committee will decide whether a hearing is necessary or not. When, however, the application relates to a gross violation of human rights, there shall be a hearing.

(c) If the crime in respect of which amnesty is sought falls within the criteria of an act associated with a political objective, amnesty shall be granted. If it does not, amnesty shall be refused. In other words, amnesty is not automatic, though the provisions are quite liberal.

The second area of the work of the commission is to establish a complete picture of gross violations of human rights between 1 march 1960 and the cut-off date. This includes an investigation of its causes and the perspective of victims as well as the making of recommendations of measures to prevent future violations of human rights.

Thirdly, the concerns of victims are addressed via a special committee dealing with reparation and the rehabilitation of victims. This third committee must also decide on practical steps to be taken in an endeavour to restore the human and civil dignity of victims.

The rationale for requiring perpetrators to apply specifically for amnesty rather than granting a general amnesty is to establish the principle of accountability. Every person must be held accountable for his or her actions or conduct. In criminal law, accountability is established through apprehending persons who have committed crimes, trying them in courts and punishing them if they are found guilty. That is the requirement of justice. The greatest deterrence to crime, as the judges of the constitutional court pointed out in the historic abolition of the death penalty judgement, lies in the certainty that criminals will be apprehended, tried and punished if found guilty.

In South Africa today, where our war is now a fight against a wave of violent crime, this wisdom is central. The need is to ensure that criminals are apprehended and punished. This is an essential condition for bringing crime under control and in entrenching rule of law.

Therefore the truth and reconciliation commission does not and cannot offer a substitute for criminal trials. Criminal trials may only be suspended pending applications for amnesty in consultation with the attorney general concerned.

These then are some of major provisions of the National Unity and Reconciliation Act. Although there have been a number of truth commissions in different parts of the world, ours is different from all the others because it is rooted in our own historical conditions. In our situation, we cannot focus on the past for its own sake. We need to deal with our past, not because of a desire for revenge or victimisation, but because we need to make a break with the past and build a future based on respect for life, for the dignity of each person and for the right of all people to live in safety, peace and security, in an environment free from violence.

We are, I believe, addressing this matter in a unique way - one which will assist the democratisation process in South Africa. It is also a way which totally encompasses human rights

HUMAN RIGHTS

Those who have followed the course of events in the sphere of human rights world-wide will recall that there have been several paradigm shifts from the initial promotional stage to the current enforcement and implementation processes. They will remember also the interesting and sometimes controversial classification of rights along generational lines into those pertaining to the civil and political endeavours of human beings and those affecting their economic, social and cultural wants. To these classifications have been added new era rights which are of great importance to people in South Africa—such as the right to education, health, work, clean and safe environment, food, clothing and shelter. This right as you know has found expression in the form of article 11, paragraph 1, of the International Ccovenant on Economic, Social and Cultural Rights which provides that:

> "The States parties to the present Covenant recognise the right of everyone to an adequate standard of living for himself and his family, including adequate food, clothing and housing, and to the continuous improvement of living conditions. The States parties will take appropriate steps to ensure the realisation of this right, recognising to this effect the essential importance of international co-operation based on free consent."

Suffice to say this evolution of a human rights discourse along the lines of paradigms has unleashed certain drawbacks. For one thing, it has led to the emergence of a perception that rights are divisible and that some rights are more important than others—for example, in some quarters the right to vote and to speak freely is given greater weight than the right to work education and clean air. Indeed even the right to counsel and trial by an independent court is treated by some as secondary in importance to the rights of worship and movement. But as you know these rights cannot really be split up, for what good does it do to a person to tell her she has a right to vote or to speak as she likes when she does not have the energy to walk to the polling booth or to open her mouth. What good is a right to education where there are no schools or employment opportunities. Moreover this division of rights has in large measure caused the pursuit of human rights' objectives to be undertaken in relative isolation from the mass efforts which have been devoted to the elusive quest for development. The result as we all know has been that a lot of the initiatives which were adopted to serve the cause of human rights have foundered. They have foundered for the simple reason that by adopting the distinction that I have alluded to, they were in fact treating the symptoms of repression rather than paying regard to the deeper structural problems which gave rise to them. In many instances these problems are rooted in under-development or mal-development rather than in the absence of knowledge about what is just and what is not.

DEVELOPMENTAL PROGRAMMES

Alongside the problem of untreated causes of violation has of course, been the failure of many developmental programmes to make any significant headway. This has again been largely due to the overriding preoccupation of those programmes with macro-economic matters, to the exclusion of the human factor. Even today, the vast majority of economists and development planners look upon human rights issues as extraneous and largely irrelevant The consideration of which can only hinder efficiency and provoke political controversy. Quite clearly that distinction has been a mistake and has cost the world time, resources and, most unfortunately, human lives.

That there is a necessary and inevitable linkage between human rights, the rule of law and economic prosperity is clear for all to see. In all the countries where men and women of talent are free to exercise their skills in the knowledge that wrongs against them or their property will be prevented and punished by free courts and that business needs will be promoted, protected and rewarded by a democratically elected government—prosperity has occurred. In those places where lawlessness and corruption reign high, even the little promise of growth that might have occurred has never seen the light of day.

As Professor Ibrahim J. Wani, an African scholar from the Sudan who is currently teaching at the University of Missouri in Kansas, recently pointed out in his article on The Rule of Law and Economic Development in Africa:

> "While there are some conceptual and empirical questions about the relationship between the rule of law and economic development – there are strong indications that the more democratic countries have a relatively strong basis in the rule of law and tend to exhibit stronger economic performances."

The state of our own continent, I am sorry to say, bears testimony to this assertion. Promising economies have seen both foreign and local investors go under due to excessive misuse of discretion, arbitrary application of rules and regulations and corruption. Other common practices cited by frustrated investors are the holding up of renewals of business permits by clerks awaiting bribes, the arbitrary and capricious handling of import licence applications and the undue delays in approving projects because government officials seem to apply different rules and regulations to each application. In those countries where the administration of justice is slow and not free from executive interference and bribery, economic life has, as you can imagine, become equally chaotic. These points are echoed by the World Bank in its report, Sub-Saharan Africa: From Crisis to Sustainable Growth. In that report the bank points to arbitrariness, lack of public accountability and disrespect for individual rights as the leading causes of economic malaise.

In addition, other institutions like USAID and other donor agencies and countries now recognise and acknowledge the dichotomy between the rule of law and prosperity. Indeed even developing countries themselves are now following suit. Many are beginning to demand transparency and accountability by governments. Quite clearly a consensus has emerged on the impact of governance and economic performance. Governance, in this regard, meaning the rule of law or in political terms, democracy.

Adherence to the rule of law also means government has a duty to provide a cushion against the effects of unequal forces. Indeed as Sir Shridath Ramphal, that great son of Guyana in South America and former Commonwealth Secretary-General, stated at the 1981 Conference of the ICJ on Development, Human Rights and the Rule of Law:

> "None of the modern industrial economies expose their citizens to the unmitigated effects of the forces unleashed by the market system. The incomes of farmers, for instance, are stabilised in those countries through subsidies and levies. Similarly when their citizens lose jobs through technological or other changes, unemployment relief is available. No obstacle is placed on the movement of factors of production and the retaining or relocation of labour is subsidised. In addition, jobs are freely moved closer to the sources of labour incentives, government contracts and other public measures. More systematically, monopolists are not allowed to exact their free toll on the public. Restrictive business practices and antitrust legislation keep them in check at all national levels."

It follows that a major responsibility rests upon developing countries to generate through the rule of law at home an environment propitious to real development and prosperity. They must strike a balance between the needs of the business community and the expectations of the poor and the workers.

To conclude, let me echo what Sir Shridath Ramphal also stated in his exposition of the accomplishments made so far in the world's efforts to bring about peace. On this point he said:

> "It is not only an international setting freed from war and crises that development needs, it needs in an acute degree, the application of the rule of law to international relations - an international legal order that upholds the objectives of economic and social justice world-wide."

This is what the new international economic order has been all about. It is what economic prosperity entails too. It is a recognition that while advocating for fairness and justice in the municipal systems, the international lending community, and the trading countries of the world cannot ignore the rules of equity and fairness. Lawlessness and injustice are just that, whether they occur in a small backward country or in a western metropole. The same result of underdevelopment and economic malaise will still take root whether the causes of injustices are local or international. It is the duty of all of us to ensure justice in all its forms.

With democracy now firmly entrenched in South Africa, it is of the utmost importance that not only the government but each citizen fulfill his or her role in nurturing it. With the contribution of everyone the well-being of our people will be assured for we have committed ourselves as a government and as a nation to a future in which human rights will not only be respected, but upheld.

South Africa is fortunate to emerge into the world in such interesting times. The irony of our late entry into international affairs is that we can reap the fruits of a world defining itself. This particular conference has, in particular, indicated the importance of sharing knowledge on common issues and problems relating not only to the law, but also to economic progress.

Against this background I and South Africa in general thank the IBA for allowing us to play a role within that organisation, and for offering a hand of friendship to criminal justice systems all over the world in order to assist in the creation of a just and peaceful environment for all humanity.

*The Role of Lawyers in the Fight against Corruption**

Monty Raphael

It is entirely appropriate that, at its half centenary, the IBA should concentrate ever more closely on the ethical conduct of lawyers. The OECD, the Council of Europe, and the European Community, are all studying ways of introducing a homogeneous code of behaviour, which will bind national signatories to stamp out corruption in international trade. Transparency International has been formed as an organisation to raise global consciousness to confront this same widespread evil.

On the 1st June 1996, in Madrid, the IBA Council adopted a resolution to encourage governments to introduce all necessary measures to deter corrupt practices, including all necessary penal sanctions and the removal of tax advantages from the payment of so called commissions

Indeed, this essay coincides with the publication by the Law Commission, a body set up by the UK Government to promote law reform, of a Consultative Paper on Corruption.

It is from this paper that I borrow its quoted definition of the verb "to corrupt": "To destroy or pervert the integrity or fidelity of [a person] in his discharge of duty; to induce to act dishonestly or unfaithfully; to make venal; to bribe." The adjective "corrupt" is given as, "Perverted from uprightness and fidelity in the discharge of duty, influenced by bribery or the like; venal".

The paper goes on to describe the development of the UK statutory and common law on corruption and to make proposals for its reform. It is significant, is it not, that the UK with its long established legal system and strong adherence to the rule of law should still, in 1997, find itself with a penal "code" inadequate to the task. Public and private bodies are imprecisely defined and needlessly distinguished, the funding of political parties, the corruption of MPs and the bribery of foreign public officials are all inadequately confronted.

With these shortcomings exposed in a developed system, it is clear that mere adherence to the rule of law is not sufficient. Members of the IBA are bound constitutionally "to promote the administration of justice under the rule of law among the peoples of the world". What do these laudatory aims mean to the workaday lawyer and upon what jurisprudential pedestal do they stand. Thomas Aquinas said that law was "an ordinance of reason for the common good." It is just only when it follows the law of nature. When it departs from it, "it is no longer a law, but a version of law". Thus, unjust laws made by man are a perversion of the ideal of law. Laws are unjust when they fail to serve the common good. Those laws do not bind in conscience and need only be obeyed "in order to avoid scandal or disturbance". Thus, law as a fact is always susceptible to moral judgment.

John Austin, writing seven centuries later for the newly emerging industrialised society came to a similar conclusion. He too recognised a higher reality, derived from divine guidance, which might not coincide with a morality which was temporarily fashionable. Both philosophers drew their inspiration from a belief in a Christian God, but their views are shared by many who trust in some albeit non-Christian divine being to provide a set of moral values.

Nor is a belief in a god necessary for adherence to the view that moral standards can be objectively valid. The "godless" Jeremy

Bentham believed that laws should serve the welfare of those they affect. It is commonly accepted that corruption keeps a society in a state of amoral servility. It substitutes bribes for proper wages, it undermines the ethical fibre of institutions, it creates unfairness in world trade, and it is an open sesame to all kinds of illegality, not least the predations of organised crime.

I must assume that those reading this essay subscribe to that set of moral values which is embodied in the Charter of the United Nations and in the European Convention on Human Rights. Those ethical nihilists who question either or both should read no further. They would have us believe that law is "value free" and thus not susceptible to moral judgment. The constitution of the IBA implies the very opposite.

I do not suggest that a lawyer may simply advise his client to disobey a "bad" law, in the pursuance of some higher morality. However by the same token, a lawyer need not become a professional accomplice to his client's grossly immoral acts, simply because they can all be prescribed within the framework of a given law, or by the acknowledgement that no appropriate legal sanction exists to forbid such conduct. Like any individual in society, a lawyer must have some moral restrictions upon his behaviour. Does adherence to this principle entitle the lawyer to influence his client either by persuasion or by refusal to act? I believe it does.

Many will ask whether these questions are really relevant to the lawyer in advising his commercial client. After all, does not the rule of law pre-suppose strict and impartial adherence to a body of rules made by governments, domestic or supra national, and should the lawyer trouble himself with questions which depart from the practical and enter into the realm of metaphysics?

If only the practice of law could be regarded this simply. In a perfect world, the law would serve the interests of all, the weak and the strong, the rich and the poor, it would indeed be for the benefit of all. Clearly, this is not the case. The rich and powerful have a disproportionate access to justice, the poor and weak have a lesser chance of pursuing their claims, however just. Vast areas of the globe are unfree politically and thus deprived of anything we would recognise as the rule of law.

In this depressing reality, how is the business lawyer to behave?

Again, I believe that these are solutions for each lawyer to devise for himself and I would hope that imposing the following questions, the answers will suggest themselves in a uniformly ethical manner. I ask these questions in the hope that a common standard may be created, which will serve to underline the objects of those who founded our professional body.

1. If you are professionally regulated in a country which imposes high ethical standards, should you abandon any of those standards to gain commercial advantage when practising in a country with lower or underdeveloped professional standards
2. Should you lend your professional skills to enterprises which are illegal in your own home country, but not illegal in the country where those enterprises are to be conducted e.g. thinly disguised money laundering activities or conduct involving environmental hazard?
3. Should business lawyers quiescently shelter behind the prevailing culture where the client does business, or should they judgementally refuse to act where the culture is morally distasteful? In a commercial world which has shrunk to the reach of telephonic communication, these and many other moral dilemmas face the commercial lawyer daily.

Any consideration of justice and the rule of law, and how the former should inform the latter, must trespass on the old debate about the extent to which morality and the law do, or should, influence one another in the conduct of business. Clearly, the business lawyer is not concerned with the regulation of morality, but he is surely concerned with the morality of regulation or often the very absence of it. There are few, if any jurisdictions, where a commercial bargain may not be lawfully struck, using domestic law as a yardstick and the lawyer must then consider whether the bargain is enforceable in the event of breach. If the answer is yes, is that the full extent of the commercial lawyer's responsibility? What if there are shortcomings in the local administration of justice? Is it sufficient to warn the client and then have him take the risk? What if the lawyer knows that local public officials involved in a business deal are corrupt, and the judicial system is similarly undermined. Does the business lawyer simply shrug his well tailored shoulders, collect his fees, and pass on?

Lawyers do not create corrupt societies, but they can promote corrupt practices simply by choosing to ignore them. Similarly, lawyers do not start wars, but they do nothing to discourage them by taking part in illicit arms deals, even where they break no domestic law.

Quite clearly there will be those who read this and say, that provided one is acting lawfully and one is not offending the professional ethics of one's own Bar Association, one should not interfere in other realms. They will say that it is not for the business lawyer to concern himself with the culture, politics or morality of his client, however distasteful any of these may be. And yet, it may equally strongly be argued that without such interference by individual lawyers, or by Bar Associations or, indeed by nations, evils will continue unchecked and the world will become a poorer place. Can anyone really deny that penetration of the world's financial and political systems by organised crime can be achieved without some assistance from highly sophisticated, highly competent business lawyers, all or most of whom are presumably going about their "lawful" business.

The last decade has seen unprecedented cooperation in cross-border investigations, driven by the war on drugs, drug traffickers, and money launderers. It has also seen the targeting of lawyers, their files and ledgers. The two developments are connected. Money laundering by trickery is ever more difficult and risky, money laundering by the use of the financial and commercial markets, executed by lawyers and duplicated by corruption is much easier, safer and in the long run more profitable.

Lawyers need not police corruption, but they should discourage it and make it ever more difficult to facilitate and disguise.

The next few years will see an intensive search for a solution to the international cancer of corruption of public officials. The United States has been criticised in the past for the purported extra-territorial reach of its Foreign Corrupt Practices Act. This seeks to penalise companies who have their presence in the United States, but who indulge in corrupt practices in the conduct of overseas trade, even though few if any overt acts are taking place in US territory. It now seems more likely than not that international organisations will regard this extraterritorial reach more benignly, and we shall see the construction of an international legal order where the narrow constraints of domestic penal law or the existence of national frontiers will not prevent the hunting down and bringing to justice of corrupters, be they individuals or multinational companies.

Meanwhile, however, fresh bribery scandals break out almost weekly in one industrialised society after another and it is, I submit, inconceivable that on all these occasions, the legal profession who are necessarily involved in the negotiating and concluding of contracts are somehow innocent of all blame.

The International Bar Association was not set up simply to encourage the mechanical excellence of practitioners or to ensure that they did not offend against the terms of their professional indemnity policies. Surely, whether it is individuals or collectively the members of this Association have a responsibility to demonstrate that the rule of law is something more than a pious expression of an age old principle, and that in their everyday work in their offices around the world, they should seek not only to uphold but to actively promote a higher better more civilised order of conduct.

Globalisation of Laws - Tearing down the Walls

Peter Goldsmith QC

"On a political map, the boundaries between countries are as clear as ever. But on a competitive map, a map showing the real flows of financial activity, those boundaries have largely disappeared"

" 'Global citizenship' is no longer just a phrase in the lexicon of futurologists. It is every bit as real and concrete as measurable changes in GNP or trade flows"

Kenichi Omhae
Management consultant and leading writer on business:
The Borderless World

Recently I visited one of the legal bookshops near the Law Courts in London. This is not a University book shop catering to the tastes of academics and research students. Its customers are working lawyers, barristers or solicitors or those completing the vocational training of these professions who want practitioners' textbooks to help them with the actual practice of law. I looked at the section on European law. 10 years ago I would have expected to see only some selected treatises written by English academics on the European Communities and perhaps some old standards on comparative law. This time I lost count of the books on purely domestic laws of other European laws: French Constitutional Law, Swiss

Company Law, Doing Business in Romania, Business Law in Spain, French Real Property and Succession Law, Employment Laws in Europe, The German Law of Torts, European Financing Laws and many others.

This explosion of interest in the domestic laws of other countries is one manifestation of the growth business of globalisation, a phenomenon described by Professor Rosabeth Moss Kanter of the Harvard Business School as "*one of the most powerful and pervasive influences on nations, businesses, workplaces, communities, and lives at the end of the twentieth century.*"[1]

The purpose of this chapter is to consider how the globalisation of the economy affects the practice of law and asks the question whether we as lawyers are rising to the challenges raised by the economic and social restructuring of globalisation.

WHAT IS GLOBALISATION?

The changes in economic boundaries written about by the leading business writer Kenichi Omhae which are referred to in the quotation at the start of this article have been amongst the most remarkable of events since the last World War. It is particularly in the past few years that their effect has been greatest. The increase in the availability of international travel has been one of the major influences. Japan, not that long ago a closed society, is an object lesson. As Omhae has pointed out, 10 million Japanese now travel annually. They have seen first hand how people in other countries live, the styles of fashion, the sports and the life styles. For the first time they have the information to tell the government what it must do for them. Availability of information from and about other States without leaving home at all is the other great influence. Telecom-

---

1 *World Class: Thriving Locally in the Global Economy*, Simon & Schuster 1995

munications which can, for example, by satellite beam CNN into living rooms in Europe, Asia or Australia give to people around the world instantaneous reports of events taking place far away. More recently, the explosion in information technology through personal computers and the Internet have opened the world's eyes creating a true global village. We can visit libraries and databases half way across the world for the cost of a local telephone call. We can talk freely to people with common interests in another continent. As the use of the Internet becomes more commercial, the opportunities expand. So a businessman in Manchester can display his services through a web site to potential customers in Singapore, Sydney or Sacramento.

For these people, and increasingly for all of us, traditional geographical barriers cease to have their traditional meanings. These trends can only continue. In the UK, for example the Labour Party has promised that if elected it will see every school, college and place of education in the country connected free to the Information Superhighway. The five-year-olds of the future will be able to examine the treasures of museums thousands of miles away on a screen in their classroom or discuss homework assignments with school children the other side of the word as easily as if they were in the next town.

The political and economic upheaval these events have is hard to understate. They have broken down traditional geographical barriers in the world of business. It has become harder to pinpoint the nationality of products or the companies which make them. Are Honda cars assembled in Ohio American or Japanese cars? What nationality are Reebok sneakers made in Korea? Or Sony videotapes produced in Alabama and shipped to Europe? Are skis made by the French company Rossignol in Spain still French? The manufacturers of the quintessentially American product, Coca Cola, has 70% of the Japanese soft drinks market. What nationality are these drinks? There is a McDonalds on every street corner in Singapore's shopping centres. Are they not now as Singaporean as the other restaurants?

As a result, the managers of businesses are having to make business decisions which transcend national boundaries. They are concerned with where to find their markets, where their supplies, where best to manufacture and whom to employ. Meanwhile consumers with greater than ever choice are buying across borders, travelling and working in other countries.

This must have a major impact on the law and its practice. Law is classically a national affair, built up on national lines to meets national needs and administered by national courts. For all of Omhae's "global citizens" law should be an aid to facilitate their business and their affairs. But how can it be so if the business is stateless, no respecter of the political boundary, whilst law is narrowly confined within the national frontier? In the 20 minutes it now takes for the Euro shuttle to pass under the Channel from Kent to Calais the traveller passes from one legal system to another markedly different with different courts, and a different legal profession where only a few would be qualified to advise him on his rights and obligations under the system has just left. As he continued his journey East to Germany, south to Spain or north to Belgium and Holland, he would find in each case a new legal system distinct from the one he was leaving and distinct from the other he would have found if he had travelled in the other direction.

The fact is that users of legal services continue to be faced with a bewildering lack of uniformity in laws affecting their cross border transactions. If the great multinationals become frustrated by the difference between the legal systems and the confusing difference in procedural and substantive law which leads to forum shopping, how much greater are these problems for the consumer?

The balance of this article is concerned to consider how in practice globalisation has affected the law and legal practice and what further steps might be taken.

GLOBALISATION CREATES WORK FOR LAWYERS

Nobody who has made even the most cursory study of the changing face of the practice of law in the last past of the century could fail to have noticed how this phenomenon has changed the practice of law.

An OECD survey of the impact of legal services provided internationally showed that between them the net trade balances in respect of legal services of the USA and the UK was little short of US$2 billion.[2] This shows the significance of the international market for legal services. It becomes even clearer if one examines the case of the UK alone. UK lawyers accounted for nearly 50% of that US$2 billion; a figure of US$830 million. Given that the size of the legal profession in the UK is perhaps only a 10th of that in the USA (which is estimated to have close to 900, 000 lawyers) the size of the British lawyers contribution to the balance of trade, nearly 15% of the entire net trade balance from services, is indicative of the scale of the international activities of these lawyers in Europe and beyond. Moreover there has been a substantial increase in the past decade, with a doubling of the export earnings of the earnings of lawyers in just 6 years[3]. The physical evidence of this internationalisation is easy to see. Offices of these London based law firms are opening throughout the world. Having started often with only small offices in Paris or Brussels at the time the UK joined the Common Market in the early 1970's, many now have offices in many European centres, in the Far East and increasingly in the opening markets of China and the former Soviet bloc countries.

---

2 Source: OECD Documents: International Trade in Professional Services, Assessing Barriers and encouraging reform.

3 Source: Law Society of England & Wales returns; Commercial Bar Association returns of barristers' export services; City of London Solicitors Company estimates.

BUT THERE REMAINS A WIDE GULF

Whilst these figures are impressive, they risk obscuring the fact that generally the law remains a parochial and domestic affair. The big US and UK law firms are the exception. Most law firms are much smaller and equipped only to deal with legal problems under the national laws of their own country.

Much work is being done to improve the possibilities for lawyers to open up offices in other countries to service their clients with international problems. But there are substantial difficulties which limit this as a route to providing clients with the wealth of expertise in different laws which globalisation of the economy requires.

The need to ensure that the profession of lawyer is only exercised by those with proper training and who maintain high ethical standards and, it has to be conceded, a high degree of protectionism, have impeded the growth of law as an international profession. Even after 18 years there are only now signs that a directive of the European Union will be brought into law to give to lawyers qualified in one of the member States the right to establish a legal practice in another. Outside the confines of the Union (where there are strong political means to force a system of mutual recognition even on unwilling lawyers) the problems are even greater. Attempts to produce agreement amongst national bars on model standards for foreign legal consultants—lawyers from a different jurisdiction setting up to practice their home law and international law essentially—have proved highly controversial and look no closer to conclusion in 1997 than they did five years before.

In any event even when these rights are fully established they will be of use to only a small percentage of the law firms affected by them. Only the largest of the firms can afford to open offices in several other countries—an expensive and risky venture. For the rest they will only ever contemplate practising from offices in their own country. Other methods will therefore have to be found if their clients are to find solutions to their cross border legal problems.

TRAINING THE WORLD LAWYER?

Training is a Part of the Solution

Accountancy, banking and even the Church have become globalised professions. This has been greatly facilitated by the similarity of the practice of these activities in different countries so that the training in one country will fit someone for practice in another.

The intricacies and differences of the world's legal systems makes it an extraordinarily difficult task to master the laws of more than one country. Comparative lawyers have been able to divide the law into different legal families. Arminjon, Nolde and Wolff[4] identified seven distinct legal families in private law: the French, German, Scandinavian, English, Russian, Islamic and Hindu. Yet this is only to identify the main characteristics. Even within the family the differences may be enormous. It may arise as a result of divergence created by the development of a common law by judges or as a result of legislative intervention to modify the common law or to create new rights or obligations to meet the perceived social and economic needs of the country. An examination of the differences between US, Australian, Canadian, New Zealand and Singapore law, for example in the area of company law, will produce many important differences even though all may subscribe to the same basic principles of corporate identity.

It is difficult therefore enough for a lawyer to become proficient in the laws of another country whose laws are within the same legal family. To expect that students should attempt to master the laws from different legal families where the fundamental principles and concepts are different is to expect too much.

Nonetheless, there are important and developing signs of global law schools in the USA. For example, New York University School of Law established the Global Law School which has developed ties with faculties abroad; students spend a period training at foreign law

---

4 Traité de droit comparé I (1950).

schools and there are frequent faculty exchanges. A similarly innovative programme operates at Saint Louis University.[5] There has been a growing emphasis on an international approach in the Universities of European countries too. In 1995, for example, some 21 British Universities offered degree programmes combining law with a foreign language and often with some study of the law of the other country as well. Moreover there are an increasing number of law students who are spending some time studying in the law faculty of a University in another country. This has been especially encouraged by the European Commission through programmes such as ERAS MUS (European Action Scheme for Mobility of University Students), a programme adopted in 1987 under which students spend at least three months at a recognized University in another member State of the European Community. A similar programme (SOCRATES) operates for staff visits and exchanges, and the TEMPUS programme has been initiated for the benefit of students originating from the Universities of Eastern Europe. Still, the concept of training the European lawyer so long as there is no real common law of Europe is a long way off.

THE USE OF THE NEW TECHNOLOGY

Just as the new technologies have been the instruments of the global restructuring we have seen, so those selfsame technologies will be part of the solution to the new legal problems they have thrown away. They offer the ability to reach clients outside the lawyers' normal catchment area. They also provide means for lawyers in one country and one legal system to discover appropriate collaborators in other countries. These would be especially beneficial for lawyers who do not have the resources or the inclination to establish

5 For further information see Journal of Legal Education vol 46 no 3, Sept 1996, published by the Association of American Law Schools.

themselves in a variety of different parts of the world but whose clients need help with cross border problems.

Although lawyers are beginning to use the Internet as a marketing tool, development of systems which would provide a more structured information network system has at best only just begun.

DIVERGENCE OF THE LAW

Against this background, it should be considered how laws diverge and how more can be done to make them converge so as to reduce the legal uncertainty.

This may be illustrated by considering the approach taken by some of the different legal systems to the question of the responsibility of manufacturers of defective products which cause damage to a consumer. With the rise in the manufacturing industry and the increasing sophistication of products and their ability to cause harm if misused or if defectively produced the question of the responsibility of the ultimate manufacturer became in the 20th century an important legal issue. To have a claim against the manufacturer may be of special interest to the victim. He may have a claim against the seller but his rights may be restricted, modified, subject to a monetary limit or even excluded altogether by the contract of sale. The seller may be of limited means and unable to satisfy a substantial judgement. Or the victim may not be the buyer himself but a member of the family of the buyer who cannot claim to be the contracting party. Or he may be a complete stranger to the contract of sale, such as a pedestrian who is injured by a defective vehicle which suddenly crashes due to a defect in the brakes with no fault on the part of the driver.[6]

---

6 See generally on this topic Zweigert and Koetz, An introduction to Comparative Law, translated by Weir, Clarendon Press 1987.

The Common Law systems did not accept the possibility of the liability of the manufacturer to the consumer of defective goods until into the 20th century[7] save in the very limited case of inherently dangerous goods like poisons. But in 1916 the New York Court of Appeals decided in the seminal case of *MacPherson* v *Buick Motor Co*[8] that a motor car was dangerous and that the manufacturer owed a duty of care not only to the person who bought it but to any user of the car and was liable to a user who was injured by the negligence of the manufacturer. This was an important step in the development of the common law. Yet it took the English courts nearly another 20 years to take a similar route when, in the celebrated decision of *Donoghue* v *Stevenson*,[9] the House of Lords held that in principle the pursuer who had suffered (allegedly) nervous shock on finding a decomposed snail in the bottle of ginger beer purchased for her by her friend could sue the manufacturers of the beer, the defendants.[10]

Yet this was to be by no means the end of the development of the law of product liability, for the Courts had to grapple with the question whether the victim need prove fault on the part of the manufacturer. The need to prove this element can often be a daunting, uncertain and expensive task for the victim involving detailed and expert investigation into the manufacturing processes of the defendant

In the United States there was success in removing this element in the case where the consumer was injured by goods which were defective when judged objectively. After individual courts had first

---

7 See, for example, *Le Lievre v Gould* [1893] 1 QB 491 where liability which was not founded on contract in the case of negligent advice was rejected on the basis that "A man is entitled to be as negligent as he pleases towards the whole world if he owes no duty to them."

8 217 NY 382, 111 NE 1050 (1916).

9 [1932] AC 562.

10 It continues to be a matter of controversy in British legal circles whether there was ever a snail at all as the case reached the House of Lords on assumed facts.

pointed in this direction[11] the Restatement (Second) of Torts was promulgated with this as a principle in 1965 as § 402A. Since then it has been adopted by courts in most States.[12]

The English courts did not, however, take the same route. Despite powerful attempts to produce a change in the law[13] the Courts continued to insist on the need for fault to be proved.

Meanwhile, in European countries, special rules for the liability of the manufacturer were also being developed. In France court interpretations of Article 1645 of the Civil Code—under which the seller of defective goods is liable to the buyer for all harm due to the defect if he knew of the defect in the object sold—increased the protection. First, the Courts held that a seller in the course of his business of defective goods is treated as if he was aware of the defect.[14] Secondly, they have allowed the consumer to leapfrog to claim against the manufacturer although the theory is that the claim is against the seller who is allowed to bring a claim ("appel en garantie") against the next in the contractual chain.[15]

The German courts appear to have gone through a similar process of evolution but by a still further route. After a period of doubt whether to base the manufacturers' liability in contract or tort the Bundesgerichthof in Germany decided that the claim must be in tort where there was no contractual relationship between the victim and the manufacturer whereas the Austrian Oberster Gerichtshof took the contractual route. [16] Nonetheless the German courts were able to avoid the conclusion that the responsibility lay with the victim to show negligence on the part of the manufacturer by allowing

---

11 See eg *Escola* v *Coca-Cola Bottling Co* 24 Cal.2d 453 150 P 2d 436; *Greenman v Yuba Power Products* 59 Cal. 2d 57, 377 P 2d 897.

12 See Zweigert and Koetz, op cit. p 715.

13 The Law Commission's *Report on Liability for Defective Products* (1977) and the Report of the Pearson *Commission on Civil Liability and Compensation for Personal Injury* cap 22 (1978).

14 See Civ.17 Feb. 1965, Bull. Civ. 1965. III. 112.

15 Civ. 5 Jan 1972, JCP 1973 II. 17340.

16 See Zweigert and Koetz, op cit p 718.

an exception in the case of products liability that the manufacturer had to prove how the defect arose and that no blame attached to the firm or its staff.[17]

Thus the courts of four major trading and consuming nations had by the mid-80s reached somewhat different views on the extent and basis for the liability of producers of defective goods. At least so far as the European countries were concerned a legislative solution was then imposed which brought a high degree of divergence.[18] After the Council of Europe had produced a draft "European Treaty on Products Liability" the European Communities eventually produced a Directive of 25 July 1985 requiring member States to ensure that their laws provided that the producer should be liable independently of any fault for the harm caused by a defect in goods produced by him.

This illustrates, therefore, both the tendency for national laws to produce different solutions to the same problem even where they are members of the same legal family and the way that concerted harmonisation initiatives can produce convergence.

EXISTING INITIATIVES IN CONVERGENCE IN LAWS

There is therefore nothing novel in recognising that the pressures lead to the desirability of provoking a greater uniformity in the law. The rich diversity of our national laws brings with it no

---

17 The so-called "fowl pest" decision BGHZ 51, 91 discussed in Zweigert and Koetz, op cit p 719.

18 Even then not complete because the contracting States were allowed a degree of leeway as to what was introduced. For example, it was possible to allow the defence of development risk which allows a manufacturer to escape liability in some cases by relying on the state of knowledge at the time. The UK allowed the defence in all cases, France, Belgium and Luxembourg in none and Germany had different rules for the development of drugs.

doubt many benefits. In particular, they provide us with the opportunity to mould legal solutions to the particular social, political and economic circumstances of our respective countries. Yet they also bring disadvantages: the uncertainty created by diversity of legal rights and obligations. Greater uniformity of law is therefore a desirable aim in the interests of the better legal protection of the citizens of our countries, greater legal certainty and increased trade.

The Courts do themselves produce some convergence. This occurs when there is parallel evolution of neighbouring legal systems trying to produce solutions to new fact-situations and borrowing from each other. A good example is to be found in a recent important decision of the House of Lords in the UK on the responsibilities of a lawyer who fails to give effect to the wishes of the testator towards the disappointed beneficiaries. In finding the solution to this problem the House of Lords not only examined the jurisprudence of other Common Law countries—by no means a rare thing to do—but considered at some length the help to be gained from German jurisprudence[19].

There are Important Institutionalised Initiatives

On the international plane there are organisations involved with the harmonisation of laws. The work they have produced principally by the production of conventions or of model laws is of great significance. They include conventions on Civil Procedure, the Service Abroad of Judicial and Extra Judicial Documents and the Taking of Evidence Abroad in Civil and Commercial Matters by The Hague Conference on Private International Law; on the Travel Contract, on a Uniform Law on the form of an international will and on International Financial Leasing by Unidroit, the International Institute for the Unification of Private Law; and the international trade conventions developed by Unictral, the United Nations Commission on International Trade Law, such as the Conventions

---

19 See *White v Jones* [1995] 2 AC 605.

on Contracts for the International Sale of Goods and on International Bills of Exchange and International Promissory Notes.

Within more localised groupings there are more sustained initiatives. A strong example is shown by the European Union. In the process of drafting a common market, ever-increasing areas of the law of the member States are unified by regulations or harmonised by directives. Examples where the European Community has taken an active role are in the field of company law, product liability, and consumer protection. Convergence also results from common norms developed within the framework of the Council of Europe (notably within the field of human rights) but also in the dense network of other, more specialised international treaties linking the countries of Europe. By way of example, the Brussels Convention on Jurisdiction and Reciprocal Enforcement of Judgements in Commercial Matters has had a profound effect in England in private international law producing a parallel system alongside the existing common law principles of *forum non conveniens*.

THE ROLE OF LAWYERS IN THIS PROCESS

The involvement of practising lawyers in the developments discussed above has been sporadic at best. Many of the representatives and experts at the international negotiating table are government officials and academic lawyers. The involvement of practising lawyers is in many cases a method of chance. Yet practising lawyers need to be involved in much of this process to ensure that the result is workable. They have an unrivalled perspective on the practical requirements of their clients, the "consumers" of the law. They have as a result a special ability to ensure that proposed reforms work in practice. They also have an ability to identify areas of priority and need.

The International Bar Association has already demonstrated that it can bring to bear on these problems the resources available through the network of highly experienced lawyers who constitute its membership. For example, a Concordat on Cross Border Insolvency developed by Section J of the Business Law section has been already applied by judges

The Standing Committee on Globalisation of Laws (established by the IBA in Berlin in 1996) is another endeavour to harness these resources so as to support the existing institutionalised initiatives and at the same time encourage our own programme of globalisation of laws. If we can take advantage of the enormous experience of the widespread membership of the IBA we hope to be able to play our role in the overall process.

CONCLUSION

Globalisation of the economy has irreversibly torn down barriers between nations as the Berlin Wall was torn down in 1989. Professor Moss Kanter argues that world business leaders now have an obligation to

> "tear down the invisible walls between countries, companies, cultures, customers and suppliers, and departments and levels within organisations, replacing walls that divide with bridges that link".

Those invisible walls include national laws which divide and confuse. Lawyers and lawmakers need to look at how they can play their part in tearing down those walls. It is appropriate that the Standing Committee on Globalisation of Laws was established at the IBA's Council in Berlin because globalisation of laws is part of that task.

*Multidisciplinary Practices – The Future**

Ward Bower

Accounting firms for years have practised more tax law than law firms, throughout the world. However, increasingly they are hiring lawyers to offer business-related legal advice to clients in areas including employee benefits, business planning and organization, insolvency, bankruptcy, and loan restructuring/work-outs. More recently, major accounting firms have acquired litigation support service companies in the US and some have hired experienced litigators to attempt to preempt dispute resolution and front-end litigation services (investigation, valuation, discovery) by the law firm and to assist in application of ADR to avoid litigation. Consider the text of a recent full-page, color, glossy ad from a Big Six firm, directed to US in-house, corporate counsel entitled—"When You Seek New Solutions to Tough Disputes." It goes on, "Today, we advise corporate counsel ... through an expanding array of litigation alternatives ... So, *before* you shoot it out in court, call Price Waterhouse." The clear implication here is that the erstwhile client may not even need to engage a law firm to solve his dispute.

The movement of accounting firms into the traditional preserves of private law practice is giving rise to the creation of MDPs—Multidisciplinary Practices (or "Multidisciplinary Partnerships"), recognized legally in some jurisdictions. MDPs are characterized by an ownership group including both lawyers and non-lawyers, often other licensed professionals, such as Chartered Accountants (CPAs). In other jurisdictions, where not legally recognized, MDPs are emerging in a *de facto* format.

MDPS AND OTHER NON-TRADITIONAL LEGAL SERVICE PROVIDERS

Although US lawyers so far have chosen to ignore the issue of MDPs, it is of significance elsewhere in the world. For example, the legal services components and affiliates of the Big Six accounting firms are major service providers in European countries, especially France, and they are gaining increasing market share elsewhere on the Continent, as evidenced by Arthur Andersen's announced 1996 "acquisition" of J&A Garrigues, one of Spain's largest law firms. One of the more aggressive of the Big Six, Arthur Andersen established a "captive" law firm in London (Garrett & Co.) in 1994, employing a well-known, former corporation counsel. Garrett & Co. now has over 140 solicitors in cities throughout the UK. Anecdotally, British lawyers report Garrett & Co. representing parties who would have no way of finding them, but for the fact Arthur Andersen happens to be their auditor. The English legal profession has been unable or unwilling to stem the invasion by Andersen, and Price Waterhouse has responded by opening its own London "captive." Ernst & Young and KPMG have publicly announced intentions to follow AA's lead. And the Labour Party vows its intention to legislate MDPs formally into existence if they prevail in the next UK election. Big Six accounting firms also have employed local lawyers to practice law in developing Eastern European and former Soviet bloc countries.

In New South Wales (Australia) multidisciplinary partnerships were approved legislatively in July of 1994, and by September Arthur Andersen and KPMG had opened their law offices in Sydney. Others are following. Other Australian states (notably Victoria) and New Zealand are reportedly considering such a move. In Latin American, Asia and Africa, sporadic reports emerge regarding activity of the Big Six accountancies in law practice. It is notable that the large accountancies now refer to themselves as "professional service firms."

To be fair, it is not only accounting firms that are invading the traditional preserve of the independent law firm. Consider, for example:

- In the state of Florida, independent paralegal firms serve clients directly in a limited range of low-end legal services (Social Security and Medicare claims, first party insurance claims, etc.). These firms are owned by non-lawyers and the paralegals are not supervised by lawyers. Proposals that would allow independent paralegal firms have been put forward in California.
- In Washington, DC non-lawyers (generally, office administrators, economists, and consultants) may take an ownership position in a law firm and share in profits.
- In many jurisdictions labor, environmental and employee benefits consulting firms hire lawyers to provide the same services to the consultancy's clients that those lawyers previously provided to their law firm's clients.
- Banks, insurance companies and financial planning firms all hire lawyers to perform estate planning and estate administration services.

Historically, the legal profession might have fought such incursions into its marketplace in courts of equity, seeking injunctions against unauthorized practice. However, that remedy is increasingly less available in most jurisdictions, worldwide, where movements towards deregulation, consumerism, and open marketplace competition are in vogue. This is especially true when the protagonists are wealthy, powerful and where they are hiring qualified lawyers to offer the legal services they provide.

A CONTEMPORARY SURVEY

In late 1996 Professor Ross Harper, IBA President, created a Standing Committee on MDPs. His first act was to survey IBA Councillors regarding the status of MDPs in their jurisdictions. Although response was disappointing, it was instructive:

- 45% of responding countries reported that they have legislation or regulation regarding MDPs, of which three-quarters prohibit them.
- 52% had no legislation or regulation, but three-fifths of that group are considering the issue, the one-third of them currently allow MDPs.
- In 20% of responding jurisdictions, non-lawyers may own an equity interest in an organization that delivers legal services.
- In 24% of responding jurisdictions, non-lawyers can share in fees and profits from the delivery of legal services.
- In 72% of responding jurisdictions, organizations other than law firms are currently providing legal service to others:
  - In 55% of those jurisdictions by accountants
  - In 34%, by consulting firms
  - In 41%, by banks
  - In 34%, by insurance companies
  - In 24%, by others, including trust companies, licensed conveyancers and trade unions
- In 20% of jurisdictions where organizations other than law firms provide legal services, they do so in violation of rules of professional conduct.
- Remedies available in countries where MDP legislation or regulation exists, include:
  - Criminal prosecution—10%
  - Injunction against unauthorised practice—7%

- Civil fine or penalty—7%
- In 83% of responding jurisdictions, lawyers can provide services other than pure legal representation (e.g., consulting, economic analysis, etc.).
- In 45% of responding jurisdictions, lawyers can become owners in accounting firms; in 38% of jurisdictions, they cannot.
- In responding jurisdictions, the following activities which relate to means by which MDPs are functioning in some jurisdictions are condoned, to the degree indicated below:
  - Referral to law firm by non-lawyer or other entity—69%
  - Payment of management fee to landlord/other entity in exchange for legal referrals—52%
  - Payment to other entity for referrals—24%
  - Reciprocal referral agreement with other entity—62%

Councillors identified the greatest threats to independent law firms by MDPs to be:

- Loss of independence
- Direct competition for clients

The greatest threats to the public, as seen by the Councillors, were:

- Loss of independence of their lawyer
- Potential conflicts of interest

Councillors did not identify potential loss of client privilege as a threat posed by MDPs, although the IBA Standing Committee sees that as a potential problem.

BLURRED BOUNDARIES

One likely result of all of this is the possible erosion of lines of distinction between service providers oriented toward the prevention and solving of problems for both private, individual and business clients, in much the same way that lines of distinction between banks, brokerage houses and insurance companies have blurred during the gradual de-regulation of those industries in recent decades. Today, it makes little difference to consumers whether they are dealing with a bank, brokerage house or insurance company in the sense that all three can invest their money, provide regular statements, issue checkbooks, credit cards and the like, or some combination of those services. Likewise, it is possible that in the near future law, accounting and consulting firms will be functionally indistinguishable, in the sense that all three are able to offer multidisciplinary advice on business, tax, investment, dispute resolution, retirement and benefits planning, and employ individuals licensed in many professions or disciplines. Boundaries already have blurred in jurisdictions where "multidisciplinary partnerships" are emerging, as in the European Union and in Australia. In February, 1997 Price Waterhouse and the Washington, DC law firm Miller & Chevalier announced a "strategic alliance" whereby clients can avail themselves of multidisciplinary advice on tax and business issues in the US.

COMPETITIVE ADVANTAGE OF ACCOUNTING FIRMS

A major threat to law firms arising from this incursion into the marketplace derives from the competitive advantage of the "Big Six" accountants. Consider the following:

- *Institutional Client Base.* Major accounting firms provide audit services to hundreds of clients, worldwide. However, declining profitability of that work, combined with its liability exposure, has forced them to refocus their efforts on development of tax, management advisory and now, legal services, all of which are "sold" to their base of audit clients.
- *Cross-Marketing.* Accounting firms are adept at cross-selling management advisory and tax services to their audit clients and can be expected to be just as effective in cross-selling legal services.

- *Size.* Accounting firms have tens of thousands of employees, both professional and support staff, worldwide, all of whom are potential and actual marketers of the firm's professional services.
- *Leverage.* Accounting firms are very highly leveraged and find means by which legions of non-CPA (non-C.A.) employees can generate profits for the owners.
  Most lawyers are/would be non-CPA employees of the accounting firm that employs them (unless, of course, the lawyer is also a CPA).
- *Availability of Capital.* The sheer size of accounting firms means that capital is available from thousands of partners, rather than only hundreds of partners in even the very largest of the law firms in the world.
- *Brand Names.* Big Six accounting firms enjoy brand name recognition, increasingly an advantage in a sophisticated, maturing legal marketplace, especially in situations where those engaging outside counsel are accountable for their choice. Recent studies appear to show brand name recognition to be worth a significant premium on fees in a professional services marketplace.
- *Institutional Advertising, Sophisticated Marketing.* Accounting firms spend multiples of what law firms do on advertising and marketing, and have years more experience in the marketing of intangible services to individuals of means and businesses. They have developed very significant, very effective advertising campaigns to reinforce their brands.
- *Cutting Edge Technology.* Accounting firms are leaders in the use of technology in professional services. The technology investments of even the largest law firms pale in comparison to those of accounting firms. They employ technology and process reengineering techniques internally to maximize the efficiency of service production, reduce costs and increase margins.
- *R&D Budgets and Activities.* Accounting firms invest significantly in research and development, not only in technology

but in cutting edge areas like quality management, process redesign and business process re-engineering.

- *International Capabilities.* All Big Six accounting firms are worldwide, and most second tier accounting firms are also international, a clear advantage in marketing "one-stop shopping" to multi-national clients.

THE WORLD VIEW

The worldwide proliferation of MDP activity (*de facto* and *de jure*) is further confused by the apparent legal authority of the World Trade Organization (WTO) in Geneva to exert regulatory control over "professional services" (including lawyers) as a result of the adoption of the Uruguay Round of GATS (General Agreement on Trade in Services) in 1993. Even the most casual WTO observer recognizes an apparent bias against regulation, for *laissez-faire, caveat emptor* and free trade in everything emanating from the rule-making and dispute-resolution activities of that body. Protectionist regulation is anathema to the WTO and even regulation in the public interest is subject to severe scrutiny.

A WTO working group is currently (1997) addressing worldwide regulation of the accountancies, as the first of the "professions" it is studying. An October 1996 WTO briefing of IBA leaders, in Geneva, indicates that the legal profession will be next, "in a few years" (1998 or after). The effectiveness of WTO rules will depend on many factors, but liberality without consideration of public and client interests could set back the professionalism of lawyers by centuries if traditional client protections assuring lawyer loyalty and preserving privilege are compromised. And WTO regulators only will understand these issues if the organized bar informs them. They are bureaucrats and economists, not lawyers or accountants.

THE THREAT TO INDEPENDENT LAW FIRMS

The emergence of multidisciplinary practices as competitors to traditional, independent law firms by virtue of their incursion into the traditional legal quasi-monopoly presents a significant threat which has yet to pierce the consciousness of many lawyers. Law firms are threatened by multidisciplinary professional service firms in labor, environmental, tax, regulatory and business practice, but more importantly in the future, it appears they will also be vulnerable in areas of "big ticket" litigation. The magnitude of that threat alone could jeopardies as much as thirty billion dollars in annual fee revenues to US law firms, alone.

In Europe and the UK, the accountancies are dismissed by many lawyers as "second tier commercial practices," threatening only mid-sized and smaller law firms practising in the domestic commercial arena, and employing only "second class" lawyers. Recent acquisitions of lateral hires by Garrett & Co. in the UK suggest otherwise, and recent approaches by Big Six firms to major US and Australian firms engaged in "first tier" international project finance, infrastructure, privatization, M&A and corporate finance practices reflects the apparent intention to compete with US and UK-based international law firms at the very highest levels. It is premature and potentially foolish to discount or underestimate either the will or the ability of the accountancies to acquire the resources to enable them to compete at the most sophisticated levels of law practice, on a world-wide scale, in a relatively short period of time. Their brand appeal could prove compelling, especially in emerging markets and in developing countries.

THE THREAT TO CLIENTS AND THE PUBLIC

The potential impact of multidisciplinary practices on the public also has not been recognized widely. Professional rules calculated to protect clients traditionally have militated against non-lawyer ownership in entities providing legal services to the public. For example, the protection of lawyer-client privilege generally is waived if the client divulges otherwise confidential information to anyone other than his lawyer. Law firms generally are charged with imputed knowledge of client confidences, firmwide. Thus, it just may be that clients who engage multidisciplinary firms for legal services place themselves in jeopardy of relinquishing their privilege, if knowledge of confidential information is imputed to non-lawyer professionals in the firm to whom client privilege is not extended by law. The fact that clients take this risk seems not to matter. Even sophisticated clients whose in-house lawyers choose outside counsel are engaging MDPs and "captives" of the Big Six, in apparent disregard of the possible impact of such a choice on the lawyer-client privilege.

Likewise, rules against sharing legal fees and profits with non-lawyers are designed to preserve the loyalty and independence of the lawyer. Rules regarding conflicts are seemingly different for accounting and consulting firms in the sense they apparently allow representation of clients by accounting firms that would present a clear conflict of interest and possible disqualification for an independent law firm. The fact that "sophisticated" clients represented by in-house lawyers hire multidisciplinary practices where they can seems to indicate that clients are unconcerned about the protections afforded by the rules helping to assure loyalty and independence of their lawyers, as well.

Clearly, *caveat emptor* is currently in order for legal clients of MDPs. The potential for loss of client privilege or lawyer independence is real.

JOINDER OF THE DEBATE

The debate on the subject of MDPs which is slowly emerging is misunderstood by many as an argument between lawyers and the Chartered Accountants, which it is not, altogether. Rather, it is predominately a debate between lawyers—those lawyers who believe the provision of legal services to the public should be restricted to lawyers practising independently in traditional firms and those who would be employed by another professional entity to practice law, or those who would support the right of other lawyers to do so. In this sense, the typical lawyer's defensive response to MDPs—that UPL (Unauthorized Practice of Law) sanctions be invoked—is irrelevant. Generally, MDPs employ qualified lawyers to deliver legal services to their clients.

STRATEGIC CHOICES

Law firms and the legal profession, generally, have a number of strategies available to address the challenge of MDPs. This first requires that the threat of non-traditional competition be recognized and acknowledged by lawyers.

Strategies which might be employed include the following:

- Formation of an affiliation or strategic alliance on a local, regional, national or worldwide basis between major service providers—e.g. Skadden, Arps/Deloitte & Touche, Baker & McKenzie/Arthur Andersen, etc. The 1997 "strategic alliance" between Price Waterhouse and Miller & Chevalier falls short of this—it is national to the US, at best, and reportedly not exclusive.
- Entry into true multidisciplinary partnerships (MDPs) in jurisdictions where so permitted, in effect allowing the law firm to become acquired by its larger, accounting firm partner. This might be expected in Australia were it not for legislation requiring a majority ownership interest in a legal MDP to be held by lawyers.
- Initiating "unauthorized practice" suits in equity, brought by the organized bar, in carefully selected areas where courts are more likely to issue an injunction in a given jurisdiction, and where the legal service is rendered by a non-lawyer.
- Reconsideration of the referral relationship between law and

specific accounting firms, when those accounting firms become competitively active in one's local legal market. This might require establishing outbound referral policies and procedures so that accounting firms which are engaging in legal services are not recipients of law firm referrals, and tracking inbound referrals to assure that the law firm is receiving its *quid pro quo* on out-bound referrals to each accounting firm.

- Discontinuing participation in economic surveys conducted by some major accounting firms, in recognition that accounting firm incursion into the legal market has been in areas of greatest profitability, whether by coincidence or not.
- Using independent legal management consulting firms rather than the management advisory services of major accounting firms, or consultancies affiliated with major accounting firms, again for protection of strategic economic information.
- Competing directly by creating management advisory, damage valuation and tax capabilities to rival those of the accountants and other service providers.
- Changing relationships from Big Six to local accounting firms less likely to compete for legal business.
- Identifying and exploiting sources of meaningful differentiation in the open marketplace, including (1) meaningful differences in the ethical rules (conflicts of interest, client confidences, etc.) between lawyers and accountants; (2) the omnipresent litigation threat in dispute resolution, which might weaken the negotiation position of clients represented in ADR by accounting firms; (3) the "switching costs" involved in shifting dispute resolution from an accounting firm to a law firm in order to litigate.[1]

---

1 However, these differentiation strategies must be pursued from the perspective of client and public interests, rather than self-interest of the profession. Nary a tear will be shed by the business community or the public if law firms are displaced by accounting firms and other service

- Using legal process redesign/re-engineering, automation and ADR to streamline legal processes, especially in the litigation area, enabling direct competition with accountants on the basis of price, efficiency and responsiveness.
- Pressing the organized bar to inform the public of the value of the ethical code subscribed to by lawyers and the protection of public and individual interests in the delivery of legal services by private law firms, especially the lawyer/client privilege and assurance of the independence and loyalty of the lawyer and firm to the client.
- Ask the bar and law societies to consider ways in which it can make lawyers better able to compete by levelling the playing field—making it easier for law firms to raise capital (non-lawyer owners? public ownership?), revisiting some of the rules regarding professional independence, conflict of interests and the like in relation to comparable standards for accountants, placing meaningful image advertising on behalf of the profession, and making it easier for lawyers and law firms to inform the public of the superior value of their services through various media.
- Do nothing and see what happens.[2]

---

providers in these areas of activity. Marketplace acceptance of non-traditional providers suggests that the public currently places little apparent value on the protections afforded individual rights as a result of representation by trained, professional lawyers and firms of lawyers in the public court systems, as opposed to accountants, consultants or others in ADR.

2 This likely would result in the abdication of significant areas of legal practice to the accounting firms. This occurred in the case of tax law when law firms abdicated preparation of individual 1040 income tax returns to accountants when they no longer became profitable, after which the accountants automated the tax return process, gaining the associated tax-related legal advice and services to individuals of means, closely-held corporations and corporations for whose executives tax returns were prepared. Ignoring the current threat could result in such a scenario.

PLANNING IMPLICATIONS

Individual law firms which have not included "non-traditional" sources of competition in their planning assumptions should revisit their strategic plans, including accountants, consultants, financial institutions and the like in their competitive analysis. Differentiation strategies based on efficiencies, public interest and quality standards should be developed, where appropriate. In addition, firm resources might be volunteered to assist in professional association efforts toward image enhancement, education and rules review.

CONCLUSION

A scenario in which the major accounting firms have taken over the worldwide provision of international corporate legal services is not implausible, in the marketplace today. All of the necessary warning signs are there. What independent law firms need to do is to integrate the threat from MDPs into their strategic planning and assure themselves and their clients that: (1) their law firms can practice law better, faster and more efficiently than accounting firms, and (2) the rules by which lawyers are required to practice in independent law firms afford clients protections which may not be available when multidisciplinary practices are engaged. Ultimately, the marketplace will tell us whether they buy the argument of those lawyers committed to and promoting independent law firms, or those allied with the accountants and other service providers.

Professional Regulation and Globalization: Toward a Better Balance

*Bernard L. Greer, Jr.**

Awareness is growing that some regulations may be inappropriate in a globalised world and that a better balance should be struck between the need for regulation and the necessity to ensure competition. *Organization for Economic Cooperation and Development, Regulatory Reform Project, Draft Chapter on Professional Business Services, October 22, 1996, at 4.*

I. THE IMPACT OF GLOBALISATION.

Perhaps the best way to illustrate the thesis of this article is to begin with an imperfect analogy. First, imagine a standard political map of the world, with each country represented by a different color. In each of these countries there is at least one legal system or jurisdiction—sometimes more than one—and within each jurisdiction there is at least one regulated legal profession. Obviously there are some differences among these various professions, but all of the

* The assistance of Felipe Núñez is gratefully acknowledged.

bodies which regulate their conduct are concerned with the regulation of what most of us would consider the practice of law within the historic borders of their jurisdiction, and each regulated profession has its own rules governing admission, conduct and practice. Because these professions are linked to the administration of justice and because the proper discharge of their duties is integral to the efficient ordering of private affairs, each profession has a privileged status within its jurisdiction, and entry into the profession and its unauthorized, i.e., unlicensed, practice have been restricted. While these controls may restrict competition, sound policy reasons support their existence and enforcement. It is important, however, to remember that these professional regimes are historically based on, and traditionally have been administered within, the framework of geographical borders.

As a second step, with the imaginary political map still in mind, superimpose upon it a diagram depicting the world's weather patterns, showing—with arrows and other symbols—the main forces which influence the weather worldwide. A comparison of this weather map with the political map shows that the weather does not respect borders, and that its main trends are influenced by developments which often take place far beyond the affected area.

Now take a final step. Replace the weather patterns with the forces which underlie the process generally referred to as "globalisation"—the increasing movement of people, capital, goods and services across national borders. Globalisation has been made possible by the revolutions in communication, information and other technologies and by sweeping political change. The result has been the rapid development of new markets for business and the expansion of developed economies throughout the world. This process seems irreversible and—as with the weather—the power of traditional political and other institutions—including the bodies which regulate the legal profession—to control it limited.

A. The New Practice Environment

Those who practice our profession have adapted quickly to this new environment, and globalisation has wrought a radical change in the way in which law is practised. With the dramatic increase of international trade and investment, the extent to which clients and companies are traveling and doing business internationally would have been difficult to imagine even a few years ago. Consequently, the tasks these clients and companies are asking their lawyers to perform have changed to reflect this remarkable change. To give one example, it is increasingly common for business transactions to be negotiated in one jurisdiction, consummated in another and financed from one or more additional jurisdictions. Increasingly, the criteria used by clients to select their lawyers are derived from factors other than their formal qualifications and the jurisdictions in which they are licensed. From my own recent experience, I can cite the following examples:

- I know an American lawyer in Paris, who is licensed only in New York and France, but whose current practice involves representation of clients from the Middle East and Europe in Eastern Europe.
- An American firm, which has no branch offices outside the United States, recently represented a French company in a joint venture with a German company in Brazil, the financing for which was provided by French and Japanese lenders.
- One of the partners in our firm's International Practice Group represented a German company in an International Chamber of Commerce arbitration in Zurich arising from claims against the government of a Middle Eastern country.

All of us can point to similar examples. The reason for engagements such as those described above is simple: a client, not unreasonably, chooses as its lawyers those who know the client's business and whom it believes to be the best qualified to provide specific services in a timely and cost-effective manner.

The adaptation of our profession to this new cross-border practice environment has been generally referred to as the "internationalization" of legal services. Although some law firms are following expansion strategies which anticipate clients' needs and demands in new "legal markets," internationalization is more accurately described as a reactive process. As noted above, it is a fact of contemporary life that individuals and companies are traveling and doing business abroad more than ever before. In this environment lawyers (and their firms) are simply following their clients and responding to, or anticipating, their needs. Barring worldwide economic depression or general war—neither of which appears to be imminent—this cross-border activity is certain to increase.

Lawyers and their firms have adapted to these developments in a number of ways:

1. Where permitted, they are establishing foreign branch offices;
2. They are constantly upgrading their telecommunications capacity, enhancing their ability to communicate almost anywhere in the world instantaneously—(international video conferencing will soon be routine);
3. They are traveling abroad much more than in the past—and to more places—on what can be described as a "temporary services" basis;
4. They are forming regional and worldwide alliances with firms in other countries ranging from loose affiliations of independent firms to more exclusive relationships, including "joint ventures"; and
5. They are diversifying the qualifications of their professional staff so that they can function effectively in more legal systems and in a greater variety of cultural settings.

The combination of these factors has made legal services much more "portable" and exportable than ever before.

B. The Unchanging Lawyer-Client Relationship.

It is important to remember, however, that, while this new environment has radically changed the arena in which lawyers practice, the basic nature of the relationship of lawyers to their clients remains in essence the same. In fact, the nature of the relationship may assume even greater importance in the context of the greater mobility of people, money, goods and services. The lawyer-client relationship remains based upon a foundation of trust and confidence. Once these have been achieved, one often finds that the client will ask the lawyer (or the law firm) to perform a wider range of services in more places.

It would be inaccurate to view this process as one involving only large firms from developed countries. In fact, no lawyer or firm is immune to the effects of globalisation. It is would be difficult to find in any part of the world a lawyer whose practice could be viewed as purely "local." More often, all countries depend upon international trade. Export transactions and international investments are growing rapidly. Dispute resolution is becoming more international in nature. Moreover, this involvement is not limited to business practice. Transnational issues may arise in domestic practice, such as divorce or child custody cases. As individual property holdings have become more diversified, multi-jurisdictional taxation and estate planning as well as bankruptcy and other insolvency issues are encountered by local practitioners much more often than in the past.[1] It has been said that, as distance increases, relationships assume greater importance. In the context of cross-border legal practice, the need for trust and confidence—the bedrock of the lawyer-client relationship—becomes even more essential.

---

1 It is important to note also that globalisation affects developing as well as developed countries. In major commercial centres such as New York and London—where the regimes permit the establishment of foreign branch offices—many lawyers from developing countries have established such offices.

II. THE CHALLENGE TO THE REGULATED PROFESSION

A. Critical Unresolved Issues

This very brief and general sketch of the landscape only hints at the complexity of the questions facing our profession as a result of what can only be described as revolutionary and ongoing change. This new environment has challenged not only practitioners but the authorities which license and regulate our profession. For these bodies, the challenge is to blend the traditional concerns of the regulated profession—competence, ethical conduct and discipline—with the need to address the demands and realities of today's cross-border environment. This, in turn, involves the balancing of old and time-honored public interests with the necessity to modernize the framework within which we practice law. It is appropriate for us to ask how well these bodies are responding to the developments described above and to compare the relevance of professional regimes to day-to-day practice. Put another way, are professional regimes addressing the issues posed by globalisation in a manner which recognizes the need to facilitate the conduct of transnational business in tandem with the need to maintain clear and rigorous professional standards? Regrettably, the answer to that question is that, with a few exceptions, they do not, and it is clear that the bodies which regulate the legal profession world-wide have not addressed the issues arising from the globalisation of legal practice in a thoughtful and comprehensive way.

These issues are abundant and varied, and they have at least some relevance to all jurisdictions. A partial listing includes:

1. *Adequacy of Education.* Are law schools and continuing legal education requirements preparing law students and active practitioners for practice in the global environment?
2. *Flexibility of Requirements.* Are bar admission requirements sufficiently flexible to permit the admission of candidates trained in other legal systems?

3. *Licensing.* Do bar examinations adequately test the competence of lawyers to perform effectively in today's transnational environment?
4. *Regulation of Transnational Firms.* Do contemporary regimes address the phenomenon of multinational and multi-jurisdictional firms in a consistent manner?
5. *Transparency.* Do restrictions on local practice in professional regimes address the phenomenon of cross-border practice—traveling lawyers and branch offices—in a fair and nondiscriminatory way?
6. *Professional Privileges.* Are traveling lawyers and those in branch offices entitled to professional privileges, including the protection of confidentiality of client communications, under local professional regimes?
7. *Professional Ethics.* Would we benefit from commonly accepted standards of professional responsibility, and are there clear guidelines concerning the standards applicable to lawyers whose practice takes them temporarily or permanently to other jurisdictions?
8. *Conflicts of Interest.* Given the proliferation of multinational firms and cross border activities of all kinds, have we developed rules for avoiding conflicts of interest which serve the interest of clients and law firms?
9. *Professional Liability.* Are there commonly accepted standards of professional performance by which our increasingly mobile profession is to be measured?
10. *Company Counsel.* Are lawyers employed by corporations and other business entities accorded professional status and privileges?

B. The Need for a Coordinated Approach

Issues of this sort have only recently begun to receive the attention that they deserve.[2] Though these issues are important and worthy of critical examination, to date no comprehensive examination has been conducted by the organized legal profession, at least not on the scale that seems required. It also seems self-evident that such an examination should not be conducted in a vacuum but should be coordinated by appropriate professional organizations worldwide with a view toward establishing the basis for a more uniform professional regime which provides not only certainty in uniformity but also a measure of flexibility necessary to accommodate the transnational delivery of legal services without the interposition of unfair or discriminatory barriers. I am not arguing that standards should be relaxed, only that they should not unreasonably impede the natural course of performance of professional duties and that they should be made clear to all practitioners. When the need arises lawyers will find ways to provide the services required by their clients—if necessary without reference to the formal professional regime. Certainly, this would be lamentable; but if this proposition is true, we should consider whether or not rules which may be widely ignored should not be re-examined.

To date, the response of professional regulatory bodies worldwide does not give cause for great comfort. It is no exaggeration to note that, to the extent it exists, regulation of transnational practices is a patchwork of varying requirements which has not adapted readily to the reality of modern practice. In a few jurisdictions, such as England and Wales and Hong Kong, open regimes have been adopted.[3] In others, for example, the United States, the situation is muddled; some states have addressed some of the issues listed above, in particular that of the establishment of foreign branch

---

2 *See*, Robert Lutz, *Ethics and International Practice: A Guide to the Professional Responsibilities of Practitioners*, 16 Fordham Int'l L. J. 53 (1992/1993); Roger J. Goebel, *Professional Qualifications and Educational Requirements for Law Practice in a Foreign Country: Bridging the Cultural Gap*, 63 Tul. L. Rev. 443 (1989).

3 Ronald C. King, *Foreign Lawyers in Foreign Jurisdictions: Rights of Practice and Establishment*, 63 Def. Couns. J. 363 (July 1996); Darryl D. Chiang, *Foreign Lawyer Provisions in Hong Kong and the Republic of China on Taiwan*, 13 U.C.L.A. Pac. Basin L. J. 306 (1995).

offices and admission to practice of foreign trained lawyers, while others have not taken any steps to adapt their regimes.[4] Still others, for example France, have adopted rules—including an examination in the local language—which are more restrictive than before.[5] Finally—and most disturbing—some jurisdictions, *e.g.*, India, have taken active steps to force foreign lawyers to cease practice after such firms have taken good faith steps to comply with local licensing requirements.[6] Thus, it is fair to say that the legal professions of the world are a long way from achieving consensus on the treatment of cross-border practice—and, in fact, at least in some jurisdictions,— are moving away from accord on the matter. Against a backdrop of increasing transnational activity of all kinds, this failure to address the essential elements of cross-border practice makes it almost certain that the already significant gulf between the reality of modern practice and the bodies which govern legal practice will grow even wider.

C. The Elements of Consensus

At a minimum, I suggest that a professional regime should address the following:

- The lawyer or law firm from one jurisdiction establishing an office or a permanent presence in another jurisdiction to practice the law of the home jurisdiction;
- The lawyer or law firm from a jurisdiction traveling to another on a temporary basis to render legal advice or perform other professional services;

---

4 *See, generally,* American Bar Association Section of Legal Education and Admissions to the Bar and the National Conference of Bar Examiners, *Comprehensive Guide to Bar Admission Requirements* (1989).

5 American Bar Association Section of International Law and Practice, Report to the House of Delegates, *Model Rule for the Licensing of Legal Consultants,* 28 Int'l Law. 207, 216 (Spring 1994); *see generally,* John M. Grimes, *"Une et Indivisible"—The Reform of the Legal Profession in France: The Effect on U.S. Attorneys,* 24 N.Y.U. J. Int'l L. & Pol. 1757 (1992).

6 Ronald C. King, *Foreign Lawyers in Foreign Jurisdictions: Rights of Practice and Establishment,* 63 Def. Couns. J. 363, 365 (July 1996).

- The permitted scope of practice of a permanent or visiting foreign lawyer, *i.e.*, what legal advice he/she will be authorized to render and what services may be performed;
- The nature and extent of the duties of a visiting lawyer to the host governing body;
- The nature and extent of the rights and privileges accorded to foreign lawyers—including confidentiality of client communications;
- The status of company lawyers; and
- The status of foreign lawyers appearing as counsel before an arbitral tribunal.[7]

Very few jurisdictions have addressed these issues in a systematic way.[8] Although there is no general database which provides a systematic analysis of the ways professional regimes have adapted to the process of globalisation, the development of a general consensus among the regulatory bodies of the world would create a much more positive practice environment from which clients and the legal profession would derive great benefit.

D. The IBA Experience

Achieving such a consensus will prove extremely difficult. The experience of the International Bar Association ("IBA") on only one of these issues—the status of foreign legal "practitioners" or "consultants"—illustrates that difficulty.

---

7 Please note that this list of issues deals only with the establishment of some sort of physical presence by lawyers and/or their firms in another jurisdiction. No less important—but beyond the scope of this paper—are the issues posed by the revolution in technology. Through the use of computers and advanced telecommunications equipment, it is already possible and will soon become commonplace for lawyers in one jurisdiction to deliver services in another without ever physically entering the jurisdiction.

8 The best work I know of has been done in Canada, by the Inter-Jurisdictional Practice Committee of the Federation of Law Societies; *see, e.g.*, *The Inter-Jurisdictional Practice of Law*, (January 22, 1990).

As a federation of national bar associations, numbering among its institutional members virtually all of the national governing bodies in our profession, it would seem appropriate for the IBA—acting through its Council—to provide leadership on cross-border practice issues as it has in other areas, such as promotion of human rights and development of consensus on professional ethics (the IBA Code of Ethics). For more than three years an IBA Committee has been working to develop a set of guidelines on this subject for its member organizations. If endorsed by a significant majority of the IBA's Council, such guidelines would play an important role in the development of a consensus on the treatment of foreign lawyers practising the laws of their home jurisdiction, i.e., the law which their home licenses authorize them to practice, when they are resident in—and subject to the regulation of—a host jurisdiction. Rules based upon these guidelines would, among other benefits, expressly confirm the right of the host jurisdiction to regulate such practice[9] and, at the same time, would facilitate delivery of transnational legal services.

Although there is general support for the proposition that the IBA Council should endorse a set of principles, the Committee's work has not yet produced the necessary consensus in support of these guidelines. It is hoped that this consensus can be achieved in 1997 and that adoption of the guidelines by the IBA's Council will promote the development of a broader consensus among the IBA's member organizations on the other important issues outlined above.

The importance of a consensus on these issues seems to be beyond question. It would, at a minimum:

1. Promote the rationalization of the regulatory process, thereby enhancing certainty, reducing risks to practitioners and promoting respect for the regulatory process;

---

9 The International Bar Association, *Guidelines for Foreign Legal Consultants*, (Draft guidelines dated April 4, 1996).

2. Bolster the independence and freedom from conflicts of interest which have been the hallmarks of the legal profession;
3. Enhance public confidence and economic development by facilitating the delivery of legal services in a way which protects clients' interests; and
4. In the process of discussing these issues and the profession's responses to the phenomenon of globalisation, contribute to the education of the public and the profession at large.

The arguments made in defense of local rules which impede cross-border practice—the maintenance of discipline, establishment of competence and minimum educational standards—address serious concerns. But in practice—and this should be faced squarely—these restrictions are often used to limit competition and are enforced in a manner designed to protect the local practice environment. In today's environment, it is simply unrealistic to believe that, in the long term, such rules will successfully protect local practitioners or the local bar from the perceived competitive "threat" represented by the foreign lawyer. In the longer term, these restrictions will make it *more difficult* for local lawyers to compete because, in the future, the ability to act effectively on a wider stage will be the primary determinant of success.

III. THE NEED FOR ACTION

Ten years ago, when I first began commenting on the issues discussed in this paper,[10] I noted that, while they were of some importance, there appeared to be no specific crisis looming on the horizon as a result. Today the landscape has changed, and while "crisis" may

10 Bernard L. Greer, Jr., *The EEC and the Trend Toward Internationalization of Legal Services: Some Observations* in Symposium, Private Investors Abroad: Problems and Solutions, at §13.05 (International Comparative Law Center, 1987).

not precisely describe the current situation, it is of immediate importance for the bodies which govern our profession to develop coordinated regimes which address cross-border practice issues.

Why has this become so important? There are, of course, many long-standing reasons for the legal profession to put its own house in order, not least of which is the uncomfortable irony of the fact that while lawyers are advising their clients to obey the law, they are often finding ways to "wink at" or avoid complying with local practice rules which may be unreasonable and arbitrary. But apart from this, certain recent developments have added greater urgency to the need for national legal professions to develop fair and realistic rules which accommodate the reality of modern practice.

The first of these is the fact that the regulation of professional services—including legal services—is now under the scrutiny of at least one international organization which has the power to determine the future of such regulation. Under the General Agreement on Trade in Services ("GATS"), professional regulation must be "transparent," *i.e.*, the rules governing admission and conduct of practice must be clear, and any restrictions on access must be objective and justifiable in the public interest.[11] The World Trade Organization ("WTO"), which will administer the GATS provisions on professional services has the power to issue binding regulations or "disciplines" which supersede national regulatory regimes which are deemed to be anti-competitive. Similarly, as noted in the introductory quotation, the Organization for Economic Cooperation and Development ("OECD") is studying the economic impact of professional regulation on competition and efficiency. If the outcome of these efforts is the conclusion by the member governments of these two organizations that professional regulation is anti-competitive, then the pressure on the bodies which regulate the legal profession to adjust their regulations will increase enormously, and

---

11 General Agreement on Trade in Services, Annex 1B to the Marrakesh Agreement Establishing the World Trade Organization, April 15, 1994, Part II, Art. VI(4)(a).

in the end, reform may be forced upon them as the result of outright intervention.

A related development is the entry by the so-called "accounting firms"—more accurately, business service firms—into the field of legal practice. These organizations have made the strategic election to practice law, and they are doing so on an increasing scale—legally where they can, by stealth almost everywhere. In entering the field of legal services, these firms argue that professional regimes which do not accept so-called "multidisciplinary partnerships" ("MDPs") are anti-competitive. There are, in fact, many serious questions of public policy inherent in the combination of the legal, accounting and other professionals in one organization, and in these circumstances it is not at all clear that the fundamental duties of counsel—confidentiality, independence, i.e., the freedom from conflicts of interest, and competence—can be maintained in a "one stop shopping" environment. The failure of national bars to develop rules which promote the delivery of legal services in ways which preserve the essence of these duties can only strengthen the arguments of those who favor MDPs that restrictive regulation is a mask for protectionism. In absence of meaningful change, we can be certain that these arguments will be made to the WTO and the OECD. It is increasingly likely that they will be made before courts as well.

In all events, these developments make clear that the regulation of lawyers worldwide will be subjected to increased scrutiny in the coming years and that regulatory restrictions will have to be justifiable in the public interest if they are to be allowed to remain in place.

We began by noting that the forces which underlie the globalisation of the world's economy are beyond the power of the world's traditional institutions to control; the best to be hoped for is constructive adaptation to a radically changed environment. The process of adaptation will not be accomplished in a vacuum. To the contrary, because of the attention focused on professional regulation by the WTO and the OECD and the coming debate over MDPs, every aspect of the regulation of our profession will be the subject of intense examination and, in the end, will have to be justified, not by protectionist concerns, but by public interests, including the interests of the increasing number of direct participants in the global economy. If that is true, would it not be better for our profession—working through the IBA and its national regulatory bodies—to begin working now to ensure that the fundamental character and independence of our profession are preserved by promoting realistic and flexible regulation which accommodates the realities of the global economy?

The Role of Lawyers in the Information Society[1]

Professor Richard Susskind FRSE

Since early 1981, when I stumbled into the field as a legal undergraduate, I have been fascinated by the possibilities of using information technology in the law. I quickly became convinced that IT would radically transform modern legal systems; and well within my lifetime. Today, I am more certain than ever that a revolution in legal life is upon us. Indeed I believe that the practice of law and the administration of justice will be more radically affected in the coming 50 years by IT than by any other single factor of which we can be aware today.

In this chapter, I seek to substantiate these rather sweeping claims. First of all, I endeavour to show that the advent of the so-called information society will transform our legal system. Then, I present a vision of what the effects of this transformation will be in practice. And, finally, I make some predictions about the long term future of law and lawyers.

---

1 The central arguments advanced in this paper are taken from the author's more detailed work, *The Future of Law* (Oxford University Press, Oxford, 1996).

I

Vital to understanding the future of law is the connection between the law on the one hand and what I call the "information substructure" in society, on the other. The information substructure is the dominant mechanism by which information is transmitted and conveyed in a society. The academic literature suggests a model for this substructure useful for our analysis—the model proposes four phases of information substructure, where societies are dependent, respectively, on orality, script, print, and then on IT. [2]

It is clear from research and writings on the history and development of communication as well as from legal anthropology and sociology, that the information substructure of society impacts considerably on each of these four fundamental stages of development and communications. And when we examine this impact, I believe we can then project with some confidence about future developments in the administration of justice and the practice of law; and can begin to see how the shortcomings of today may be overcome tomorrow.

It is hard today to conceive of what a society stripped of script, print and IT might have been like. As Walter Ong puts it, in his splendid study, *Orality and Literacy:* "Try to imagine a culture where no-one has ever 'looked up' anything. In a primary oral culture, the expression 'to look up something' is an empty phrase: it would have no conceivable meaning." Nonetheless, we can infer, from what might be regarded as the natural constraints inherent in a community only capable of oral communication, some likely features of the law during the phase of orality.

Although it is probable that the memories of human beings were better exercised and more retentive, it was surely not possible for there to have been huge quantities of detailed regulation covering all aspects of human life. No-one could have remembered the

---

2 See, for example, Ong, W.J., *Orality & Literacy* (Routledge, London, 1988) and Katsh, M.E., *The Electronic Media and the Transformation of Law* (Oxford University Press, Oxford, 1989).

equivalent even of tiny fractions of the quantity of law in force today. Rather, the thrust of the rules of conduct were expressed in fairly general terms, as broad principles of whose content most people were generally aware.

Change in the law would have been fairly infrequent, in large part because there were no mechanisms for formally recording and promulgating such change.

Mastery of the law would have been given to only a few, senior elders of the community, of almost mystical status, who could recite the obligations and prohibitions in force and were called upon to apply them in situations of doubt. They too were responsible for passing down the law from generation to generation.

When we turn to reflect on the era of script as the information substructure, Walter Ong tells us: "Writing ... was a very late development in human history. *Homo sapiens* has been on earth perhaps some 50,000 years ... The first script, or true writing, that we know, was developed around the year 3500 BC." And again: "of all the many thousands of languages spoken in the course of human history, only around 106 have ever been committed to writing to a degree sufficient to have produced literature, and most of them have never been written at all."

With the advent of script, in agrarian society, it became possible in writing (and other pictorial representations) to augment the capacity of human memories and so the quantity of law could and did increase. As it became articulated in a fixed form which was open to scrutiny (admittedly only by the relative few who could read), the law itself came to be expressed with greater precision and rigour. Legal jargon and shorthand evolved as mechanisms for expressing concepts which were frequently deployed and so a new level of complexity was introduced.

Although the recording of change in the law was facilitated by script, the inability to reproduce material and disseminate it widely other than by manual transcription (which was, in any event, error prone) became a natural constraint on the frequency of change.

Again, however, it was necessary to have access to specialists—those who had a grasp of the evolving body of legal concepts and jargon (where the average citizen did not have). These individuals were both sources of advice on conduct and also called upon to settle disputes when the law, as articulated, was in doubt or disagreed upon. These individuals were lawyers.

With the advent of the printing press, in the middle of the fifteenth century, came a revolution in legal as well as social life. With print, not only did it become easier to produce text, but, crucially, the capability to reproduce and disseminate printed material, exerted a radical influence. The quantity of legal materials was able to expand rapidly, extending into many more areas of social and commercial life.

With printing's capacity to reproduce and disseminate massive amounts of information came the facility for change in the law. Indeed, the mechanisms for change became more formalised, both in legislating and in the development of case law through the doctrine of precedent.

More than ever, then, there was, in what became a print-based industrial society, a pressing need for specialist help to handle the increase in quality, complexity as well as the volatility of the law. Advisory and judicial roles became more clearly distinguished and a dedicated legal *profession* and judiciary evolved. Gradually, only suitably trained individuals were permitted, by law, to offer legal advice in certain circumstances, while the dispute resolution process became increasingly formal.

Our move into the age of IT has brought the capability for everyone to become printers in their own right. With powerful word processors available, legislators and draftsmen are not contained in their capacity to generate the printed word. The reproduction of printed material has also entered a new era: first with photocopying technology; later with transferable word processing files and high capacity laser printers; and, more recently, with telecommunications technology, text can be transmitted and disseminated electronically and at minimal cost.

IT cannot be blamed entirely for the huge quantity of legislation and case law which are now available (both in print and in electronic form in massive databases), but it has certainly not helped to check the verbosity of legislators around the world. Similarly, in the age of IT we have unparalleled complexity in our legal provisions. The specificity and detail of so much legal material today so often renders the law impenetrable and too complex.

What is more, IT facilitates change in the law. In contrast with the eras of orality and script when change was a rarity, with IT available, the prevailing attitude towards documentation is that it is dynamic *by nature*, and subject to regular alteration, rather than static. At all stages in the life cycle in the generation and application of the law, IT supports rather than inhibits change.

With more legal source material than ever before and with the added challenge of some of this being available in legal databases that are themselves impenetrable, are specialist lawyers more or less in demand in the era of IT? In fact, it appears to have led to an increasingly lawyered society.

On this view, should we not conclude that IT is having a tragic effect on the law? I think not, for to do so is to make the mistaken assumption that we have completed the move from the industrial print-based society into what is called the IT-based information society. I believe instead that we are still in a transitional phase between these two eras and what you have just heard are some of the rather unfortunate consequences or features of being in this transition.

The reality today is that our ability to use IT to capture, store, retrieve and reproduce information wildly surpasses our ability to use technology to help analyse, refine, and manage the mass of information which conventional "data processing" has itself created for us. We are great at getting information into systems and sending it around, but not so good at extracting *all but only* the information that we want. I call this disparity *The Technology Lag*. It is the all-important lag between what technologists call "data processing" and "knowledge processing."

The point about *The Technology Lag* is not only that we are not yet getting computers to behave more intelligently. It is also that good old-fashioned data processing, through such technologies as photocopiers and scanning machines, has actually created problems for us and these are problems which the latest, so-called "knowledge-based systems" are not yet sophisticated enough to overcome. In law, senior barristers and judges regularly reminisce about trials in the past when complete document sets could be held under the arm or in a briefcase. They curse the photocopier and attribute today's escalating costs and delays in the courtroom to the document analysis and management tasks which that technology seems to bring for us. Current litigation support systems, based on data processing, only go some small way to conquering the document mountains but it will be some years yet before advanced knowledge-based techniques (such as conceptual retrieval, expert systems and hypertext) are refined and applied successfully to help manage the difficulties which earlier technology has left as its legacy.

So, until *The Technology Lag* is overcome, I believe we will remain in a confusing transitional position between the print-based industrial world and the IT-based information society; a position where IT might sometimes be thought to be doing more harm than good. But when the transition is complete (say, in 20 years' time), the legal world, in its turn, will have changed as radically as it did when society moved, first, from being one based on orality to one in which script was the principal means of communicating; and later from a script-based culture to one dominated by print.

The shortcomings of the transitional phase to which I refer are all fine illustrations of the way in which our data processing capabilities have, so far, surpassed our knowledge processing capacity. But we are now refining our techniques in the field of knowledge processing and gradually developing systems which will help us analyse and manage the vast bodies of information we have created for ourselves. And these systems will themselves help us pinpoint *all but only* the material relevant to our particular purposes as users.

Once these technologies are in place, quantity becomes a non-issue because users will be assisted with accuracy in the retrieval of manageable amounts of legal materials; complexity will largely be hidden from them, as systems will effortlessly guide hitherto perplexed users through the labyrinths of the law; and change will either be hidden from the user with updating a continuous phenomenon or, more proactively, be brought to the attention of users by systems which themselves have the ability to monitor all relevant developments for individuals.

Perhaps even more radically, as I explain shortly, knowledge processing will spawn a multitude of legal information products and services for direct consultation by non-lawyers and so, in the information society, there will be less rather than more reliance on specialist legal advice.

I must stress that this vision of a transformed legal service on the strength of knowledge processing is not one which is likely to be realised in the next few years. Researchers have battled for a quarter of a century in trying to develop knowledge-based systems for lawyers and the results so far have been modest. Elsewhere, however, the investment in using IT to harness the power of information is enormous. I have some considerable confidence (some might say faith) that advances in knowledge processing will be stunning in the coming 25 years, thus easing us from this transitional period into the fully fledged, IT-based information society.

Let me offer one illustration of an emerging technology which gives me cause for such optimism. One of the emerging and most intriguing techniques for overcoming the problems of basic information retrieval is that of "intelligent agents"—programs which can be instructed to roam around specified bodies of new information in search of materials which are likely to be of interest to those who instruct them. Like tireless and ever-willing paralegals, these agents monitor the content of documents as they are loaded and draw attention to those that seem relevant.

On one model, intelligent agents could work like this. A user would build up a detailed profile of her social and business interests selecting these from a rich set of categories which have been articulated in advance. At the same time, the information services community would commit not just to loading the entire text of documents but also to providing further information which classifies all searchable materials, using the same category set as that employed for users' profiles. The intelligent agents can be instructed for a specified or indefinite period to monitor all new materials and to identify all matches, in effect, between the interests of the user and the subject matter of the new information. Thus, a user passionate about 19th century French painting and paranoid about European environmental regulations relating to waste might log on to her machine in the morning to learn of an auction in her locality and a high powered meeting of ministers in Brussels.

Alternatively, such information would be ready and waiting on the breakfast table, embodied in that same user's *Daily Me*. This is the fascinating notion, as described so well by Nicholas Negroponte in his stimulating book, *Being Digital*, of a personalised newspaper which is generated each day but is filled only with items which have been specified in advance as being of interest to the particular reader.[3] (The prospect of never receiving a newspaper stuffed with reports of cricket or football is, for me, joyous beyond words. Instead, my *Daily Me* would have huge coverage of track athletics.)

There is more than a glimmer here of a useful tool to help diminish the effects of *The Technology Lag*, with technology itself being used to seek to overcome information overload.

In relation to the law, intelligent agents are a promising technique to help encourage promulgation, in that new legal developments could be brought automatically to the attention of lawyers and non-lawyers. There is the basis here also for an innovative information service for clients—as lawyers add materials to their own in-house know-how systems, these could also be classified and then relevant materials could immediately be routed to clients with matching profiles. And where clients are operating on the same system as their lawyers—through groupware, for example—notification of the arrival of this information could pop up on their screens and the details could be accessed there and then. There would be no need to dial up periodically to see if anything new had arrived.

---

3 Negroponte, N., *Being Digital* (Hodder & Stoughton, London, 1995).

More generally, fascinating work on a variety of enabling technologies (including workflow systems, groupware, hypertext, intelligent checklisting, project management) is currently being conducted. Increasingly, the influence of these developments will be felt by lawyers and my bet is that from around the turn of the millennium onwards (that is, within the time frame of most lawyers' current strategic planning), the world of practising lawyers will become a very different place—we will all (without exception) be using the global "information highway," communicating with one another electronically, using all manner of information services (domestically and in business), there will be no practical limitations on the amount of information we can store and distribute, and the systems themselves will become more and more useful.

What does all of this mean in practice? I turn now, in the second part of this paper, to provide one view.

II

I envisage in the world to come that much of the lawyer's work will shift from being advisory in nature to becoming, in large part, a form of information service, a kind of legal service which might meet most of the needs of individual citizens and businesses and yet differ markedly from the traditional means of working as a lawyer.

Legal service will become a form of information service in two broad ways. First, as various technologies are refined, much of today's conventional legal work will be systematised, routinised and proceduralised and then made available on the much-vaunted information highway as one amongst many consultative information services. The second dimension is potentially far more significant and this is the use of IT to help realise what I call the *latent legal market*—the myriad of circumstances, in domestic and business life, in which non-lawyers today are generally unable to benefit from the legal input they require because conventional legal service is too expensive or impractical in the circumstances. IT will help bring legal guidance to this *latent legal market.*

In both instances, there will be a major change in the underlying relationship between those who are involved in delivering legal service and those who receive it. On the traditional model, we have had lawyers and their clients, with the contractual commitment upon the legal adviser to offer some kind of advisory-based service, to their individual clients alone, on the basis of some more or less agreed charging structure (invariably, in the past, charging by the hour or day). When legal service becomes information service, there is a change, but not simply from the delivery of advice to the provision of information. Much more, a new set of relationships are established, under which those who are guided become *users,* the lawyers who analyse and organise the material become the *legal information engineers* and the organisations who develop and market the legal information products and services become the *providers.*

The users of legal information services of the future will consult, navigate about and be empowered to apply legal information made more readily accessible and financially acceptable than in the past. Legal information will be but one of countless sorts of information available on the global information highway, although the compartmentalisation of information into legal and other such conventional categories will itself in time fade away. The information products and services available—and available, in due course, to all citizens—will be packaged and oriented towards providing practical and directly implementable guidance with little or no distinction between the disciplines from which the final information product has been derived. A user who has a problem which traditionally may have needed, say, accounting and banking expertise as well as legal, may consult a service which provides a synthesis of these three sources of guidance; but there will be no particular need for, or benefit in, the overall guidance being broken down into units which reflect their original structure. This kind of compartmentalisation may be a practical necessity of today but will have less place in the IT-based information society.

The basis for charging users for legal service will shift from being fixed in the number of hours expended by the lawyer towards a fee that is more likely to reflect the overall market value of the information to the user.

The number of such users will be vastly greater than the number of conventional clients of today; and the frequency with which these legal information services will be consulted will greatly outstrip the frequency of consultations with lawyers today. The difference will lie in the emergence and realisation of the *latent legal market*, as innumerable situations in domestic and business life are enlightened by the law when this would or could not have happened in the past. For example, when a citizen crashes his car, purchases faulty goods or considers taking out a loan, he will have at his fingertips practical, focused and applicable guidance which, it is likely, would not have been realistically available in absence of some IT-based information service. Similarly, in the commercial world, in preliminary negotiations, in on-the-spot procurement or in business planning and legal risk management generally, a layer of legal counsel will be available when previously it may have been regarded as too cumbersome or costly to obtain legal input. Like guidance on medical matters, property, investments and leisure, legal guidance will be available on the information highway.

At first glance, this may seem like tragic news for the average lawyer and be thought to be a harbinger of the end of the legal profession—asking the legal practitioner to buy into this model of the future may seem akin to inviting the proverbial turkey to vote for an early Christmas.

In fact, it will mean fundamental change and a very different market for legal knowledge and expertise will emerge. Those lawyers who fail to recognise and plan for this massive shift may well cease to trade profitably; whereas those of vision and entrepreneurial flare are already planning today for an exciting commercial future. The liberation and emergence of the hitherto *latent legal market* will create a range of opportunities for lawyers to package and sell their expertise in innovative ways.

What, then, might the lawyer's role be as an engineer of legal information? The main task, in the first instance, will be that of analyst—it will be for the lawyers, with their unparalleled knowledge of the legal system, to interpret and repackage the formal sources of law (legislation and case law) and articulate it in structured format suitable for implementation as part of a legal information service. Trained lawyers will continue to have unique insight into the law and legal process. In the information society, they will repackage this insight and sell it *not* through one-to-one advisory work, but in the creation of legal information products and services.

Who will be the providers? In print-based society, lawyers have enjoyed a dual role, combining that of being legal information engineers as well as providers. In fact, the two functions have become intertwined as one—those who gained expertise in law, in a world based on print and paper, were the only individuals who were in a practical position to apply it in particular circumstances in providing advice.

In the IT-based information society, in contrast, the process of analysis and formulation of information can and will be separated from that of the provision of legal information service. Knowing the law and being able to articulate legal information will no longer necessarily lead to domination in the sale of that information.

Lawyers will by no means be the only workers affected by this break from the past—many of the middlemen known as brokers or agents or intermediaries or the like who have also enjoyed their monopoly over various information services (estate agency, insurance broking and travel agency, for example) will find they may no longer dominate their markets. Where the service being delivered is essentially information-based, other imaginative providers will enter the markets and strive to use IT to deliver greatly improved service on the information highway. "Disintermediation" will be the order of the day and the middlemen will need to find new, imaginative ways of adding value.

In this, we see perhaps the greatest commercial challenge of all for lawyers, because with the shift in the nature of legal service comes their loss of a monopoly over the provision of legal services.

While at first glance, today's lawyer may be most apprehensive about moving from an advisory role to that of an engineer and analyst, the far graver and fundamental challenge is actually that of retaining market share in the provision of legal information.

In the past, conventional legal publishers have delivering products (textbooks and journals, generally) which clarify formal legal sources and put them in their wider legal, business and social contexts. The market for these products was confined mainly to lawyers themselves, as the nature of printing imposed a natural constraint on the range of individuals who could directly derive benefit from books and articles. In short, legal publishing was for lawyers because no-one else could really understand law books.

However, as legal publishers have diversified into electronic legal publishing and are gradually exploiting crucial enabling techniques such as hypertext, document assembly, enhanced text retrieval and groupware, then the products they produce demand less legal expertise on the part of the users and so appeal to a wider user base. As these techniques are refined, legal publishers will slowly come to vie with practising lawyers in the market for legal information. It is entirely conceivable, for example, that a leading legal practitioner may be invited to collaborate, even on a permanent basis, with imaginative electronic legal publishers who may retain the services of this lawyer at rates which could match or exceed the fee-income which would be generated by traditional work on an hourly billing basis. At the same time, innovative lawyers will package their conventional work product, such as a well drafted document, in electronic form, using techniques such as hypertext to enhance and clarify contractual and other materials and to provide ready access to relevant legal sources.

As the markets of publishers and lawyers converge, both must also look beyond their own rivalry if they are together to dominate the market for the provision of legal information systems. For they are likely to have to confront and avert threats in the commercial world far graver than one another. I have in mind the large accounting and consulting firms, whose vast information systems resource will prepare them far sooner for the delivery of professional services on the global information highway. It is entirely conceivable that the recruitment of legal specialists to act as sources for information service providers is as likely to occur at the instance of these multinational players as from the legal publishers. With mastery of the information services market which will outstrip the most technically advanced of lawyers, it is entirely conceivable that an accounting and consulting giant could cultivate and then dominate the *latent legal market.* On this model, lawyers would be relegated to the role of back-room technician, while the other professionals enjoy the glamour and profit of delivering the information service to business and society generally.

Equally, the same *latent legal market* may be recognised by the increasingly powerful telecommunications providers whose great experience of the information infrastructure would stand them in splendid stead to exploit the legal market.

All of that said, I accept that an important market for legal service delivered in the traditional, advisory manner will remain (although streamlined through IT), because there will be a variety of situations in which it will not be possible or appropriate for legal information systems to supplant or replace the conventional approach. In all the excitement (or horror) of anticipating a shift from advisory to information service, it is vital not to overlook these areas of legal life which will remain the province of lawyers—high value, socially significant or complex legal work, for example.

For most law firms, however, one of the biggest long-term strategic questions is whether they can survive by advisory work alone; or perhaps by information service in isolation; or whether a mutually supportive mix of both will always be needed.

III

Looking ahead now, I believe that our rapid progress towards the information society will bring about a shift in legal paradigm and that after this fundamental change has come about, many features of legal service and legal process of today will be displaced by a new way of legal life underpinned by a fresh set of basic assumptions about the law and lawyers.

I have argued here that this shift in legal paradigm can and will only happen when we emerge, from the transitional confusion in which we find ourselves, into the fully fledged IT-based information society. Only then will *The Technology Lag* be overcome and will our capacity to manage legal information be more than equal to our ability to create and disseminate it.

As to providing some detail of the shift to this new legal paradigm, I suggest in this final section of the paper how various features of legal service and legal process of today might change in years to come. These changes are summarised in the following table.[4]

THE SHIFT IN LEGAL PARADIGM	
Today's Legal Paradigm	*Tomorrow's Legal Paradigm*
advisory service	information service
time-based billing	commodity pricing
restrictive	empowering
defensive	pragmatic
legal focus	business focus
dispute resolution	dispute pre-emption
a dedicated legal profession	legal specialists and information engineers
print-based	IT-based legal systems

4 For a fuller listing and analysis of the changes, see the author's book, *The Future of Law* (Oxford University Press, Oxford, 1996).

From Advisory to Information Service

If I have any single, unifying theme in my work in this area it is that IT will eventually enable and encourage legal service to change from being a form of advisory service to a type of information service. While most of the work of the lawyer in today's paradigm is advisory and consultative in nature, the emphasis will shift radically in the information society as many lawyers assume the role of legal information engineer and devote much of their professional lives to the design and development of legal information services and products. With the exception of specialist lawyers and judges, the work of lawyers will gradually become forms of information service, both serving and liberating the *latent legal market.* The ultimate deliverable will be reusable legal guidance and information services pitched at a level of generality considerably higher than the focused advice which characterises legal advisory work of today.

From Time-Based Billing to Commodity Pricing

When legal service becomes information service, the work product of lawyers becomes reusable. In turn, the time and effort expended cannot sensibly be allocated amongst those who are paying for the service, and so there can be no question of hourly billing. In fact hourly billing, the charging regime of today, which can penalise the efficient and reward the indolent, will have no place in tomorrow's legal paradigm. Many commentators assume hourly billing will be displaced by some form of value billing which entails charging for the value of some service to the client. Others go further and suggest lawyers will be able to charge for time saved rather than for time spent (although I have never heard a client accept this suggestion with relish). Value billing may, however, prevail during the transitional period between the print-based industrial society and the IT-based information society, but I doubt it will survive in its pure form in the new legal paradigm when it is more likely that legal information services will be akin to commodities, for sale in the *latent legal market* and subject to the more prosaic economic models of supply and demand which apply to physical goods today. Gradually, access to legal service packaged as information service will sell in high volumes for mass consumption at low prices.

From Restrictive to Empowering

Today, the law is often perceived as setting up obstacles in the path of domestic, social or commercial aspirations. With the demystification of the law and its far wider availability will come the perception that the law helps rather than hinders. Instead of regarding the law as restrictive, users of legal information services will gradually appreciate that the law can be a source of empowerment and a powerful weapon which can be marshalled in support of the exploitation of opportunities and the attainment of all manner of objectives. While the business person would characterise this future feature of the law as empowering and catalysing, the citizen should come to regard this as meaning the law has become more helpful and supportive.

From Defensive to Pragmatic

One of the great debates which awaits us is over the extent to which legal liability can be attached to those who develop and market legal information services. While the courts have not indicated where they will draw the line, in liability terms, on the continuum between the professional adviser and the published book, as a matter of public and social policy it is likely that the state will want (or want to be seen to want) to promote and encourage the development of legal information systems and the realisation of the *latent legal market*. But uncertainty over liability could well inhibit the growth of legal information services.

In any event, by their very nature, legal information services are pitched at a higher level of generality than legal advice. And so, while it may be reasonable for users to rely on the guidance offered, we have to accept that on those (rare) occasions where the guidance is inappropriate and gives rise to problems, the pragmatic social compromise will be not to attach liability to the developers other than in exceptional circumstances. Otherwise, all services would be emblazoned with disclaimers warning that the guidance should not be relied upon without taking conventional, professional advice. The essence of liberating the *latent legal market*, however, is precisely that such additional professional guidance is not sought.

The availability of legal information services will give rise to improvement but not perfection in making the law more usable and available and the marketplace itself will establish mechanisms for drawing attention to unreliable or defective services (perhaps allowing users—both disgruntled and content—to leave accessible evaluations of the systems on the service for future users to peruse). Legal information engineers may not often be held liable in the future but they will find their market severely eroded if their systems fail to do the job.

From Legal Focus to Business Focus

The successful information services of the future will be those that provide legal guidance which is packaged and integrated with more general commercial assistance. While I would not go so far as to suggest that the "man of affairs" will mutate into some "information system of affairs," it will surely be both beneficial for users and commercially astute for legal information engineers, to embed some street wisdom and business acuity into the legal services they provide. On this model, legal advice will be bundled with and embedded in more general business advice; other than for the legal specialists in their advisory role, who will probably retain the mantle of ivory tower legal analysts.

Legal service as information service will also have far greater business focus in another sense. The products and packages which will be developed will not be devoted exclusively to the conventional areas of law, as taught in today's law schools, or practised within individual departments of law firms. Nor will the services correspond to the subject matter of today's legal textbooks. Rather, the business focus will require that the guidance transcends many of our conventional legal boundaries and, no doubt, into other disciplines as well. Even if multi-disciplinary practices do not come to fruition, multi-disciplinary information systems most certainly will.

From Dispute Resolution to Dispute Pre-emption

Where legal information systems are being deployed to help manage legal risks more effectively, it is likely there will be an overall reduction in the need for formal dispute resolution. The effective control of legal risks prior to their escalation and realisation as problems will mean that disputes will be pre-empted and avoided and so will not progress to any formal or alternative resolution process.

Furthermore, in a society which sustains the social compromise of not attaching liability to defective legal information systems, users will tend, on the first time round, to follow and accept the guidance offered by the "living law." Here I borrow a term coined by the legal sociologist Eugen Ehrlich, earlier this century—when he referred to the "living law" he was meaning the law which *actually* reflects and conditions behaviour in society.[5]

The broad, generic representations of the law as embodied in legal information systems could themselves create a culture in which there will be little incentive to pursue legal matters at the high level of specificity and in the strictly literal terms which are so characteristic of today's legal paradigm. For all practical purposes, the law in action will be the law as held in legal information systems; less rigorous, less formal and less adversarial than contemporary, common law jurisdictions. By a quite different route, and following entirely different principles, common law jurisdictions of tomorrow may come in line in spirit with civil law jurisdictions of today.

---

5 Ehrlich, E., *Fundamental Principles of the Sociology of Law*, reprint edition (Arno Press, New York, 1975).

From a Dedicated Legal Profession to Legal Specialists and Information Engineers

The information society will always need access to legal knowledge and expertise. What will not be sustainable is any continuation from the position in today's legal paradigm whereby the legal profession enjoys an exclusive position as the interface between individuals and businesses on the one hand and access to the rule of law on the other.

In place of lawyers at this interface, will lie ever more flexible, powerful and accessible IT-based information systems serving both the *latent legal market* of the past and other areas of law amenable to systematisation. For problems of great complexity or high value, legal specialists will continue to operate in their traditional advisory role. But they will represent a relatively small fraction of the legal profession of tomorrow. A far larger number of lawyers will have reoriented their careers and will become the legal information engineers whose knowledge forms the basis of the legal information services. Thus, the legal profession of the future will be constituted of two tiers, not the solicitors and barristers of today, but the legal specialists and legal information engineers of the information society. Whether or not the profession has sufficient entrepreneurial talent and general foresight to be involved in the third discipline of marketing as providers of the legal information services and products is a great unanswered question of today.

From Print-based to IT-based Legal Systems

Finally, and in summary, legal practice and the administration of justice will no longer be dominated by print and paper in tomorrow's legal paradigm. Instead, legal systems of the information society will evolve rapidly under the considerable influence of ever more powerful information technologies. We will no longer suffer from the excessive quantity and complexity of legal material. There will be mechanisms in place to give everyone fair warning of the existence of new law and changes in old. Legal risks will be managed in advance of problems occurring and so dispute pre-emption rather than dispute resolution will be the order of the day. Our law will thus become far more fully integrated with our domestic, social and business lives.

The future of law, then, is exciting and full of promise. The future for lawyers very much depends on the legal profession's ability to adapt to the demands of the information society.

The Lawyer's Role in International Business Practice

Francis Neate

Since I first started life as a business lawyer at the beginning of 1964, the world has become a very different place: some profound changes have taken place, both in the political and in the business world, and these have had a significant effect on the practice of international business law. Accordingly, the opportunity presented by the invitation to contribute to this publication, to look back on more than 30 years of legal practice and to reflect on these changes, proved irresistible. I do so from the perspective of an English solicitor practising international business law in London. My perspective is necessarily partial, probably narrow. It certainly omits a number of important developments which have affected the legal practices of others more than they have affected mine. I acknowledge these limitations at the outset.

The first and probably most important development was already well under way when I started to practise the law, namely the consolidation of the American business empire which succeeded the British colonial empire immediately after the end of World War II. There are those, including the Americans themselves, who would argue that this empire (if it ever existed at all) has long since ceased to be dominant. This may be true. It is, however, easy to forget how dominant was American business and American investment immediately after World War II and onwards into the 1950s and 1960s, much of it (remembering the Marshall Plan) crucial to the reconstruction of Europe.

From the lawyer's point of view, this dominance had two important consequences which remain with us today. The first, and by far the more important, was that the English language became the dominant language not only in the British Commonwealth, but also in other parts of the free world, and in due course was established as the international business and legal language. A second feature of the dominance of American business and American investment during this period was that the American businessman tended to take his lawyer with him when he went abroad. This contributed at a crucial time to the introduction of American approaches and attitudes to the practice of international business law.

American overseas trade and investment gave rise to the Eurodollar. I have read historical studies which have dated the first appearance of the Eurodollar to 1954 and it is commonly suggested that the American deficit created by its involvement in the Vietnam war was a major contributor to the rise of the Eurodollar and the ultimate creation of the Eurodollar market. Be that as it may, what came to be known as "the Eurodollar market" only really emerged as such in London in the early 1970s, before exploding in a welter of lending to sovereign states in the second half of the 1970s. This coincided with the development of the North Sea oilfields, a very large part of which was funded from the Eurodollar market and led to the introduction to English lawyers of a variety of American financing techniques and, in particular, American style loan agreements. The English lawyers learned quickly and it was not long before they were producing loan agreements every bit as long and as complicated as their American brethren. It was these developments of the 1970s which gave birth to the global capital market as we know it today. The process of parturition was completed at the end of the 1970s when the new Tory government in the U.K. abolished exchange controls.

The Section on Business Law of the International Bar Association was formed at the start of the decade. The founders of the Section were prescient. Other events also occurred during the 1970s which, while not directly related to the development of the global capital market which we have today, nevertheless also influenced the development of international legal practice. Perhaps the most important of these was the United Kingdom joining the European Economic Community in 1973. One consequence was to complete the introduction of English lawyers to a supra-national law (European law) which could be as relevant to the transaction in which they were engaged as their own law or any other country's law. English lawyers had already been affected by and focused on Articles 85 and 86 of the Treaty of Rome and, for some time after the U.K. joined the EEC, the focus remained on those two Articles, although it is now becoming obvious to all that European law applies to a far wider field than merely freedom of trade. Another consequence of the U.K. joining the EEC was that English law firms began to wonder whether or not they should make closer contact with the Continent of Europe. Before 1970 not more than 2 or 3 English law firms had offices in Paris and their offices elsewhere were insignificant. In the mid 1970s, however, a number of other English law firms established offices in Paris and a few elsewhere on the Continent. Why the majority chose Paris is a mystery. One might have expected Brussels to be the first choice, but the extensive establishment of foreign law firms in Brussels came later. In any event, the English law firms in Paris developed viable practices with surprising speed. It is difficult to guess at the reasons for this relative success. Possibly, the French legal profession were slow to respond to the competitive challenge; certainly, they have responded vigorously in more recent years. There may have been a surge of investment in France from U.K. companies coincidental to the U.K. joining the EEC. If I remember correctly, there was substantial British investment in property in Paris at about this time. Another element, more directly related to the developing global capital market, was the interest of former French colonies in Africa and elsewhere in raising Eurodollar funds. They preferred to do this through Paris, even if English law was applicable, as it was for most Eurodollar funding transactions at that time.

At about the same time as the English law firms were establishing themselves in Paris, they also began to do so in Hong Kong. This was entirely opportunistic. There was no grand strategy which foresaw the development of the global capital market and the rise of the economies of Asia which was the talk of the early 1990s. In the mid 1970s, all that was seen was an opportunity presented by the explosive growth of the Hong Kong economy and the very limited number of local law firms available to service it. An opportunity was seen and seized. At the time, China and the Chinese economy were almost an irrelevance. The use of the English language and English law was far more important.

So, at the end of the 1970s, all the building blocks for the global capital market were in place, the American and English law firms were dipping their toes in the water with overseas offices and there was a huge and rapidly developing Eurodollar market in London. During the 1980s, the global capital market became a reality. I would not dare to attempt to explain how or why this came about, but it is relevant to my theme to highlight certain developments which affected the practice of international business law. The American banks caught a severe cold in their sovereign lending, especially but not only in South America. So did almost all the consortium banks which had been formed in the mid 1970s to take advantage of the opportunities offered by the London Eurodollar market to fund large Eurodollar loans to different parts of the world: almost every consortium bank formed in London in the 1970s was either publicly or very quietly bust by the mid 1980s. This led the banks to look for other ways to make money than by borrowing and relending excess Eurodollars and in time contributed to an increase in the issue of marketable debt instruments and the creation of a market in them. In addition, the currency swap (which had only been invented in 1977) suddenly became popular, was closely followed by the interest rate swap and other variations, to such an extent that a whole new market was developed. An indication of the speed with which swap transactions became commonplace is that a very limited number had been entered into before 1980, yet by 1985 the International Swap Dealers Association was being formed, one of its first tasks being to develop standard forms of swap contract to enable the swap market to operate more efficiently.

The London Stock Exchange decided to jump on the bandwagon. Once they realised that the Thatcher government was serious about challenging their restrictive practices, they decided to turn the situation to their advantage. The principal purpose of Big Bang in 1986 was to enable London to become (or to maintain its position as) the leading international financial centre. Simultaneously, the Thatcher government was privatising large parts of British industry. This gave rise to some of the largest international equity issues ever undertaken. These issues were so large that they had to be offered internationally: the U.K. market alone was simply not big enough to absorb them. It was these issues, surely, which established the global capital market as a reality.

Strange things were also happening in the political world. The socialist countries (both democratic and non-democratic) began to liberalise their economies, China, the USSR and India being prime examples. With extraordinary rapidity, economic liberalisation was followed in the USSR by political liberalisation. Against the background of these astonishing events, the democratisation of South Africa, which simultaneously espoused liberal economic principles, was almost a side-show, although it was perhaps the most extraordinary development of all and one which may yet provide leadership and hope for other parts of Africa. At the same time as these political developments were taking place, the attention of investors was being concentrated on the rapidly developing economies of Asia, not only Japan, but also South Korea, Taiwan, Hong Kong, Malaysia, Singapore, as well as China itself. These economies began to be talked about as the engine rooms of economic growth in the next century.

The last, but by no means the least, development relevant to my theme has been the advance of communications technology, without which many of the legal and financial transactions which are commonplace today simply could not take place at all.

One could amuse oneself by inventing a new parlour game in which the participants had to list those who have been the principal beneficiaries of these events. There is little doubt that lawyers, particularly the leading English and American law firms, should be close to the top of every list. The leading London law firms experienced phenomenal rates of growth during the 1980s. These were accelerating as the decade came to an end. There was a slight shift during the decade in the approach to the establishment of overseas offices. Offices were opened in New York, Tokyo and Singapore, from which a pattern could be deduced that the London firms were tracking the development of the global capital market into the leading financial centres. This pattern seemed to be confirmed towards the end of the decade when offices were also opened in Frankfurt. Numerous foreign firms were, of course, also opening offices during this period in Brussels, because of the growing importance of being close to the European Commission. However, around about 1989 or 1990 there occurred a significant change in approach from some of the leading London firms. With the benefit of hindsight, it is now clear that, at about this time, these firms took a new and major strategic decision to expand their international practices vigorously. This decision was not unlike that of the London Stock Exchange which led to Big Bang five years earlier, namely that if there was a major international market developing, in this case for legal services, then London would be at the forefront of those servicing that market. As a consequence, the 1990s have seen two different types of overseas expansion from the leading London law firms. One has involved the acquisition of local law capability in sophisticated jurisdictions like Frankfurt and New York, where English law firms have entered into direct competition with the established firms in those jurisdictions. The second has been the establishment, mainly by the same London law firms, of offices in far less sophisticated jurisdictions, mainly in the former USSR but also in some countries in Asia, where previously there has been little or no established legal system or independent legal profession. The London firms' move to practising New York law has been matched by a significant number of New York firms moving into the practice of English law, not only in London but in other jurisdictions around the world. It is this aggressive expansion on the part of the Anglo-American law firms which has created a degree of turmoil among those practising international business law. Whether or not the end result will be the creation of a number of global law firms which will dominate the international legal market place, is not a question which I propose to address. It is a braver man than I who would be prepared to engage in crystal-ball-gazing of this nature. Nor do I intend to address the reasons why the firms in question decided to embark on this expansionary strategy, or whether or not those reasons were good ones or still hold good today. There are, however, a number of ways in which these decisions are already affecting the practice of business law around the world and I would like to examine one or two of these.

One of the reasons why I began with an historical survey was to draw attention to the fundamental importance of the development of the English language into the accepted international business and legal language. This was closely followed by the development of the Eurodollar market which led to English law or New York law becoming at an early stage the chosen law for many international financial transactions. English and New York lawyers were the beneficiaries of these trends, but they did not create them. A lot of nonsense has been talked about the merits of the common law as a system to govern commercial transactions. I have heard the virtues of the trust extolled as an example of English legal creativity denied to our Continental brethren, yet I cannot believe that civil lawyers could not have been equally creative with their concept of fiduciary obligations if given the opportunity. I have heard the flexibility of the floating charge praised as being English law's unique contribution to financing techniques, notwithstanding that it provides the clearing banks with a stranglehold over the business activities of many of their customers. If I were a civil lawyer, I would find this kind of patronising trumpet-blowing extremely irritating, and many civil lawyers do. The fact of the matter is that the common lawyers cannot claim any particular credit for the dominant position in which they now find themselves. They are merely very fortunate to have found themselves able, unlike their contemporaries in other countries, to take advantage of historical trends which have developed in their favour. I think it is important to emphasise that these trends are not the fault of the Anglo-American lawyers, because many of these developments still cause widespread resentment in other countries. This resentment is not, of course, limited to the legal profession and it is far more deeply rooted than a mere dislike of competition, because at a fundamental level they are perceived as a threat to local language and local culture. However, what that means is that wherever these resentments surface, they must be taken seriously and dealt with carefully. The international legal profession now finds itself at the forefront of coping with this problem.

One particular feature of this problem, which the legal profession has so far shown itself incapable of resolving, is the question of the conditions under which foreign lawyers should be admitted to practise law in another country. The European Bar Associations have been wrestling with this for some years and have so far failed to find a solution to it. Recently, it has surfaced in other countries, for example, in Poland and India. Once again, it is important to emphasise that the problem is not merely one of fear of competition. At a fundamental level, it is a cultural problem. That is why it is so intractable. It is also an aspect of the problem which proponents of free market economic theory find difficult, if not impossible, to understand. If lawyers do not wish this problem to be perceived simply as one of competitive economic activity, they need to examine carefully how far their law is embedded in their culture and how far their culture and their system of administration of justice are intertwined.

Another aspect of the same problem is the growing tendency of the leading international firms of accountants to practise law in many jurisdictions throughout the world. Again, this is resented and resisted by many members of the legal profession. Once again, however, one cannot forget that it is free enterprise economic theory which has apparently won the battle with socialism and which favours competition and freedom of establishment. If the legal profession is to resist these developments, it must find reasons for doing so which are not rooted merely in fear of competition but are perceived to be based on more fundamental cultural or policy considerations. I rather suspect that support for this resistance will not come from the international business lawyers. They will tend to see it as a simple issue of how to ensure that their sophisticated clients can conduct their business and conclude their transactions in the most effective way. If there are other arguments to be deployed, they are more likely to be found in the need to provide protection for less sophisticated clients from exploitation, or in the need to underpin the administration of justice through the courts with a common system of values and culture shared between the judiciary and the advocates. These considerations are of little relevance to the practise of international business law.

Another reason for rehearsing the history of these developments is to emphasise the relatively limited field in which English and New York law has come to be dominant, namely international financial transactions. There is far more to the practise of international law than that and, even in international financial transactions, the local law of the participants is likely to remain relevant. There is, therefore, plenty of scope for lawyers from other countries to practise international business law, even if English or New York law tends to be the chosen law of the contract in international financial transactions. Sadly, however, the vigorous pursuit by English and American lawyers of international financial work has led them to establish offices in other countries and to practise local law in direct competition with the local firms and with the clear purpose of taking the more profitable financial and corporate work from them. The result is that the local firms seem to be faced with only one question, namely: if you cannot beat them, do you join them? So far, the leading local firms in many countries seem to have rejected this option. Instead, at least in Europe, their reaction has tended to be to join with other firms (neither English nor American) in other countries to create various types of association, some looser than others, a development which many see as a kind of interim defensive manoeuvre (not dissimilar to gathering the wagons into the corral) which will not last.

I am saddened to realise that I have started to use the language of warfare to describe what is happening. Nevertheless, it is appropriate language in which to draw attention to the dangers inherent in the present situation. Several observations occur to me.

I mentioned earlier that in the 1980s the rate of growth of law firms in London was phenomenal, totally unprecedented. One has to question to what extent it is wise to make decisions on the basis that such a rate of growth can be maintained, or even that it is desirable to do so. That was, unquestionably, one of the considerations that underlay the decision of some London firms to expand internationally. Some have expressly acknowledged that they saw little prospect of maintaining their rates of growth if they remained based principally in London: the only sensible course was to look for further growth overseas. However, I wonder whether it really makes sense for lawyers to get trapped into the vicious circle of the search for growth in which so many of our clients are forced to engage. They are producers and traders of commodities. Are we lawyers engaged in a different kind of trade? Is the continuous pursuit of growth a sensible ambition for us? and even if it is, is the market in which we operate (the market for legal services in international financial transactions) capable of growing to the extent necessary to sustain the required rate of growth?

At present, competition in the market-place for international legal services is ferocious. In my view, there is no reason to expect that to change in the foreseeable future. There are far too many lawyers eager to enter the market-place and no real likelihood of the market expanding fast enough to accommodate all of them. In this context, one has to ask what will happen to professional standards. That is, of course, the question which the proponents of undiluted free enterprise and of the benefits of free market forces have never been able to answer satisfactorily. It is also the question which the legal profession has never been able to answer satisfactorily: the successful lawyer is by no means always the lawyer who gives the right advice, more often it is the lawyer who gives the most plausible or the most palatable advice.

In this situation, the Section on Business Law of the International Bar Association can play a role of considerable potential value. The Section has, over its short life, developed a "family atmosphere," very much in the tradition of a select private club, which is treasured by many of its members. Many close friendships have been established through membership of the Section which go beyond mere business relationships. In bringing its members together in this kind of atmosphere and enabling them to forge relationships of this nature, I believe that the Section can play a valuable role in mitigating the potential consequences of the ferocious competition in which many of its members are engaged and in ensuring the maintenance of high professional standards in the face of that competition.

Perhaps the most pernicious of the developments in legal practice prompted by the development of the global capital market is the increasing trend towards specialisation. Many factors have contributed to this. The demanding timescale imposed by increasingly sophisticated clients and the competitive pressures on price mean that specialisation is the only way to respond. The increasing volume of transactions means that specialisation is a feasible way of continuing to make a living in the face of reducing prices. Another way of achieving the same result is to work ever longer hours. For all these reasons, the trend towards specialisation seems to be inevitable, but it also means that international business lawyers are becoming increasingly narrow-minded and, in London, the trend towards ever earlier retirement also seems to be irreversible. The undesirability of these trends tends to be talked about in terms of lack of job satisfaction, but what is more disturbing and arguably more pernicious is the production of so many highly paid lawyers with so narrow a focus.

The public at large might well react to all these developments with the consoling thought that, if the worst comes to the worst, it is the lawyers who will suffer, condemned to work ever longer hours to meet ever more absurd timescales set by ever more demanding clients for less and less return. That would be a facile reaction, because the quality, status, independence and professionalism of the legal profession are matters of fundamental importance to all of us. However, it is also clear that there will be winners as well as losers who will emerge from the present maelstrom, and they will all be lawyers. What this means is that, if there are problems to be addressed as I have suggested above, they must be addressed by the lawyers themselves.

There is an alternative, more positive way of looking at the impact of the international legal profession in many of the countries in which they have established themselves in recent years, particularly in those countries of the former USSR and elsewhere where a legal system barely existed a few years ago. In these countries, it can be argued that the international law firms which have established offices there are effectively paying for the establishment and training of an independent legal profession and contributing substantially to the establishment of a workable legal system. It would be ridiculous to argue that this is being done at the cost of the country concerned because, even if one acknowledges that the purpose in establishing an office there is not altruistic, it is almost certainly not done in the expectation of being able to withdraw serious profits in the foreseeable future, if ever.

There is another less obvious but certainly more important role for the international legal profession in the world of the 1990s. The apparent victory of free market economic theory in almost all parts of the world carries with it great hope for all of us, not because a free market economic system is a good thing in itself (it is no more than the least bad economic system mankind has yet been able to devise), but because such a system brings with it other benefits, not least the Rule of Law. You cannot have a free market economy without the Rule of Law. Furthermore, if your free market economy wishes to attract investment from the global capital market, its law must be seen to be stable, sensible and impartial. Today's international business lawyers have a valuable role to play in ensuring that those fundamental truths are understood and turned into reality in many parts of the world where they are relatively novel concepts and not necessarily well understood.

Just as you cannot have a free market economy without the Rule of Law, so you cannot have democracy without the Rule of Law. In each case, you cannot have one without the other. The big question for the 1990s is whether or not you can have two without the third - are they three sides of an equilateral triangle which, without one of its sides, will collapse? President Mandela argued powerfully in his lecture to mark the 25th Anniversary of the IBA's Section on Business Law (reproduced in this volume) that the three were necessarily and inextricably interlinked. Mikhail Gorbachev and F.W. de Klerk would no doubt agree with him. The Chinese, on the other hand, seem determined at present to prove the opposite. The international business lawyer has a valuable role to play in the next few years in helping the world to resolve this very crucial issue, by introducing people at a very mundane level to the Rule of Law and the values it represents.

Value of the International Business Lawyer

Willem J. L. Calkoen

In these cynical times it is unusual for anyone to speak favourably of lawyers. To suggest that lawyers are a benefit to society and that international business lawyers have a particularly valuable place in world affairs is to invite scorn and derision for one's views. The overwhelming tide of public opinion is anti-lawyer. Polls in the US show that lawyers are increasingly unpopular. Anecdotes are legion of disputes exacerbated by legal quibbling, of sky-rocketing costs and of businesses driven into bankruptcy by the expenses of litigation.

It is with some hesitation therefore that I put forward the proposition that international business lawyers as a whole play a positive role in the world community and that many provide 'added value' far beyond their duties as litigants and advisers. Unfashionable as it might be to say it, I believe that international business lawyers are a good and worthy species and that many of them practise with the same high ideals that I certainly started out with, some 25 years ago.

To support my case I will look at the work of lawyers in general, international lawyers and international *business* lawyers.

LAWYERS IN GENERAL

Lawyers or advocates[1] have existed for a very long time. You find them everywhere in societies of many sorts. The lawyer's chief purpose is to defend people's rights. This is a legitimate and honourable purpose; a purpose and a need that concerns many people in a fundamental way.

If you want to defend someone's rights there must of course be rights and law. That there must be law is self-evident—and not only to lawyers. '*Ubi judicia deficiunt, incipit bellum.*' Free translation: 'Where the judiciary fails, a mess is created'. Society needs order and regularity of the law. A society cannot do without legal dispute resolution as a safety valve. The prosperous development of a society certainly depends on a proper functioning of the judiciary. Just look at countries where the judiciary has been neglected or is even non existent.

There is a need for lawyers, but that does not mean they are popular.

Lawyers are not Popular

Europe's most important writers through the ages have written about lawyers in a derogatory way.[2] The anecdotes of litigation going too far and costing too much do much to explain the general dislike for lawyers, but there are other reasons. For one thing, lawyers are often perceived as being stubborn, critical and difficult. This view is not without a basis in truth; many of us probably have lawyers like these as our partners. Indeed these attributes may well produce the best lawyers: lawyers with a real commitment to their clients, who will fight to defend their rights, whatever the circumstances.

---

1 Advocatus (Latin): someone, who assists a litigating party, usually a respectable citizen, in the Emperor's period the advocate-procurer, licero and others; advocate, call to help, especially in a procedure.

2 The well-known words: 'Let's kill all lawyers' in Shakespeare's Henry VI are not words of the King but of an accomplice of the farmer-rebel Cade, see part 2, Act IV, scene 2. Goethe said: 'Er erben sich Gesetz und Recht wie eine ewige Krankheit fort.' Also the plays of Molière make fun of lawyers.

Another possible cause of lawyer unpopularity is the fact that lawyers are often called upon to speak for unpopular clients and causes. The lawyer might have to argue against existing legal notions, against what the judge may think and against public opinion. This is difficult, but it is what clients expect their lawyer to do.

The classic example from fiction of a lawyer fighting for an impossible cause is the movie 'To Kill a Mockingbird', in which Gregory Peck plays a lawyer who must defending a black client in one of the Southern States of the US. The client is accused of the rape of a white woman. It is impressive to see how the lawyer struggles against the prejudice of his surroundings and against his own prejudice. It is a great movie. Happily enough, there are real lawyers who fight for similar causes, although they may be less handsome.

'Positive' Qualities of a Lawyer

Apart from being stubborn, critical and difficult, lawyers must also be trustworthy and independent, flexible and creative. They must have fighting spirit and the wisdom to know when it is better to conciliate rather than to fight. They must consider the emotions of the client, the opposing side, the other players, the lawyers, and themselves. They must be sensitive, but must also have a thick hide.

An overriding requirement is that the lawyer is absolutely trustworthy in: (a) attending to the interests of the client; and (b) in upholding the rule of law. It is essential that the client can trust his lawyer. The client does not know the law but must be sure that the lawyer will do what is best for him. For this the lawyer must be independent from any outside influences that might compromise his defence of his client's rights, by the same virtue he must also be sufficiently independent of the client to resist any pressure to use unfair practices in the client's defence.

Creativity and flexibility are needed because most legal problems are not straightforward and cannot be solved in a routine manner. Lawyers are constantly called upon to come up with tailor-made creative arguments and solutions.

So the ideal lawyer must have the fighting spirit of a knight, the sensitivity of a priest, the diplomacy of an ambassador and the creativity of an inventor. Do such paragons exist? Perhaps not, but a few come close. I would point to the example of our own IBA President, Mr Desmond Fernando of Sri Lanka, who showed great commitment, independence and sensible fighting spirit when organising the defence of anti-government protesters. At a time when lawyers had been murdered for handling such cases.

INTERNATIONAL LAWYERS

There are many definitions of what precisely constitutes an *international* lawyer. Within many law firms there is a debate as to what percentage of the work in the firm is *international* work. Whatever definition is used however, the sheer quantity of international work is undeniably growing, because of the ever-increasing growth in international trade and investment.

International work can be divided into a number of distinct categories:

Inbound Work

Most good lawyers have been consulted by foreign investors in their countries and by foreign lawyers for the benefit of their foreign clients. The foreign investors want advice about agency or distributorship, import, investment and foreign exchange laws, mergers and acquisitions, competition, environmental and tax laws as well as dispute resolution and many other fields. The local lawyers have been approached because of their knowledge of their own law and in that sense they are not international lawyers. However, there are quite a lot of lawyers who are better at giving this advice to international clients, because their advice comes with the extra benefits of their language skills and their understanding of foreign laws, cultures and relationships with foreign contacts (who they have quite possibly established through their involvement with the International Bar Association).

Outbound Work

Here the lawyer helps their, usually home-based, clients in their activities overseas: foreign investments, mergers and acquisitions, competition, dispute resolution and taxes. Usually the lawyer starts off with a limited knowledge of the laws of the foreign country.

The lawyer must find and work together with a lawyer of the foreign country. The real challenge of such work is to find such a lawyer of sufficient quality and trustworthiness. Various methods of finding such overseas contacts have evolved over the last 30 years:

- information clubs: clubs of five up to 100 law firms that meet each other twice a year, exchange information and give each other free telephone advice; they refer clients to each other, but are non-exclusive;
- alliances of five up to 100 law firms that refer to each other exclusively;
- international law firms with offices in many but not in all countries.

Partners in all such firms will also actively seek out contacts in other ways. They will go to conferences and meetings of international lawyers with the prime intention of establishing foreign links—'networking' as it has come to be known. It is in this field of international networking that the International Bar Association (IBA) and its Section on Business Law has grown to play such a vital role.

The IBA was founded in 1947 as an association of bars rather than as an individual lawyers' organisation. For its first 23 years, the IBA was a meeting place for council members of national bars, who were interested in their own national problems rather than in international development or legal cooperation. It was only in 1970, when the IBA acted upon George Seward's repeated proposal and established the Section on Business Law, that international lawyers were welcomed into the IBA as members.

The character of the meetings of the IBA changed instantly. Rather than the social gatherings of 30 or so members that had gone before, Conferences were organised with separate meetings for Committees interested in specialised areas of law. The individual lawyers who joined did so because their practice was already international and they were interested in learning about foreign laws and cultures, and especially in finding out who the good lawyers in other countries were.

A regular visitor to Conferences of the IBA not only meets international lawyers from all over the world, but really gets to know them and can find out how he/she thinks legally, and what his or her 'yes', 'no' and 'maybe' really mean. In this way the IBA member builds up a network of social and legal contacts and is thus able to provide greater experience and resources to his client's problems.

The Lawyer who Accompanies his Client Abroad

In this case the international lawyer goes a step further than the outbound work discussed above, but the same points apply. The lawyer needs to know what to ask and who to ask—there is the same need to find the best lawyers abroad.

Although there may be an extra cost for the client in taking along a lawyer from his home country, that cost is usually saved by the greater efficiency of their work together once they are abroad. If a client from the US wants to know whether or not to make an investment in India, he will be able to rely on the opinions of the US lawyer who has come with him and of an Indian lawyer recommended by the US lawyer. The time and anxiety saved by such an arrangement is invaluable—a clear example of international lawyers providing 'added value' for their clients and to international investment in general.

I would stress that the lawyer visiting a foreign country really does need a guide to the local legal regime and thus really should appoint a local lawyer to help him.

Foreign Practitioners

This is the lawyer who sets up an office in a foreign country without taking a law degree or bar exam in that country. Such a lawyer only practises and advises on his or her own law, providing the services of 'inbound' and 'outbound' practice. A French lawyer at a French firm in New York will advise US clients about French law (inbound practice) and help French clients in the US to find the right New York lawyers and ask the right questions (outbound practice).

There are many such branch offices all over the world, especially in the financial centres. These lawyers provide the 'added value' described above and are on hand to attend meetings quickly. A US corporation wishing to buy a pan-European group may wish to meet lawyers from all the relevant countries at the same time. Such a meeting could be arranged with foreign lawyers based in, for example, New York.

The only problem here is one of competition. The English or American lawyer setting up in Tokyo, Moscow or New Delhi may well take work away from local lawyers. I would recommend that lawyers practising abroad should use local lawyers as much as possible. In this way, local lawyers will learn about the foreign practitioner's legal system and will be able to work more effectively on the local side of the transaction. This shared learning provides a benefit to the legal community as a whole.

From the Dutch experience I can say that English and American lawyers have taught us all about lengthy M&A agreements, warranties, guarantees, due diligence and disclosure letters and all about project financing agreements in the North Sea. In the early years they introduced their clients to us and were very much in the driving seat. Now Dutch lawyers can compete on the same terms. The English and American lawyers benefited, their clients benefited and so did we.

Truly International Law Firm

This is the law firm that sets up offices in many countries and practises local law, usually employing or entering into partnership with local lawyers.

There is 'added value' in this arrangement for certain clients, who wish to have a single calling point for legal services and is not interested in the legal niceties of each country it invests in. Again, I would recommend cooperating with local firms and using them as much as possible. A lawyer from one of the biggest international firms, who is the resident partner of the firm's Vietnam office, stressed at an SBL Regional Conference in Singapore how important it is to involve local lawyers. At the same time, the international firms should not set out to 'buy up' the best members of the local bar.

International Business Lawyers

The profile of the lawyer in general applies to business lawyers as well. Most business lawyers, and especially the older ones, have worked on family and criminal cases and know what it is to work for emotional clients or clients who confess that they have done wrong, but still have a right to the best defence. Business problems can of course have the same emotional and confessional aspects.

The only special aspect of business lawyers is that their clients are in business. It might also be said that business lawyers are in business and other lawyers are in a profession. Indeed, business lawyers are perceived as having become more commercial than in the 'good old days'. This is another element in the declining popularity of lawyers.

I would argue against this view. Lawyers have always had to pay attention to the commercial aspects of their profession. The fact that lawyers think about budgets, costs, rent, salaries, and the buying or leasing of computers and other infrastructure, does not mean they have forgotten about their values. It simply shows they are living in the real world: to be blind to reality does not make anyone more idealistic.

Society has a right to lawyers who can render good legal assistance. The law has become complicated. There are often difficult questions, the urgency is usually eminent. Clients do not go to lawyers with easy problems. The lawyer needs good training and continued legal education specialisation—hence larger partnerships—and a good infrastructure. The lawyer must invest and must therefore also send invoices.

Parasites of Society

Business lawyers and large law firms are perhaps especially unpopular. As the Australian former Governor-General of Australia, the Rt. Hon. Sir Ninian Stephen AK, GCMG, GCVO, KBE, said at the opening of the Melbourne IBA Conference in 1994: "No one likes lawyers, but many want their children to become lawyers". Supreme Court Justice Blackmen said: "You have two types of lawyers: parasites of society and engineers of society."

Let me give you some examples of parasites of society.

(a) My father experienced a parasite when he started working as a lawyer in the recession of the 1930s and drafted a straightforward contract. His older colleague commented: "The draft is too clear, you will not see it back for litigation."

(b) Similarly, a young lawyer in Los Angeles representing a movie star drafted a two-page agreement which covered all the necessary elements and sent it to the experienced lawyer of the producer, the older lawyer phoned by return and said: "I cannot even send the draft to my client. The draft should be at least 25 pages. You are driving both of us out of business."

(c) A businessman is involved in litigation. He gets fed up, phones the opposing businessman and settles the case. He phones his lawyer proudly and tells him proudly of his achievement. The parasite lawyer reacts: "You cannot do that, I am in charge, I could have obtained a bigger settlement and would have made my invoice higher. I will have to sue you, my client."

The impression that many people have is that lawyers take more than they give, and this certainly true of some lawyers. However, most international business lawyers I know are so busy that they give more than they take. They love their work, do it day by day with full commitment for their clients.

Engineers of Society

In the rest of this chapter I would like to list some examples of international business lawyers giving 'added value' to their practice and to their clients.

1. A Belgian lawyer helped his client in a takeover in Germany and used a lawyer from first-rate German law firm. The other side argued a point and it seemed useful to get a second opinion from another German law firm. The Belgian lawyer, through his contacts in the IBA, knew a lawyer from another law firm and was able to get a second opinion very quickly. It was interesting to see that the law firms in Germany were not irritated by this sequence of events at all and were perfectly prepared to work with each other on giving the second opinion.

   Here the clients benefited from the good relationship the Belgian lawyer had with his IBA contacts and the readiness of the German lawyers to cooperate with each other.
2. A Danish lawyer had a Danish client who wished to sell a factory in Seattle. The client did not have the time and the resources to travel to the US. The US buyer was prepared to come for a day to London to negotiate. The Danish lawyer, through his IBA contacts, knew a very good lawyer from Seattle who could help his client in the negotiations. The lawyer from Seattle stayed in Seattle and was reachable by phone during the negotiations between the American buyer, the buyer's lawyers who were present in London and the Danish lawyer and his client.

3. A French lawyer was asked by his client for an address of a lawyer in Malaysia. He said that it would be better if he introduced the Malaysian lawyer, but the client said that that was not necessary. The French lawyer gave the address and a day later the client phoned back to say that the Malaysian contact had no time for him. The French lawyer knew the Malaysian lawyer through his IBA contacts and asked him to give his client a better service. In the end the Malaysian lawyer fetched the client from the airport and gave him the best service possible.
4. The general counsel for an American client called his American lawyer and asked if he could help with the relocation of a manufacturing plant to Central America with special reference to questions about labour and tax laws. The American lawyer immediately told the general counsel of his IBA contact in the foreign jurisdiction. The IBA contact was able to very quickly answer the general counsel's questions

   The same American lawyer received the call from a colleague in Spain seeking a similar referral to a different jurisdiction in the US. The American lawyer was able to give the Spanish colleague a good contact.

   The American lawyer also received a call from a New York lawyer seeking a lawyer for a high-tech acquisition in the UK and was promptly able to give a well-qualified source who he could vouch for personally.

   These exchanges demonstrated the efforts of an international business lawyer to see that the client received the services needed, often without receiving any personal benefit for doing so.
5. In 1989, Sir James Goldsmith's company Hoylake launched a $20 billion-plus takeover bid for BAT, an English company which owned the Farmers Group of insurance companies in the United States. Under the UK Takeover Code, offers have to go fully unconditional within 81 days. If not, the bid lapses, and normally the bidder is not allowed to rebid for 12 months thereafter.

The problem was that the bidder would have violated the insurance laws of each of the nine US states in which Farmers insurance companies were domiciled if the bidder acquired control of BAT without first having obtained approval of the insurance regulators of those states.

The task of the bidder's lawyer was to work with Sir James Goldsmith's UK counsel in educating the Takeover Panel as to the US regulatory regime, and to convince them to permit Hoylake to lapse its bid, with permission to reinstitute the bid once insurance approvals were obtained. The basic pitch to the Takeover Panel was: "If you do not allow us to lapse our bid and recommence it once the regulatory problem is solved, you will render takeover-proof every UK-headquartered multi-national company that has a regulatory issue in a non-UK jurisdiction. And that will hurt UK shareholders."

The value added by the Hoylake lawyer was in identifying the differences in the regulatory regimes, and in explaining them to one set of regulators in a way that enabled an appropriate creative solution to be fashioned.

6. In 1984, the Republic of Korea, as a major step in the liberalisation of its capital markets, decided to authorise the launching of a US-registered investment company to invest in Korean securities. The new Fund was to receive research and advice as to Korean securities from an affiliate of Daewoo Securities, the largest securities firm in Korea.

   In US parlance, the Daewoo affiliate was to be the 'sub-adviser', but this term was not acceptable to Daewoo Securities because of its possible connotations of subordination. On the other hand, the underwriters wanted it to be made plain to investors that the investment decisions were to be made in the US, with the Daewoo affiliate having input but not decision-making authority. How to achieve the objectives of the parties, in a way that did not offend the sensibilities of Daewoo? Some creativity in nomenclature was called for: a US international business lawyer suggested that the defined term in the prospectus for the investment company would be

'Manager' and the defined term for the Daewoo affiliate would be, not 'subadviser', but 'Korean Adviser'.

Since investing in the Fund was basically a bet on Korea, it was necessary to have accurate disclosure in the prospectus of the Korean economic and political situation. This disclosure had to be done in a way that did not offend the sensibilities of the Korean government, since the Fund's prospectus was going to be widely read by the international investing community as an introduction to investment opportunities in Korea. Moreover, to help guard the underwriters and directors against Securities Act liability for an inaccurate prospectus, the Minister of Finance of Korea was to certify that the description of the Korea economic and political situation was being made on his authority.

Again, the 'added value' of the international business lawyers came from their sensitivity to the sensibilities of others, and in their careful choice of words. For example, how to tactfully communicate to investors that democracy in Korea at the time was still young, and that the Executive Branch of the government was the strongest branch? The answer was a careful recitation of recent Korean political history, which included the assassination of one President and the ascendancy of others to office without elections, and delicately phrased statements such as: 'Governmental authority in Korea is highly centralised and is concentrated in a strong presidency.'

7. In India, lawyers have always been treated with great respect. This is mainly due to the fact that lawyers in India have not considered the profession only as a means of earning a livelihood but have used their knowledge of the law for the service of the country. The term 'Social Engineer' can be aptly applied to many lawyers in India.

The legal profession in India played an outstanding and significant role in the struggle for independence from British rule. Mahatma Gandhi, Jawaharlal Nehru, Dr Rajendra Prasad, Dr B.R. Ambedkar, Subash Chandra Bose, Motilal

Nehru, Sir Tej Bahadur Sapru, Mr K.M. Munshi and other national leaders were responsible for moving public opinion in favour of the independence of India and eventually the British had to yield and leave.

Lawyers played a significant role in ensuring that the struggle for independence was a peaceful one and not violent or bloody revolution. Even after attaining independence, lawyers continued to play a dominant role in the administration and governance of the country. Dr Rajendra Prasad and Jawaharlal Nehru, both lawyers by profession, were the first President and Prime Minister of India.

Lawyers in India are not as yet commercialised as those 'in the West' in that they do not sell their time on an hourly basis and are still devoting considerable time to social work, political activities, human rights protection and legal aid etc. Business law is now an important growth area in this country and the legal profession will hopefully retain its image as a force for the preservation and promotion of the rule of law.

In their commercial and business law practice, Indian business lawyers try to follow the principle that a quick bad settlement is better than a successful but long litigation and thus keep their business clients out of the courts. Business lawyers have also been active in supporting a much better arbitration law. They are evolving from firefighters to advisers on business decisions.

8. An important international merchant bank controlled a financial institution in a Latin American country through a local holding. The holding company had, as additional shareholders, four local groups who were financially strong but very primitive and unsophisticated businesswise. The international merchant bank wanted to sell its participation in the holding as it had decided to move out of the retail business in which the financial institution was involved.

The local partners made a tremendous fuss about this decision, arguing that it caused them significant damage, because most probably the operating company would be sold to a competitor. The management of the operating company, originally appointed by the international bank, realised that their jobs were in danger and turned around against the bank. The minority shareholders together with the managers who formed part of the board, took control of the board.

The most bellicose of the local partners obtained a court injunction preventing the international bank from selling the shares in the holding company without giving a first refusal to the plaintiff for a price below the invested capital, and also preventing the bank from taking any action to change the board.

The services of a local international business lawyer were requested at this stage by the international merchant bank. The lawyer, who was known and trusted in the business community, suggested and finally convinced the bank to try to rebuild its relationship with as many of the minority shareholders as possible. Several trips were necessary to the head office of the bank.

Despite the difficult situation, he was successful in winning over three of the minority shareholders. Once he had managed this, he went to the court of appeal seeking a lifting of the injunction, arguing on legal grounds, but also pressing strongly on the bad image that such a case could cause to foreign investment in Argentina. He also persuaded the embassy of the foreign investor's country to discretely apply some pressure. The court of appeal overruled the injunction.

An aggressive litigating attorney would have escalated the legal actions against the minority shareholders. Probably, he would have achieved the same end result, but after a long and expensive battle. The constructive approach cost much less, was quicker, and was completely satisfactory to the foreign client.

9. In an international tender for a major infrastructure project in Africa funded by well-known international agencies, several contractual clauses prepared by the local authorities although well adapted to local contractors and small works were clearly

unreasonable in the light of international usages and practices, shifting too many risks to the contractor. Any experienced international contractor could only make a provision in its price in order to attempt to cover these risks. As a result, the prices proposed for the work by reliable contractors were too high and, as a result, the African country could not obtain any international funding and a badly needed infrastructure project could not be built.

The role of the international business lawyer specialising in the industry and familiar with the particular country and its laws was to explain to both parties the various legal and practical consequences of the unreasonable clauses (*force majeure*, unforeseen impediment, change in regulation, etc). It emerged that, to some extent, both sides misunderstood the actual consequences of the draft clauses. In particular, the occurrence of the risks and their practical consequences were, to a great extent, different from their *prima facie* understanding (taking into account the insurability of the risks in question).

After discussions, the parties agreed that, through more detailed clauses allocating the risks between them in a more balanced manner and linked with an equitable and efficient dispute prevention and resolution system, the price of the contract could be substantially reduced for works of same quality. As a result, the contract became viable and the project could be built in an efficient and economical manner without jeopardising the public interest on one side and the normal profit margin of the contractor on the other.

10. A complex infrastructure project had to be built in another emerging country involving foreign and local technology, foreign and local contractors as well as management contractors. Here again, the proposed price at the negotiation stage was too high due, *inter alia*, to the heavy taxation regime in the host country. Indeed, the overall customs and tax burden amounted to 25 per cent of the overall contract value. In this case, it was not possible to negotiate any tax concession and

the role of the experienced international lawyer was to modify and rearrange the initial contractual structure in such a way that the tax burden could be reduced by half. This achievement was possible thanks to a detailed analysis of the tax laws both in the host country and in the foreign country of origin. This restructuring was a significant element in the implementation of the contract.

11. A foreign client involved in a large project in an emerging country prepared a large claim against a local employer and wanted to know the reaction of an experienced international lawyer before initiating the proceedings. It was quickly apparent that, taking into account the dispute resolution clause and several precedents in the same country, most of the claims—although valid in principle—were unlikely to be entertained if presented in a developed country, or, if at all, only after years of arguments and arbitration and large costs.

    The client was advised of the conclusion and several meetings were held with the top management of the contractor organisation where the international lawyer was cross-questioned on the various elements underlying his conclusions. As a result, a substantial part of the claim was dropped and the parties managed to settle without a long battle. A new relationship started to develop between the parties in such a way that the foreign contractor managed to get new contacts with the same client to the satisfaction of all parties.

12. A new joint venture company had to be formed in an Asian country between a foreign company and a local company.

    After months of meetings, the executive of both companies agreed in principle to form a company on a 50-50 basis. After more negotiations they realised that a 50-50 situation was in fact dangerous since it would lead too often to a deadlock situation.

    Each partner, as a result, wanted to have a 51 per cent stake; after several rounds of argument, the parties could not find a solution due to their conflicting views of the consequences of the 51 per cent stake. The role of the international business lawyer familiar with both systems of law and of their practice was to defuse the conflict and to assist them in explaining, through various scenarios, the true nature of the decision-making process, the issues at stake and the various ways to resolve the matter in a satisfactory manner.

The parties eventually agreed to go back to their original 50-50 intention and to clarify their respective roles in the decision-making process, inter alia, through ad hoc clauses in a shareholder agreement and in the articles of association. They eventually entered into a joint venture which developed smoothly because several sensitive issues had been envisaged in advance, with the help of the experienced practitioner, and potential misunderstandings avoided.

13. A transaction involved three companies: a Japanese parent, the Japanese parent's semiconductor subsidiary, and a US company. This transaction exemplifies the fact that an international lawyer's value often goes beyond just having a strong grasp of various laws, good drafting skills and an ability to negotiate effectively (what might be called 'pure' lawyer skills); the more significant skills may often be the ability to understand the two cultures involved and to find creative solutions—'bridges' between the two cultures.

The transaction came about as the result, on the one hand, of the US company looking for an established Japanese company, one with personnel in place, manufacturing facilities, customers and a knowledge of the markets involved and, on the other hand, of the Japanese parent reaching the conclusion that its semiconductor subsidiary was too small to survive on its own, and that for the good of both the parent and the subsidiary, the subsidiary would have to be sold. As to the latter, in Japan merely reaching the conclusion that a subsidiary needs to be sold is a painful one as it is viewed as an admission of failure; consequently, opportunities to make an acquisition are quite rare in Japan.

It became publicly known that the parent was looking for a buyer for its subsidiary. Certainly, the parent company's management contemplated a Japanese buyer, and there was immediate interest expressed on the part of certain very large, listed Japanese companies with whom the subsidiary had been dealing. However, the US company also learned of the subsidiary being up for sale and went to a Japanese international business lawyer for legal advice.

He formulated a legal framework for the purchase, which also involved educating the US in-house lawyers as to the legal requirements. Conveying these requirements was the first bridge he had to build in order that the US company would be acquainted with his strategy for dealing with the Japanese parent company. Finally came the negotiations between the US company and the Japanese parent: in this, he played a significant function as an 'interpreter' of the cultural issues and social mores which came into play.

For the US side he had to firmly establish the importance in Japan of building long-term relationships in order to build trust, and the importance of conveying to the Japanese side that the US company would honour the relationships established by the Japanese subsidiary. Another issue, which was at first not at all acceptable to the US side but which he had to fully convey the importance of in order to both successfully complete the deal and to have a successful and smooth-running company thereafter, was Japan's policy of lifetime employment and the necessity of maintaining existing levels of fringe benefits.

An even bigger obstacle existed on the Japanese side: the social stigma of being sold out to a foreign company. This was truly a high hurdle to overcome. Fortunately, during the course of discussions it appeared that the US company had a very strong history in its past acquisitions of honouring the corporate culture of the acquired company and treating it as a respected partner and equal. On the other hand, it was also possible for the lawyer to argue that large, publicly traded Japanese companies do not have a good history regarding their treatment of smaller, acquired companies. The lawyer went to work bringing these points home to the Japanese parent. He essentially argued that it would be better to be acquired by the US company, which would agree to honour the relationships the subsidiary had built, keep in place the lifetime employment system and fringe benefits and, as would not be the case if a large Japanese company acquired the subsidiary, honour the corporate culture of the subsidiary and treat it and its employees as equals. He asserted that a large Japanese company would treat the subsidiary as a 'second class citizen', and asked company management to reflect on their experiences and knowledge of similar situations and decide whether they agreed with him. He also talked with employee representatives and asked that they consider the same points.

To almost everyone's great surprise, the US company and its Japanese international lawyer ultimately triumphed, even though they were competing with giants of Japanese industry. Now, years later, the Japanese subsidiary still retains its basic Japanese structure, with some modifications. It is a successful company and now forms the core of the US company's activities in Japan.

14. On some occasions we are even engineers in the sense that we provide the necessary input for our client to build new commercial and business relations, introducing our clients to other companies and/or investors in order to develop joint projects and/or new business. Nevertheless, it is always extremely important not to miss the point that we are the legal counsel, with the main responsibility of providing our client with the legal advice needed and required for the performance and development of their business, giving the complementary advice that will permit our client to have a better understanding of the local environment and to make the correct business decision. We should refrain from making those business decisions ourselves, as they are properly the responsibility of the client and their local management.

These examples all demonstrate the 'added value' that international business lawyers bring to their work. None of these lawyers regard these extra benefits as being beyond their normal 'call of duty' but see them as part of the service they are required to give as lawyers.

In my view, many of the most valuable attributes and skills of the international business lawyer are not learned at law school but are achieved through the experience and contacts that they acquire through attending International Bar Association and Section on Business Law Conferences. IBA members can justly celebrate the establishment of the international legal network at the 50th anniversary of the IBA and they welcome the bar leaders to celebrate with them.

The Role of Lawyers in ADR

By Robert Briner

In order to identify the role of lawyers in ADR, it is necessary to first agree on a definition of ADR. No generally recognized definition exists and even the meaning of the "A" can be controversial. Normally ADR is understood as Alternative Dispute Resolution, but it also has been described as Appropriate Dispute Resolution. Black's Law Dictionary, Sixth Edition 1990, states under ADR: "*See Alternative dispute resolution; Asset Depreciation Range.*" and after the caption "*Alternative dispute resolution,*" the definition is as follows:

> "Term refers to procedures for settling disputes by means other than litigation; e.g., by arbitration, mediation, mini-trials. Such procedures, which are usually less costly and more expeditious, are increasingly being used in commercial and labour disputes, divorce actions, in resolving motor vehicle and medical malpractice tort claims, and in other disputes that would likely otherwise involve court litigation. See also Arbitration; Mediation; Mini-trial; Trial (Summary jury trial)."

This definition is similar to all other definitions insofar as ADR is considered to constitute a dispute resolution method different and distinct from, and possibly even opposed to, litigation before state courts.

No unanimity, however, exists regarding the place of arbitration in ADR. Can it be considered as constituting part of ADR, as suggested by the definition of Black, or does it have to be excluded? Under the modern tendency arbitration is clearly distinguished from court litigation as it introduces a degree of flexibility not possible in case of litigation before state courts (see e.g. the 1996 English Arbitration Act, especially Sections 33 and 34; see also Jan Paulsson's paper "Different Approaches to International Arbitration Procedures—A Harmonization of Basic Notions".[1] Arbitration does, however, constitute a method which provides for an examination of the factual and legal situation and an authoritative, final decision giving rise to an enforceable award with *res judicata* effect. Although the form of the arbitration proceedings should, and ideally will, be different from court proceedings, the effect of the end result, the award, will be identical to a court decision.

In order to establish a clear separation between what might be called the normal or standard dispute resolution processes giving rise to an enforceable decision on the one hand and ADR (understood as *alternative* dispute resolution) on the other hand, it would seem appropriate to exclude in the following discussion arbitration from the definition of ADR, contrary to the definition given by Black. This seems especially indicated in the context of this paper as the role of lawyers in court litigation and in arbitration is clearly related and basically has as the same objective namely to convince the judge or arbitrator that his party has a better claim than the opponent. Obviously, in arbitration a lawyer often also assumes the role of the adjudicator, reserved to the state judge in court litigation. To a certain degree this role of the lawyer as arbitrator creates a bridge to some aspects of one of his roles in the context of ADR to be discussed later.

It is not necessary to deal at length in this paper with the historical development of ADR, especially since the 1970s, and its roots which have their origin primarily in the United States. Although this of course constitutes a great simplification of a very complex situation, it would seem fair to state that there exist two main reasons

---

1 Published in ADR Currents, volume 1 (1996) Nr. 2 (a publication of the American Arbitration Association), page 17

for the growth of ADR in the United States. On the one hand the courts themselves realized that many cases, especially those with low amounts at stake or within a specific field like labour and family law (see above definition in Black's) could not always be handled in an expeditious and inexpensive fashion. The parties to such litigation were therefore often no longer assured of having proper access to justice. One of the remedies developed, other than streamlining the ordinary court procedures, consists in compelling parties to try to settle their dispute by ADR and, in certain cases, also by arbitration. In some instances, recourse to ADR is declared mandatory and not just left to the discretion of the court or the will of the parties.

On the other hand, not just in smaller or mass litigation but also in large, important disputes the parties began to question the suitability of traditional American litigation, be it before courts or before an arbitrator, as the most cost and time effective method to resolve disputes. Alternate methods were identified and tried.

Eventually other common law jurisdictions also became interested in alternatives to the traditional way disputes were resolved and a close look was taken at ADR as a possible alternative to court proceedings. This went hand in hand with efforts to also modernize court proceedings (see in England e.g. the Report by Lord Woolf[2] and the in-depth and pertinent analysis made by Arthur Marriott in the 1995 Freshfields Lecture[3]). Not the only reason, but surely an important one, was the realization that time consuming court proceedings in civil litigation with extensive pre-trial discovery, cross-examination and, in the United States, a jury trial, might not always constitute the most effective method to resolve disputes.

In Continental Europe, the courts have of course also become more and more congested but ADR has not, at least so far, had a major impact on the litigation scene. Arbitration has, however, become more widely used as a method to resolve disputes and in

---

2 Access to Justice, Final Report, By The Right Honourable the Lord Woolf, Master of the Rolls to the Lord Chancellor on the civil justice system in England and Wales, London HMSO, 1996

3 13 (1996) Arbitration International 1, page 1

some countries which used to belong to the COMECON, arbitration has even become the preferred method also for domestic business disputes as the courts are often not yet capable to efficiently handle such matters. Furthermore, the historic perception of the role of the courts as the sole authorized decider of disputes is diminishing. Even in those countries where arbitration had to fight a long struggle to be recognized at least as the smaller sister of the courts, legislation has been introduced allowing arbitrators to resolve differences between parties with binding effect. But also in Europe there exist movements to encourage ADR as an alternative to court litigation, however, again, primarily not in business disputes, but in that great number of law suits which are the major contributor to the congestion of the courts e.g. family matters, debt collection, traffic accidents and other tort matters. To give but one example: President Chirac in January 1997 instructed the French Government to reform and streamline the legal system including an examination of the role which mediation and conciliation could play.

It should also be noted that state judges in a number of European countries have an obligation to explore with the parties the possibility of a settlement. Depending on the environment, the legal framework and the personality of the judge, the courts often go to some length to conciliate the parties, involving some of the same techniques often recommended by articles and manuals which have been published in the ADR field.

The picture drawn by Bryant G. Garth, director of the Chicago based American Bar Foundation,[4] according to which mediation and other ADR processes constituted a reaction to the "take-over" of U.S. litigators of international commercial arbitration, is greatly exaggerated. He describes such arbitration as "private litigation" or perhaps "off-shore" litigation. He sees the source in hyper-adversarial or "scorched earth" business litigation which according to Garth developed initially in the mid-1970s and was also employed in international commercial arbitration. It is obvious that in inter-

---

4 CPR Institute for Dispute Resolution Publication "Alternatives" (volume 15, Nr. 1, January 1997)

national arbitration American litigators, in the eyes of many observers, employ methods and tactics acquired on the American litigation scene. However, relatively few international commercial arbitrations are actually conducted according to these lines. Large Wall Street (and London City) firms do not have a decisive influence on international arbitration. Of course they play an important role but they have no monopoly nor do they usually employ American litigation tactics. Exceptions of course exist but they are not representative of international commercial arbitration. Extensive pre-trial discovery and long cross-examination are the exceptions, not the general rule of arbitration and, for all practical purposes, can really only be employed within an environment where both parties are represented by U.S. or English lawyers. The trend, as shown by Jan Paulsson in the paper referred to above (footnote 1), goes towards a blending of the common and civil law procedures always keeping in mind that the process also has to be cost effective. Undoubtedly the well published practice of the Iran-United States Claims Tribunal in The Hague also plays an important role as this tribunal was able to show that complex business disputes could be adjudicated with practically no discovery and strictly limited examination of witnesses.[5] It is not seriously disputed that international commercial arbitration continues to be the preferred method to resolve commercial disputes and is not being replaced by ADR.

The statistics of the ICC demonstrate this fact as they show a continual growth of the number of new requests for arbitration which increased from 126 in 1970 to 182 in 1975, 250 in 1980, 339 in 1985, 365 in 1990 and 433 in 1996. This observation, namely that arbitration continues to be the main method used to settle international disputes, does not only apply to Europe and North America. Also in many Latin America countries arbitration is becoming increasingly popular. The arbitration laws are changing and are more friendly towards arbitration. International investors do not

---

5 See e.g. George H. Aldrich, *The Jurisprudence of the Iran-United States Claims Tribunal - An Analysis of the Decisions of the Tribunal*, Clarendon Press Oxford, 1996

want to become entangled in domestic litigation before the courts of the host country, but want to be able to rely on arbitration to settle disputes in a binding fashion. Only arbitration offers the well known advantages e.g. the possibility to agree on the applicable law, on the language, the greater confidentiality, the great flexibility of the procedure allowing tailor-made solutions, the choice of knowledgeable arbitrators and the availability, although not always perfect, of the enforcement mechanism of the 1958 New York Convention for the Recognition and Enforcement of Arbitral Awards.

In all arbitration procedures it is perfectly conceivable that the arbitrator explores with the parties the possibility of a settlement and actively encourages the parties to come to an agreement. For the foreseeable future it, however, seems rather unlikely that ADR will become a favourite method to resolve international disputes involving developing economies.

The same considerations apply to Asia. Of course conciliation is the preferred method to resolve disputes, of course we all know that there are relatively few practising attorneys in Japan. It would, however, seem that the preference for conciliation pertains mainly to domestic matters not to international business transactions where arbitration remains the favourite method to resolve disputes.

We considered it necessary to first develop these distinctions in order to more clearly define the role of ADR as a possible, but by no means the main, method to resolve disputes and thereby identify the framework within which the lawyer will be called upon to act.

As this paper constitutes a contribution to the book published on the occasion of the 50th Anniversary of the International Bar Association, we will obviously only deal with international disputes, here defined as involving parties from different countries and involving commercial transactions. We shall therefore not deal with domestic ADR which indeed is, for the reason set out above, becoming an increasingly more accepted method on the national scene. It is, however, necessary to realise that what may be very successful in an internal relationship with one legal system and an uniform cultural background will not easily lend itself to be transferred to the international scene.

The lawyer, both in-house counsel and lawyers in private practice, can intervene in ADR proceedings in various capacities and at various stages. We will therefore identify the various stages and examine the role which lawyers should, can and do play in the ADR process.

The first possible involvement arises at the time when a company defines its general policy regarding the preferred way to resolve disputes arising from a contractual commercial relationship. Especially the in-house counsel will carry a great responsibility in formulating such corporate policy. This calls for a careful analysis of the field of business of the company, the legal environment, possible contracting parties and their legal and economic background and a weighing of the different options available. The in-house counsel also plays an important role in educating the people who actually negotiate the contracts. The drafting of standard dispute resolution clauses is part of his obligations. In this connection he carries a special obligation to avoid pathological clauses. It is remarkable how many defective clauses are constantly inserted in contracts; just a few real examples to illustrate this point:

- a construction sub-contract between a Turkish contractor and an American sub-contractor for a plant in a newly independent State in the Southern part of the former Soviet Union contained the following clause regarding the applicable law: "*The laws of the United States of America and of Turkey shall apply in case of a dispute.*"
- another clause provided: "*Disputes shall be settled in Toronto, Canada*" and furthermore, two paragraphs later, stated: "*All proceedings shall take place in New York.*"

Although not actually encountered, one could well imagine a contract containing the following clause:

> "All disputes shall be settled by arbitration. The mediator shall be appointed according to the Commercial Mediation Rules of the American Arbitration Association."

There exist no limitations to the fantasy of drafters of contracts and the variety of defective clauses which result from such drafting.

At the stage of actual contract negotiation, now possibly together with the normal outside counsel of the company and/or together with local counsel in the country of the other party, many of the same issues have to be dealt with as those identified previously when discussing the general formation of the company policy. However, this analysis now has to take into consideration the real circumstances of the envisaged transaction and the particularities of the other party. The following discussion will obviously need to include the other contracting party and its advisors. It is possible, and occurs rather frequently, that such contract negotiations are only held between the business people and the technicians of the two (or several) parties without necessarily involving in-house or outside counsel. It would, however, seem that in view of the difficulties in clearly defining the best suited ADR method and in view of the lack of internationally recognized ADR standard rules (other than for conciliation), it would be indispensable to also involve lawyers in the contract negotiations if one of the parties intends to adopt an ADR clause. Careful drafting, as always, will hopefully avoid later unpleasant surprises. This is especially important in the context of ADR. If ADR solutions are envisaged, the advantages and disadvantages of not being able to obtain an enforceable award or judgment have to be carefully weighed against the perceived savings in cost and time which an ADR process should normally produce. Much will obviously depend on the analysis which is being made of the other party, its trustworthiness and the expectation that even when a dispute has arisen the other party will in good faith collaborate in order to bring the ADR process to a fruitful conclusion and not misuse it for dilatory purposes.

The dispute has arisen. Two situations are possible. The contract already contains an ADR clause which then has to be set in motion. However, it is conceivable that the parties did not provide for any specific method to resolve their dispute or have chosen court litigation or arbitration. Once the concrete dispute exists, the parties might both agree that in view of the concrete nature of the dispute the originally envisaged method might no longer constitute the best option. It is probably at this moment in the relationship between two parties when the choice of an ADR method has the greatest chance of success. Other than adopting one of the straightforward conciliation or mediation clause using one of the internationally recognized rules, be it of UNCITRAL, of the ICC, of the World Intellectual Property Organization (WIPO), the American Arbitration Association, etc., which can be inserted in the contract itself, the choice of another ADR method will be much more complex. In this context we are not dealing with specific industry related ADR methods like Claims Appeals Committees or Disputes Review Boards sometimes encountered in the construction industry. Once the dispute has arisen, the parties, conscious of the respective positions and knowing the nature of the dispute, can now select the appropriate ADR method, provided that both parties are reasonably convinced that the other party will in good faith participate in the process. Now the resourcefulness and experience of the lawyer to find the best solution for the matter at hand can be put to full use. Now choices regarding the method best suited, be it mediation, conciliation, facilitation, mini-trial, med-arb, arb-med, medaloa, etc. need to be assessed for their suitability to solve the concrete dispute which has arisen.

During the next phase the lawyer will be called upon to participate in the implementation of the ADR method chosen. The lawyer will surely be involved in the selection of the third person who will have the duty of trying to bring about a settlement between the parties. Certain ADR processes try to directly involve the top management of the parties who should then be the main actors of the process. Even in such a scenario the lawyer, with his background and training, will have an important role to play. He will need to advise the executive as to the risks involved and, especially, he will want to compare the result of the possible settlement with the likely or probable outcome which is most probable to occur if a settlement cannot be reached and the dispute would therefore need to be adjudicated.

The lawyer who is called upon to play an active role in the ADR process will need to possess specific qualities. What is needed is not the "normal" adversarial litigation lawyer, whose adrenaline flows faster when confronted with an opponent who presents a different position. It is rather the skills of the transactional lawyer which are needed, who understands the position of the other party and who tries to see how this position can be accommodated, at the same time not losing sight of the interests and objectives of his own party. These talents of a negotiator, and not of a litigator, are undoubtedly part of the skills which many lawyers have acquired, not necessarily only in ADR proceedings, but rather in their commercial practice and which can now be put to use, refined and developed in this ADR environment.

A further obvious role of lawyers in the ADR process is that of the independent third party, as conciliator, mediator, president of a mini-trial or whatever other role the parties have agreed that he should exercise. This role might be somewhat unusual to many lawyers. The objective will not be to represent, in whatever form, a party. His duty is to find, together with the parties, a solution with which both parties can live. Specific gifts are required. Not just a developed feeling for justice and fairness, but also the intellectual flexibility which enables him to familiarize himself with a specific business environment, that of the two parties. He needs to understand their problems and aspirations and, especially, to possess enough imagination and knowledge of the specific "playground" which will allow him to propose innovative solutions which can satisfy both parties, for instance to explore possibilities for future collaboration or for the common exploitation of business opportunities. But then again, although the lawyer is usually not well trained or experienced in assuming such a non partisan role, which normally is not associated with his traditional work, many are indeed well suited to assume such an office. It is part of the normal experience of business lawyers to be constantly confronted with new situations, to have to familiarize themselves with the ever changing challenges confronting their clients in very different fields of activities and to adapt to changed circumstances in an active, positive and forward looking fashion and not adopt a defensive posture. Many arbitrators have through their exposure also been able to acquire such skills.

One of the aims of the ADR movement is to provide an alternative to court litigation and thereby to reduce the role of the lawyer who, especially in the United States and other common law jurisdictions, rightly or wrongly is accused to have contributed to the apparently unsatisfactory state of affair in the dispute resolution field. It is, however, obvious from the above analysis that many important, interesting and even essential contributions to the ADR process can and are made by lawyers.

It might even be possible to identify a further role, so far not touched upon, which lawyers play in the context of ADR. It is noteworthy that most publications dealing with ADR have been written by practising lawyers who tried, legitimately so, to direct the attention of the users of legal services to other methods suitable for the resolution of disputes. In this connection it is interesting to note that some ethical rules governing the profession of lawyers stipulate an obligation of the lawyer to draw the attention of the client to possible other methods to resolve disputes than court litigation. Some of these possibilities are genuinely new, some only present the traditional methods with a new packaging and a different ribbon around the package. ADR initially constituted a niche product which enabled "initiated" proponents of ADR to enjoy a competitive advantage. Professors, sociologists, judges and law makers of course also became interested in the subject and many have written about it. The main underlying mantra recited by the advocates of ADR seems to be that lawyers are primarily to blame for the high cost and the length of legal proceedings and that the world, especially also the business world, would be better served if top management was more directly involved in the resolution of disputes and, assisted by a facilitator or other sage person, they would be able to satisfactorily resolve all issues. Of course this idealistic picture sometimes does exist—even in real life—but reality normally tends to be different. In the real world, as we have tried to show in this paper, it would seem that the role of the lawyer continues to be a crucial one, especially also in the context of the ADR process. Some 400 years ago Shakespeare had the rebels against the establishment in Henry VI say "*The first thing we do, let's kill all the lawyers*".[6] So far this program has not been successful and it seems highly unlikely that ADR will be able to achieve this goal.

6 Dick Butcher in 2 Henry VI, IV, ii, 68

The Role of the Lawyer in Shaping the UN

John Salter

1.INTRODUCTION

The 50th anniversary of the IBA is sandwiched between that of the UN in 1995 and that of the GATT multi-lateral trading system in 1998 and almost coincides with a special session of the UN General Assembly (UNGASS) to be held in New York on 23rd to 27th June 1997 presenting the world with a unique opportunity to bring a new political momentum to the process begun in Rio in 1992 which will hopefully result in a clear agenda for future international action in relation to the environment.

The UN Charter sets out the constitution of the international community affording a juridically secured form of international co-operation. It is pre-eminent amongst multi-lateral treaties. The basic principles of the UN Charter were settled in 1945 after VE (Victory in Europe) day at a founding Conference in San Francisco.[1] The initial role for lawyers was, therefore, to be the drafters of the Charter. That meant not only providing for rules to maintain

---

1 RB Russell, *A History of the United Nations Charter*, 1958.

international peace and security but also to tackle matters which might lead to the development of major crises.

2. HUMAN RIGHTS

Generally speaking the subject of human rights did not feature as a subject of international law before 1939. Text books on international law scarcely touched upon the subject. The index of Oppenheim's International Law, 3rd edition 1920, does not contain any entry for "human rights". The recognition and development of human rights has brought about a change in the structure of the international legal order. This has been recently recognised in the establishment by the International Bar Association of the Human Rights Institute. The international legal profession has for a long time expounded human rights obligations as part of customary law.[2] Commencing with the Universal Declaration of 10th December 1940 a large number of multi-lateral human rights treaties are in force.[3] The high points were reached with agreement of the International Bill of Human Rights dealing with civil and political rights and with the 1966 International Covenant on Economic Social and Cultural rights. The importance given to this subject by the United Nations is shown by the establishment in 1993 of a UN High Commissioner for Human Rights.[4] The World Conference on Human Rights was held in Vienna. In its Declaration of June 1993 the parties declared that all human rights are universal, indivisible, interdependent and inter-related. "The international community must treat human rights globally in a fair and equal manner, on the same footing, and with the same emphasis... While the significance of

---

2 Bruno Simma and P Alston, *The Sources of Human Rights Law,* 12 Austl.Y.B. of International Law, p.82 (1992).

3 See UN Centre for Human Rights, UN Documents ST/HR/1REV5 (1994) and ST/HR/2REV4 (1994).

4 General Assembly Resolution 48/141.

national and regional particularities and various historical, cultural and religious backgrounds must be borne in mind, it is the duty of States, regardless of their political, economic and cultural systems, to promote and protect all human rights and fundamental freedoms".[5] The restoration of human rights is enforced by peer group pressure arising out of published decisions, for example, of the Working Group on Arbitrary Detention.[6] The International Bar Association plays a major role in monitoring possible violations of human rights and bringing such matters to the attention of the State concerned and the international community. Other factors which have brought about changes in the international legal order include matters relating to disarmament, environmental protection, international trade law, the law of the sea and development policies which are considered, in turn, below.

3. DISARMAMENT, ARMS CONTROL AND NON-PROLIFERATION

Under the Charter, the Security Council was designed to be the focal point for disarmament measures and for monitoring potential violations of Article 2, paragraph 4, on the non-use of force. The Council was unable to discharge these responsibilities during the cold war due to the use of the veto. The UN General Assembly set up the UN Atomic Energy Commission and the Commission on Conventional Armaments. Their work was also frustrated by the use of the Soviet's veto. The Commissions were consolidated in 1952 to form a single Disarmament Commission. In 1963 the Partial Test Ban Treaty was signed. In 1968 the Treaty on Non-proliferation of Nuclear Weapons was signed. In 1996 the

---

5 UN Department of Public Information, *World Conference on Human Rights: The Vienna Declaration and Programme of Action*, New York, 1993, para. 5.

6 See UN Document E/CN.4/1994/27.

Comprehensive Test Ban Treaty was signed. The Conference on Disarmament achieved the Chemical Weapons Convention which was concluded in 1992. Many legal instruments have been brought in to being with the help of lawyers covering nuclear and other weapons of mass destruction. Current problems relate to transparency, verification, compliance and enforcement of compliance. The UN register of arms has been established. This has, however, ended up as a register of selective and limited conventional arms. Not all Conventions contain verification mechanisms. Thus, the Security Council has not discharged its Charter responsibilities in the disarmament field. Reforms are needed to enable the Security Council to be the ultimate authority and to ensure compliance. The Major Powers have assumed such a role. Thus, the joint Declaration by the leaders of the Russian Federation, Ukraine, the United Kingdom, the United States of America of December 5th, 1994 took into account the commitment of the Ukraine to eliminate all nuclear weapons from its territory and contained obligations from the declarants to refrain from the threat or use of force against the territorial integrity or political independence of Ukraine.[7] Contracting Parties agreed to provide assistance to Ukraine as a non-nuclear weapons State if it became a victim of an act of aggression or an object of a threat of aggression in which nuclear weapons were to be used. Nuclear weapons sites in Ukraine are gradually being decommissioned. The General Assembly has adopted a Resolution[8] by which it declared that the use of nuclear weapons would be a violation of the Charter and a crime against humanity.

4. ENVIRONMENTAL PROTECTION

The need for environmental protection has brought about changes in the international legal order. The UN's five dimensions of develop-

7 UN Document A/49/765.

8 General Assembly Resolution 1653(XXI).

ment are environmental protection, peace, the economy, social justice and democracy.[9] UNCHE in 1972 in Stockholm called upon Governments to co-operate in developing international law for the protection of the environment. The lawyers under direction of politicians drafted on a sectoral basis treaties which either dealt with specific sources of pollution or specific pollutants or areas of pollution or activities causing particular concern, dealing with such matters as air, water, habitats, wastes, chemicals, safety and health. There was no UN environmental treaty overseeing all these sectoral issues. However UNCED in 1992 in Rio called upon governments to integrate the environmental dimension into their developmental policies and trade law. Environmental law is concerned with influencing processes and production methods in accordance with the emerging doctrine of producer responsibility and the promotion of best practice in waste minimisation affecting even methods of decommissioning whereas the multilateral trading system is primarily concerned and deals with products without embarking upon life cycle analysis of the design, manufacture, distribution and ultimate disposal of those products. The work of an international body concerned with trade was originally envisaged to fall within the UN system. In fact the work of World Trade Organisation is conducted from Geneva in proximity with other international institutions but is legally outside the UN system. Much of environmental policy is conducted on the world scene by resolutions, recommendations, guidelines and declarations which are not legally binding. The lawyers did however get together in a working group and prepared Legal Principles for Environmental Protection and Sustainable Development which were annexed to the Brundtland Commission's "Our common future" summarising the work of the World Commission on Environment and Development (WCED). Lawyers also got together in assisting the International Union for Conservation of Nature and Natural Resources (IUCN) in its preparation of an International Covenant on Environment and

---

9 UN Secretary-General's Agenda for Development, UN Document A/49/665, dated 11 November 1994 at para 5.

Development.[10] The environment, as a highly important natural resource base, needs protection and for twenty years between 1972 and 1992 the lawyers were very active in drafting a whole range of treaties. UNCED's important contribution in 1992 to the international scene was to bring together the economic, environmental, health, safety and social aspects of development into Agenda 21, being a programme for sustainable development. This programme, as well as dealing with sectoral areas, introduced and considered cross-cutting issues such as finance, poverty, sustainable production, technology transfer, trade and the environment and integration of environmental protection into policies and actions right across the board. CSD was asked in 1993 to monitor the implementation of Agenda 21 and to produce a strategy for its development. CSD issues an annual report. It publishes sets of indicators of sustainable development and it allows for full discussion of major issues. The UN has been careful to organise a range of major conferences on particular issues to gain information on how to react to such matters as poverty (the Copenhagen Conference) the rights of women (the Beijing Conference), the control of population (the Cairo Conference), problems relating to urban settlements (the Istanbul Conference) and the question of important food security (The Rome World Food Summit Conference).

5. INTERNATIONAL TRADE LAW

Priority areas which need financial aid, which could be combined with debt relief[11] are population growth, sustainable agriculture, forestry, bio-diversity and energy efficiency, but aid levels have dropped below the Agenda 21 Rio target of 0.7% of GNP. There is a problem for the lawyers to sort out in that it appears that some of

---

10 Circulated at UN Conference on Public International Law, New York, in March 1995.

11 See the World Bank's and the International Monetary Fund's Heavily Indebted Poor Countries Debt Initiative approved in October 1996.

the provisions of agreements forming part of the legal documentation setting up the World Trade Organisation (WTO) are in conflict with multilateral environmental treaties. These problems were not specifically addressed at the first Ministerial Conference under the World Trade Organisation Agreement held in Singapore in December 1996. There is a clear need for the World Trade Organisation to participate in the work for example of the UN Commission on Sustainable Development (CSD). A legal approach is now however being adopted by Panels and by the Appellate Body established under the WTO Agreement. There appears to be a much better dispute resolution system in place now than under the former regime. It is a matter of some concern to the legal profession that shortly their activities will be examined under provisions contained in GATS—the agreement relating to the provision of services. The International Bar Association (IBA) is consulting its member organisations about the proposals.

IBA lawyers from the Section on Business Law (SBL) are currently working hard with UNCITRAL on such matters as insolvency, receivables financing, BOT contracts and electronic commerce amongst other projects including revision of the Hamburg Rules and the New York Convention.

6. LAW OF THE SEA

The UN Convention on the Law of the Sea (UNCLOS) came into effect on 18th March 1994, the end of many years of legal effort starting with the work of the International Law Commission (ILC) in 1956 and ending with the work of the UN Secretary-General in achieving the Agreement relating to the Implementation of Part XI of UNCLOS which modified and supplemented Part XI before it came into effect.[12] The UN Secretary-General co-ordinated the work on the agreement of the Treaty with the helpful contributions

12 General Assembly Resolution 48/263 of 29 July 1994.

of FAO dealing with fisheries, IMO dealing with pollution from ships, IOC[13] dealing with matters relating to marine scientific research and UNEP dealing with the marine environment. International organisations such as Committee A Maritime and Transport Law of the IBA Section on Business Law are keen participants in the process of international law making to help the product gain wide acceptance. That is a valuable contribution that can be made by lawyers particularly through publication of their conference proceedings. The work of lawyers in formulating the Treaty was enhanced through the establishment of the Committee on the Peaceful Uses of the Sea-Bed and Ocean Floor Beyond the Limits of National Jurisdiction.[14] Had the Third UN Law of the Sea Treaty merely been a codification the lawyers could have handled the matter without difficulty but as the Treaty encompassed new concepts then help was required from politicians and those with wide practical experience of maritime issues. There is now however effective regulation of the seabed and its resources declared by General Assembly Resolution [15] to be the common heritage of mankind, and not of any one Member State, as opposed to a free-for-all for those using high seas. The work of the lawyer was ably supported by such scene setting Resolutions passed by the General Assembly.

7. DEVELOPMENT POLICIES

The primary objective of support for international development is the reduction of poverty.[16] "Development must be about

13 UNESCO's Inter-governmental Oceanographics Commission.

14 Set up by General Assembly Resolution 2467 (XX111) of 21 December 1968.

15 Declaration of Principles governing the Sea-Bed and Ocean Floor, and the Subsoil Thereof, Beyond the Limits of National Jurisdiction, General Assembly Resolution 2749 (XXV) of 17 December 1970.

16 See the World Bank's Annual Progress Report on Poverty and the World Bank's World Development Reports.

improvement of human well-being; removal of hunger, disease and ignorance; and productive employment for all. Its first goal must be to end poverty and satisfy the priority needs of all people in a way that can be productively sustained over future generations."[17] So said the United Nations' Secretary-General in his Development Report of 1994. Whereas in the political sphere the world has seen the emergence of a large number of smaller nation states, in the economic arena there has been a tendency to form regional associations such as the European Union, ASEAN, MERCOSUR and NAFTA. There is thus a great deal of economic co-operation outside the sphere of the United Nations. Yet some matters can only be dealt with on a global basis. Thus the World Bank has helped to establish and served as a trustee of the trust fund established under the Global Environment Facility, of the Ozone Trust Fund and of the Rain Forest Trust Fund. The World Bank has helped Member States to address the challenges of poverty and economic growth and to set appropriate priorities and build their own institutions to implement appropriate programmes. Lawyers are used to working with the World Bank which is an organ of the UN and has five specialist agencies namely the International Bank for Reconstruction & Development (IBRD) founded in 1944 for the purpose of guaranteeing or participating in or making loans to a Member State or to an organ of the Member State or to any business, industrial or agricultural enterprise in the territory of a Member State with the guarantee of the Member State; the International Finance Corporation (IFC) founded in 1956 for the purpose of providing finance to private bodies in a Member State without that Member State's guarantee; the International Development Agency (IDA) founded in 1960 for the purpose of providing concessional loans to public or private bodies in less developed Member States and to those Member States themselves, with or without guarantees; the International Centre for Settlement of Investment Disputes (ICSID) founded in 1966 for the purpose of settling investment disputes between Member States and nationals of other Member States; and the Multilat-

---

17 UN Secretary General's Agenda cited in note 9 above at paragraph 6.

eral Investment Guarantee Agency (MIGA) founded in 1988 for the purpose of helping foreign investment by making available guarantees against non-commercial risks for foreign investors. It helps to support the UN's five dimensions of development. Private sector developments played an important role in World Bank activities. The lawyer has long has a role in the promotion of economic growth through private sector development encouraged not only by the World Bank but by the UN itself. The UN Secretary-General's Agenda for Development provided that as part of the partnership strong private enterprise sectors, the use of market forces and market based mechanisms and the cultivation of entrepreneurship should be encouraged.[18] The International Bar Association provides a forum for the exchange of ideas on detailed matters concerning property and contract law which underpin the carrying out of economic activities. Its Eastern European Forum (EEF) and Section on Business Law (SBL) have focused on legal reforms appropriate for Central and Eastern European countries including privatisation, corporate law and judicial reform.[19]

8. PEACE KEEPING

The International Monetary Fund (IMF), the World Health Organisation (WHO), the Human Rights Commission (HRC) and the Economic and Social Council (ECOSOC) were set up to address underlying causes essential to save succeeding generations from the scourge of war.[20] One out of 130 of the world's population is currently displaced by war.[21] The Charter establishes a system of collective security under Security Council direction

---

18 UN Secretary General's Agenda cited in note 9 above at paragraph 20.

19 See World Bank, *The World Bank and Participation*, 1994.

20 First sentence of the UN Charter.

21 Thomas G. Weis, *The UN and Civil Wars*, 17 Washington Quarterly, 1309, 140 (1994).

which in effect was meant to replace the right of states to make war. The UN has deployed more than 650,000 peace keepers since 1948.[22] The Security Council was mandated to monitor observance of the newly established principle under Article 2, paragraph 4, of the non-use of force and to take protective action. Disputes were to be settled under a rule of law. Thus in 1990 it conferred a mandate[23] on the States supporting Kuwait to use all necessary means to deal with the war of aggression by Iraq but the experience of war in the former Yugoslavia and in Rwanda shows that the powers of the Security Council are inadequate and in need of reform. Article 42 envisages that military operations should be undertaken by forces of Member States of the UN. Under Article 43, these forces should be made available to the Security Council on its call and in accordance with a special agreement or agreements to be concluded between the Security Council and Member States or between the Security Council in groups of Members States. Chiefs of staff of the permanent members of the Security Council or their representatives should be responsible under the Security Council for the strategic direction of any armed forces placed at the disposal of the Security Council under Article 47. With the assistance of the military staff committee, the Security Council should have made plans for the application of armed force under Article 46. It appears that there are no agreements between the Security Council and Member States for putting any armed force at the Security Council's disposal. On two occasions the UN Secretary General has tried to persuade Member States to organise a permanent force or stand-by force. The possibility for the Security Council to take direct action depends on the conclusions of agreements on an ad-hoc basis with those Member States who are willing to supply troops. This hampers the UN response, causes delay and makes it less effective. UN interventions are in practice made by Member States themselves who have received authorisation for the use of force from the Security Council. After

22 Figures for deployment are from PS/DPI/15/Revision 7 of July 1994.

23 Resolution 678 dated 29 November 1990.

North Korea's invasion of South Korea the Security Council called on UN Member States to provide military forces and other assistance for a unified command under the United States and authorised that force, although not under the Security Council's direction, to use the UN flag and emblems. The United States took charge of what was virtually a franchise arrangement. Contrast these arrangements with the forces under a command of the UN Secretary General which consisted of an ad-hoc mix of national contingents in the cases of Angola, Cambodia and Mozambique. Separate funds could perhaps be established, one to deal with peace keeping operations, the other to cover military operations by UN forces. The challenge for the United Nations and its Member States is to make the existing order work better than it has done hitherto using the requisite powers which are in place, although there is a case for structural reform. Lawyers can assist in crystallising issues and in preparing documents to amend or supplement the UN Charter.

9. ENERGY

The UN has done much to promote energy saving and efficiency and the use of alternatives to fossil fuels. Substantial work on this subject has been undertaken by the European Community and by the IBA's Section on Energy & Natural Resources Law (SERL). In September 1996 UNESCO organised a World Solar Summit in Harare, Zimbabwe, which was attended by representatives of 107 States and 30 international organisations including 19 heads of State or of government. This formed part of a round of discussions started by UNESCO in 1993 to promote the use and development of renewable energy sources and in particular that of solar energy. The participants at the end of the summit launched a World Solar Programme 1996 to 2005 and adopted a Declaration on solar energy and sustainable development in which they committed themselves to work towards the wider use of solar energy to enhance the economic and social development of all people and to establish effective and international mechanisms that should speed up and facilitate the use of solar energy.

10. PROTECTION OF CHILDREN

The IBA's Section on General Practice (SGP) has a long record of achievement in helping to develop the law relating to children. In August 1996 a World Congress Against the Commercial Sexual Exploitation of Children was held in Stockholm. The UN Secretary-General has been asked to have the Declaration and the Plan of Action circulated to all UN Member States. The Declaration emphasises the need to promote international co-operation. The Plan of Action accompanying the Declaration is designed to highlight existing international commitments, in particular the Convention on the Rights of the Child, to identify priorities for action and for co-operation and to help implement them.

11. CRIME

The Convention on Simplified Extradition Procedure between the Member States of the European Union was signed in March 1995 and the Convention Relating to Extradition Between the Member States of the European Union was signed on the 27th October 1996. They strengthened judicial co-operation in criminal matters and improved on the current Council of Europe Convention being the 1957 Convention on Extradition and the 1977 Convention on the Suppression of Terrorism by significantly lowering the threshold for extraditable offences. The European Council on the 27th September 1996 adopted an Act drawing up the Protocol to the Convention on the Protection of the European Community's Financial Interests of 1995. It is directed specifically against corruption against Community or national officials which damages or is likely to damage the Community's financial interests. The UN has published the Basic Principles on the Role of Lawyers[24] dealing with access to lawyers and legal services, special safeguards, qualifications and training, duties and responsibilities, function guarantees, freedom of expression and association, professional matters and disciplinary proceedings. The UN has also published [25] model treaties on extradition, mutual assistance, transfer of proceedings, transfer of supervision of offenders and the prevention of crimes that infringe on the cultural heritage of peoples in the form of moveable property. The IBA has been represented at sessions of the Commission on Crime Prevention and Criminal Justice. It has contributed to recent developments in international criminal law particularly as regards the working of the International Criminal Tribunal for the Former Yugoslavia based in The Hague in The Netherlands.

12. THE INTERNATIONAL COURT

The part played by the International Court of Justice (ICJ) in enhancing the role of the lawyer in shaping the UN can be assessed by reading its judgments. For example it has interpreted Articles 10 and 11 of the Charter to give the General Assembly secondary powers over matters of peace and security[26] but has the International Court of Justice indicated a willingness to review the legality of Security Council's recourse to Chapter VII actions? In the Lockerbie case the Security Council decided that Libya's harbouring of accused terrorists who allegedly destroyed a civilian airline in flight over Scotland constituted a threat to peace and demanded that the

---

24 Adopted by the Eighth Crime Congress on the UN and Crime Prevention, New York, 1996.

25 *Compendium of UN Standards and Norms in Crime Prevention and Criminal Justice*, UN publication E.92.IV.1, ISBN 92-1-130148-3.

26 Certain expenses of the UN, 1962, ICJ at page 151.

perpetrators be extradited for trial. Libya challenged that decision and asked the International Court of Justice to stop the Security Council from taking further measures of enforcement.[27] Libya suggested judicial review of the actions of the Security Council, said to be accountable under the Charter and to the UN Member States, for alleged gross abuse of discretion. But can they be juridically reviewed? The ICJ on 14 April 1992 denied Libya's application to take interim measures. The situation has since been deadlocked. The ICJ cannot currently agree to try the accused. IBA lawyers have suggested solutions.[28]

13. REFORM

Under the Charter the General Assembly has control over finances. It is representative only of governments of participating Member States. If structural reform is envisaged the Constitution could perhaps be amended under Article 109 of the Charter to transform the General Assembly into a two-chamber body. One chamber could be directly elected. Decisions of the General Assembly could then be taken by double majority in place of the two thirds major currently required for important questions under Article 18.2 of the Charter. Lawyers no doubt will continue to suggest a range of options reform and can well assist in clarifying issues. The Security Council is not subject to review of the legality of its actions. It can thus increase its competency and has done so. Relying on its function to guarantee international peace and security, for example, it has set up international Tribunals to try persons responsible for violations of humanitarian law in 1993 with regard to the former Yugoslavia and in 1994 with regard to Rwanda. The idea for these

27 Security Council Resolution 731 (1992) of 21 January 1992. Security Council Resolution 748 (1992) of 3 March 1992 required Libya to extradite the accused by 15 April 1992.

28 See "*The Lockerbie Impasse*", International Bar News, February 1997.

international criminal tribunals no doubt came from the work of the International Law Commission (ILC) who in 1994 adopted a draft statute for an international criminal court, a proposal which has been supported by the International Bar Association. Article 39 of the Charter, dealing with threats to peace, is used by the Security Council as authority for legislating without taking into account obligations arising from other international Treaties. Resolution 748 of 31st March 1992 relating to Libya and extradition, is thought to be contrary to the Montreal Convention for the Suppression of Unlawful Acts Against the Safety of Civil Aviation of 23rd September 1971. Some of the provisions of the Charter are clearly obsolete, for example those which concern decolonisation, the trusteeship and the ex-enemy states. Some of the provisions are inadequate, such as those concerning the position of the permanent members of the Security Council and the powers and functions of ECOSOC. New provisions are needed to specify the powers of the Security Council and to define its relations with other principal organs like the General Assembly and the International Court of Justice. Lawyers can help clarify the precise terms of what is required by a body now under the new leadership of UN Secretary-General Kofi Annan.

The UN remains more than ever indispensable but needs to adapt and renew itself to serve the needs of a new century. Non-payment of dues owed—the so-called poison in the system—should cease. Mr Kofi Annan is hopeful following his meeting on 23rd January 1997 at the White House with President Clinton, who said that his federal budget would include a provision to ensure prompt payment of the debt owed to UN by USA (US$1.3bn), that Congress will accept that money is needed to re-style the organisation in preparing for the 21st Century. Republican leaders want the dues to be lowered from 25% to 20% of the UN budget. The 50th Session of the General Assembly's Declaration called for the UN to be re-directed to greater service to human kind, especially to those who are suffering and who are deeply deprived. There needs to be a process of continual modernisation of the structures and working methods of the UN. Administrative efficiency could be achieved for example by creating a single international secretariat to deal with, be responsible for and oversee each sectoral issue, take for example chemical safety, under the umbrella of an appropriate convention, for example in the case of chemical safety lawyers could assist in drawing up an appropriate Chemicals Convention. It would be much easier administratively to achieve legal protection if there was only one body charged with the responsibility for dealing with a specific issue and one body charged with co-ordination where a number of issues are involved. For example, the United Nations Commission on Sustainable Development (CSD) having monitored progress with regard to the implementation of Agenda 21and having taken into account shared experience with others tries to set out broad policy directions. It is, however, UNEP and UNDP which set out and manage programmes for implementation and the World Bank and IMF which deal with the financial aspects. There is a case for UNEP to merge with CSD into a new body say UNSDP (the United Nations Sustainable Development Programme) which should have direct linkage to the World Trade Organisations Committee on Trade and the Environment, which should co-ordinate programmes on a non-sectoral basis under ECOSOC's guidance and which should be the promoter and developer of international law with regard to sustainable development.

14. THE VIEW OF THE EUROPEAN UNION

The UN General Assembly met for its 51st session on the 23rd September 1996 in New York. The European Union has emerged as an important institution in progressing global issues. At the General Assembly meeting the European Union was represented by Mr Dick Spring, the President of the Council who felt that the UN should give top priority to disarmament, arms control and non proliferation and the campaign against anti personnel mines.[29] He

29 Bull. EU 9-1996,.2.2.1.

called for more active commitment to human rights and minorities, an increase in humanitarian assistance and a renewed effort to alleviate poverty. He reiterated the European Union's commitment to the United Nations, the only global organisation pursuing world peace, economic and social advancement, human rights, democracy and humanitarian action, whilst at the same time underlining the importance of proposals and current action for reform.

15. CONCLUSION

Lawyers have thus played major parts in shaping UN developments. They will continue to play an important part in refining the UN to be a more effective institution. Members of the International Bar Association are active in assisting the development of appropriate Treaties. Some of these are even self-initiated, as in the case of the Insolvency Concordat welcomed by Judges and the Human Genome Treaty originally suggested by HYGO and currently under review.

Role of the Lawyer in a One-Party State

Raul Mantilla Ramirez[*]

INTRODUCTION

Before starting this subject, and in order to provide a general insight to the topic, we will present some general information for better understanding.

Cuba, the largest Caribbean island, is located at the entrance of the Gulf of Mexico, in the western area of the Greater Antilles. It is a tropical country, subject to the trade winds; and there are only two seasons during the year: the rainy season, from spring to summer; and the dry season, from autumn to winter.

The Cuban population comprises a mixture of races: Siboney Indians, Spaniards, and Africans. Also, Chinese and Japanese immigrants were later integrated into this population, as well as people from other countries. Today, the total population is around 11 million people: 70% live in urban areas, and 30% live in the countryside. Forty per cent of Cubans are under 20 years of age, over 50% are between 20 and 60 years of age, and 10% over 60 years of age. Life expectancy is 76 years.

---

* The IBA is grateful to the law office of Fernando Petáez-Pier, Bentata Hoet & Asociados, for the translation into English of this chapter.

Cuba has significant deposits of iron, nickel, and cobalt, along with other rich deposits of copper, chrome, manganese, marble, limestone, kaolin and oil. Oil exploitation has increased substantially during recent years although it still is merely 1.5 million of MT.

However, Cuba's most important resource is agriculture, where sugar cane cultivation reigns, along with tobacco, citrus, coffee, tropical fruits, diverse fiber species and vegetables. Fishing is also an important sector of the economy.

During the last years, tourism has become the second source of income for the country. In the near future, a significant increase is expected in the number of tourists, due to the development of its infrastructure and tourist centers located in areas of pleasant tropical weather and beautiful beaches. In 1996, visitors totaled one million, and during the next five years 10 million visitors are expected.

Without delving too deeply into the Cuban social-economic situation and before understanding the practice of the legal profession in a country ruled by just one political party, we will refer briefly to some of the principal Cuban economy indicators, as well as data and reflections related to the social conditions of Cuban citizens.

To better understand present problems, the Cuban economy suffered two major blows in a period of 30 years, which almost halted the country's most important productive areas. The first took place in the 1960s, when the United States issued a Commercial Embargo Decree, which later degenerated into a total economic blockade of the island. This obliged Cuba, whose trade was mainly conducted with that powerful empire, to look for new markets for its import and export activities and to begin substituting its technological potential, which was mostly American, with others from various countries, with whom new relations were established.

It was necessary to reorganize the business sector, establishing new economic ties with countries as far away as Europe, and among these, with the former socialist countries. We would say that it was not only economic reasons that led Cuba to those countries. In fact, the political systems adopted by those countries at the end of World War II were an example for us. Economic relations were established, starting out as mutual assistance, and these evolved into stable economic links which proved to be secure and mutually beneficial, to the extent that Cuba established almost 85% of all its trade agreements with the above-mentioned countries, and especially with the USSR. This situation encouraged a sustained and increasing development of its economy, as well as the modernization of its industrial technology, important growth in exports of its goods, and increased imports, mainly oil which totaled between 10 and12 million tons per year.

After this first important period, came the second, which occurred during the two last years of the 1980s and the beginning of the 1990s, when the socialist world almost disappeared. Suddenly, those stable and safe trade relations, developed over 30 years, were cut. Important and vital factories were paralyzed. The planning designed to develop the national economy was drastically reduced, as well as exports and imports. Scarce financial resources were utilized to cover the population's basic needs, to invest in sectors profitable over the shortest term possible and producing freely convertible currency. The same applied to agriculture, which suffered a strong blow when vital items disappeared: fertilizers, pesticides, herbicides, animal food and others.

Reorganization of the national economy was a priority, resulting in the difficult and complex task of finding new markets. Between 1991 and 1995, the country was in a severe crisis, but at the same time the first indications of recovery were noticed. Records reflected a growth of 3% in the gross internal product; in 1996, a growth of 7.8%, and a 4 or 5% growth is expected for 1997.

The new economic order introduced the need of increasing foreign investments that had been planned since 1980. Different investors from various countries expressed interest in setting up joint ventures with Cuba. Today, the country has almost 300 foreign companies, investing their capital in various economic sectors of the island. This has strengthened our economy, although the American blockade still prevents access to the international financing sources.

Despite the political and economic ups and downs suffered by the nation, health indicators are among the highest of the world, with a death rate of 8 per one thousand births. This is a mortality rate that only few countries have accomplished. Medical attention is guaranteed through a modern and efficient hospital network with the most sophisticated equipment. Our health system guarantees medical services.

Regarding education levels, Cuba is still one of the most educated countries in the world, where every child is secured a place at school and a teacher. Both medical attention and education are free for all citizens.

Having dealt with Cuba's achievements in education, public health and other sectors, we must add that employment in Cuba is a right and an obligation for every citizen, and this is endorsed in the Constitution. Social security, retirement and pensions, as well as subsidies for temporary medical reasons, are guaranteed by the Government, even though they increase substantially the budget.

POLITICAL ORGANIZATION OF CUBAN SOCIETY

It is necessary to explain briefly the political organization of Cuban society and its governmental system, in order to understand the practice of law in the country.

In the Cuban Constitution, it is clear that the political organization has its roots in the fighting spirit, heroism, and sacrifice of our ancestors. This fighting spirit can be observed in the fact that our Indians preferred to die instead of being held under submission; later, slaves rebelled against their masters; and patriots from 1868 on initiated wars for independence and emancipation for 100 years until the revolutionary triumph.

The approved Constitutional text, which was modified in 1992, establishes the Cuban political organization, granting to Cuba's Communist Party, Martían and Marxist, an organized innovative role in the nation and the leading force in the State and society. It also bestows an important role on the Communist Young People

Association and on the social organizations—all a result of the historic fight of the Cuban people.

The existence of a single Party and the socialist system in Cuba does not condition the citizen to the State's plans. On the contrary, the individual is seen as a social entity, with rights and obligations, having all his/her individual rights secured. Socialism encourages independence and the ability to act according to one's ideological convictions.

There exists in Cuba the well-known Committees for Defense of the Revolution, the Cuban Women Federation, the Small Farmers National Association, and Cuba's Central Union (which mobilizes all workers in the health, education and economic sectors). There are others of a social nature, including professionals, artists, churches, syncretic religions, etc., amounting to more than 2,000 organizations. These social organizations have guarantees approved by the Constitution; Law N° 541 establishes the procedure for their creation and registration, each being ruled by its own by-laws. These by-laws interact with decisions from the State, yet, Cuba is a single-party country. Working women, for example, are a real bastion for opinions and recommendations when the need arises to test policies planned or under study by the State. This is a right not only reserved for this portion of the population, but for all sectors of society, social organizations and people.

THE CUBAN STATE AND ITS ELECTORAL SYSTEM

The State and its entities evolve and develop their activities according to the democratic principles expressly established in the legal text.

The National Assembly of Popular Power (Cuban Parliament), is the State's most powerful institution, which represents and expresses the people's sovereignty. It is also the only body with constituent and legislative power of the Republic. It comprises Deputies who are elected freely, directly, and secretly by electoral districts organized for these purposes, for a term of five years. When constituting a new legislature, the National Assembly elects a President, Vice-president, and a Secretary; it also elects the State Council.

The State Council comprises a President, a first Vice-president, five Vice-presidents, a Secretary, and twenty three members. Its President is, at the same time, Head of State and of Government.

The Cabinet, the highest executive and administrative entity, which constitutes the Government of the Republic, comprises the President, Head of State, a first Vice-president, the Vice-presidents, the Secretary, and other members expressly determined by law.

According to the Cuban electoral system, the electoral districts are based upon the existing population parameters in the 169 municipalities in the country. These are divided into candidate nomination areas, which choose the delegates for Municipal Assemblies of the Popular Power, which are the basis of the system.

It is at the meetings, in which neighbors gather in the above-mentioned nomination areas, that the candidate who will represent the interests of the area in the municipal government is selected The voting to appoint a candidate is by show of hands, the winner being the candidate who obtains the majority of votes. In the elections of 1995, the appointment of candidates-to-be-delegates reached the historical proportion of 80%, reflecting the interest and participation of electors. The electoral law establishes that there should be no less than two candidates in each electoral district but a respectable number of candidates are put up for elections — up to 8, this manifesting the democracy of this Cuban civil exercise.

On election day, the process is carried out through printed ballots, on which the last names of the candidates are printed in alphabetical order; electors of every district, by means of direct, secret and freely exerted choice, select the candidate of their preference; the one elected being the person who receives the majority of valid votes. Cuba has high attendance levels during elections; never under 97%.

The appointed delegates in the municipal assemblies meet whenever they decide. The constituting session appoints, after votes are validated, the president, a vice-president, and a secretary of the municipal assembly. In a later session, the assembly appoints the Municipal Administration Board, led by its president and several vice-presidents, who hold administrative positions in the area.

This phase is followed by the election of delegates for provincial assemblies, and of deputies for the National Assembly of Popular Power. This power is also based on the electorate districts. The day before elections, candidature commissions created across the country prepare their proposals from the ones issued by the social entities. Then, they present to the assembly their candidates, and wait for approval from a municipal entity with decision-making power. Every municipality has more than one electoral district, and in those where population density is too low, the municipality is a district itself. The established principle is that every area is represented in Parliament and in the provincial assemblies by at least one delegate or deputy.

The election of the president and vice-president for the municipal assemblies operates on the same basis. The same are presided by a workers' representative, and comprise members from social organizations.

After constituting these assemblies, the same is carried out for the municipal assemblies, prior presentation of the candidates by their commissions, to elect the president, vice-president, and the secretary. In a later session, they nominate for the Provincial Administration Board.

The functions of the Administration Boards in every territory, either provincial or municipal, are wide; they respond to their respective assemblies and higher entities for the social-economic development, focusing on problems affecting citizens and their well-being.

It is necessary to point out that those people elected may be removed by their electors at any time during their term in office. In municipal assemblies, the term is two and a half years; provincial assemblies delegates and deputies, five years. All these procedures are regulated by law.

The participation of the Cuban electorate in the 1992 elections reached 98%. They elected the present provincial and parliament delegates freely.

THE CUBAN COMMUNIST PARTY

The roots of the Cuban Communist Party go back to before the Revolution of January, 1959, led by Fidel Castro. Its principles are based on the ideas of José Martí, the national hero who fought for Cuban unity and identity; he organized and directed the liberation war against Spain, to create a independent Cuban state, never to be ruled by foreign empires.

On January 5, 1892, the Cuban Convention totally approved the project for the foundation of the Cuban Revolutionary Party. It was presented by Martí, who was able to persuade his countrymen of the necessary strategic, tactical, organized renovation of a single political party, in order to fight the disintegration that was devastating the country after a 10-year war. At the aforementioned 1892 Convention, Martí addressed the participants as follows:

> "Those political parties that may last, parties arising from public awareness; the parties that come to be the visible molded soul of a nation, its arm and voice, parties not interested in any benefit from any man, or group of men— they have not been organized based on personal interest, on the contrary, as the Cuban Revolutionary Party is organized, based on the free and spontaneous opinion.
>
> "Noise is not the organization. The device does not satisfy real men. To win a soul that is punished and pardoned, a soul that sins and then regrets, is far more pleasant and useful to the country, than bending and raising dust. Trees grow and can not be seen. Seas gets bigger and it is unseen until the high tide throws itself onto the beach...What matters is that all good Cubans, all active Cubans, unite with liberty and sincerity" ("Patria", New York, June 25, 1892).

In another article devoted to the anniversary of the Party's declaration, and the solidarity of Cuba with all nations of "our America", José Martí writes:

> "Beautiful is the united action of the Cuban Revolutionary Party, for the dignity, never hurt either by intrigues or flattery, of the members who comprise of it and the given authorities—for the equity of their confessed purposes, that do not see the happiness of the country in the predominance of a class over another in a new country, without the voluntary poison and humiliation, that can only be diminished with lax or excess from the ones who exert it -, and for the opportunity, about to be lost, for the slave Antilles comes to take their place in the American world, before, the most disproportionate development of the most powerful section of America makes a theater of universal greed, lands that still can be the garden for its inhabitants, and as the pointer of the world". ("Patria", New York, April 17, 1894).

This Martían ideology concerning a single and unique party for the Cuban nation had distinguished followers, among them Julio Antonio Mella and Carlos Baliño who founded the Cuban Communist Party on August 16, 1925. Mella was assassinated by "*sicarios*", but people such as Blas Roca Calderío and many others gave it life, since they maintained the party organization despite the persecution they suffered.

We, Cubans, know that the political multipartisanship from 1901 until 1959 has sad memories for our people.

On January 1, 1959 the Rebel Army won over the army troops of the Batistian tyranny. The Cuban nation, in re-unifying revolutionary organizations, formed the United Party of the Socialist Revolution on October 16, 1965, from which emerged the former Popular Socialist Party. This is today the Cuban Communist Party, which continues the one founded by José Martí in 1892.

This historical review demonstrates why the Cuban people identify with a single Party, recognizing it as a major constitutional element in the state and society.

THE PRACTICE OF LAW

The practice of law in Cuba goes far back in time with its earliest documents located in 1831, at the time of the founding of the Puerto Príncipe Bar Association. Due to political reasons, the Havana Bar Association only appeared in 1879, although the Santiago de Cuba-Trinidad-Remedios-Sancti Spíritus Bar Associations had already been constituted in 1842. These Associations, comprising 200 lawyers, received their credentials in Spain. There was a loyalty oath to the Crown.

The Havana Bar Association elected a governing body comprising a dean, acting as president, six deputies, a treasurer, and a secretary, in charge of finances and administrative control. The association held an annual meeting to present and discuss the report of the administration. The supreme authority was the General Board, which all associates attended.

As the years passed, the number of lawyers registered in the Bar grew, and in 1927, the registered total was approximately 1,500 members. Of these members, some 250 practiced law while the remainder specialised in business, politics, or other labor matters.

The governing body and the procedures for elections were left unchanged, with the General Board remaining as a body formed by all its associates, and the Government Group, who were the Association's directors. The structure of the Government Group, related to its integration and composition, was slightly changed; some new members joined both organizations. Major changes occurred at the end of 1940, with the election of deputies to the General Board. This election determined the first, second, and third deputy alternate, so, if the General Board was convoked, there was no way the lawyers could not be represented in those meetings.

Some corruption arose in those organizations. It is important to highlight the efforts of some experts at that time, who lacking interest and following their deep patriotic traditions, conducted a major fight to keep alive the spirit of José Martí, not only for the celebrations organized for the anniversary of his birth or death, but also, the University of Havana's determination to create the Martí School. A quotation of Martí's, presented in the Annual Report of the Ordinary General Board, held on June 1, 1927, explains this effort:

> "The Board accorded, as part of Dr. Zamanillo's proposal, to study the way to initiate the systematic procedure close to Public Powers and the University of Havana to create the Martí School, which will spread the Apostle's ideas to develop the civic culture. Said School later organized a law prize, called 'Martí', of international importance among Latin-American intellectuals, which was financed by the Cuban government, of equal prestige to the well-known Nobel prize of universal fame."

With the establishing of the National Order "José Martí", the Cuban government ended the daring goals of lawyers in those difficult days. This took place years after that January 1959, and besides the Martían ideas which prevailed, the lawyers organized their profession the best they could.

The services rendered by lawyers at that time were similar to current procedure: the client would arrive at the office, was attended by the lawyer he chose, and if he was able to pay the fee agreed upon, all was set. The majority of citizens who required a lawyer did not have enough money to pay for professional services, though in reality, very often such lawyers offered fees according to the means of their clients. Also, there were some cases where some of the lawyers did not charge the Bar's stamp which made their representation legal. Since law practice was private, many lawyers worked with law firms because these firms were well-known by the public, and there was the possibility for newcomers to the firm to acquire clients.

The Cuban law system worked this way until 1959 when a group of young lawyers with strong links to the Rebel Army and its underground organization in the city thought that all wrongs of the Bar could be solved by closing down the organization. Nothing further happened, since the Rebel Army, following the principles of law, declared that any defendant had the right to a defense lawyer. This led to the understanding that once the Revolution took over, neither the lawyers, nor the Bar Association, were to disappear; what was really important was that the old system had to go.

In the first years of the 1960s, a National Direction of Collective Law Firms was created, composed of a small numbers of lawyers, and immediately the collection system for the public and the payment for lawyers was reformulated. It was not until the first years of 1970 that more work was done to redefine justice and equity concepts to ensure better practice with the principle that any worker, no matter how low his income, had the right to freely appoint a lawyer desired for the legal assistance provided by law.

From 1959 until the end of 1960s, the country was absorbed in the socialization of the private sector, so that the basic productive sectors were the property of all workers, represented by the Socialist State and its institutions as guarantor of those assets. In this process, the law could not be left out. In 1973, the Cuban judicial system was restructured; and it was established that any legal assistance had to be performed solely by lawyers from the National Organization of Collective Law Offices. This way, the practice of law was institutionalized and was improved in the following years.

If we go back to Cuba's constitutional text, reading articles 58 and 59 are sufficient to show that all citizens are equal before the law, as guaranteed in the Constitution.

> *Article 58.* The freedom and inviolability of a person are guaranteed to anyone living in the national territory. Nobody shall be detained, but attended only by the procedures provided by law. The prisoner is inviolable in its personal integrity.
>
> *Article 59.* Nobody shall be charged, nor convicted, but by a legal court, according to aforementioned laws, as well as the formalities and warranties provided. Any defendant has the right to defense. Neither violence, nor coercion, of any kind shall be exerted to force people to confess. All declarations obtained breaking this precept are null, and those responsible shall incur such sanctions as are provided by law".

The Republic's Constitution was approved by popular referendum in 1976. By that time, the country had committed itself to create the necessary State institutions of power to guarantee security and stability for both current and future generations. This explains the improvements in the legal system, in the definition of governing legal dispositions and the constitution of State entities as well as better organization for all lawyers. The results obtained from the studies carried out on the background to law practice, and the conditions created, allowed the Government Board to approve Decree-Law N° 81, dated June 8, 1984. This decree established that the law practice was to give juridical assistance and provide consultations, and advice through the science and technology of law, to individuals and corporations, and to conciliate, direct, defend, and represent the legitimate interests and rights of these people before courts of justice, arbitration entities, and national and international organizations.

On the other hand, the same decree rules that the lawyer, in his practice, is free and independent, and owes his allegiance only to the law, according to the ethical principles of his profession. Under this regulation the National Organization of Collective Law Offices was established. Its supreme entity is the General Assembly with delegates elected from the collective of lawyers. The assembly chooses a board of directors for all matters concerning organization and control.

These government entities retain a great deal of similarity to the old Cuban bar associations, but with important changes with regard to integration, function and autonomy, maintaining their own juridical personality and self-financing. They are coordinated with different State entities, mainly with the Ministry of Justice, which is in charge of the inspection and supervision of the autonomous entities and non-governmental institutions.

The basis on which Cuban justice relies, is constituted by the Collective Law Offices. It is here where the lawyer is in contact with the client, informs him on procedures; on the procedural situation of defendants; notifies him of sentences, or other resolutions issued by the courts or administrative entities, and offers consultations. The National Organization of Collective Law Offices has about 200 associations of lawyers across the country, and 2,100 members.

Constitution and Decree-Law 81/84 gives the practice of law an institutional nature. Penal procedural law and civil procedures guarantee the principle that every citizen has the right to a defense lawyer.

Cuban procedural law, better known internationally as criminal law, does not differ greatly from the laws of other countries. It establishes the different stages of procedural law; that is, accusation, preparatory phase, and trial. During a criminal proceeding, criminal lawyers have access to the defendant from the moment he is charged. Even in a provisional arrest the defendant appoints his lawyer. This appointment may be made by a family member or any other person. The law does not require any relationship at all.

The appointed lawyer reviews the records of the legal proceedings, studies them, holds private interviews with his defendant, and determines evidence to be used for the defense. It is important to say that the interview with the defendant is completely confidential. Procedural law makes it obligatory that the lawyer maintain silence on the facts related to his defendant's trial, and also the ethics code of the organization requires that the lawyer keep all matters affecting the client confidential, even after his services are rendered.

The means of proof established by the defense does not preclude any possibility. A new declaration may be made by the defendant, witnesses and experts of any kind may be called in on his behalf. The lawyer proposes evidence that will help his defendant, and that is why extreme care is taken with the evidence. As known in any criminal system, the incriminating evidence is presented by the prosecutor, while the discharge of same is the role of the defense. Cuban regulations maintain and guarantee this principle.

The power of the defense to propose evidence is not confined to instructing charges. Once the accusation is presented by the prosecutor and the summary offense properly identified, the defense lawyer may present his defense, and the prosecutor his case. This is provisional. At this phase, the lawyer has the right to propose new evidence of any kind and, by law, the court has three working days to notify the defense lawyer. The rejection of any proposed evidence prompts a protest appeal; and if this is accepted, it is possible to promote resources for appeal to the next instance, or appeal to the Supreme Court if dealing with Courts of First or Second Instances. Finally, in the second phase, once the accused declares, answers the accusation questionnaires and the defense approves it (since the accused is not obliged to answer questions, or make declarations that endanger his situation), the lawyer may propose more evidence. This, at this phase, is documentary, because the evidence and witnesses from the prosecutor are proposed during the instruction or qualification. If any documentary evidence is rejected, the defense lawyer objects to it right away, and this is registered in the trial minutes.

The defense still has a major part in the criminal proceeding. Once arrest is resolved as a precautionary measure, the law permits for its modification; if not, there is the remedy of complaint before the public prosecutor who announces the resulting resolution within three days. The defense may pursue, as many times as it is necessary, the modification of the precautionary measure imposed on his client.

The instruction of charges on the accused is performed by police instructors, specialized in judicial matters. Public prosecutors exert control on the summary offense, in order to prevent excesses or defects not corresponding to legal principles established by penal law.

The defense lawyer's role will be better understood in the penal process, and the legal powers protecting him, if we read Article 1 of the Criminal Law:

> "The accused is presumed innocent while there is no convicting sentence upon him. Any criminal act must be proved separately from the accused's testimony, from that of his spouse and relatives up to fourth degree of consanguinity, and second degree of affinity. As a consequence, the sole declaration of the aforementioned people, will not abolish the obligation to perform the necessary proof process to confirm facts".

We have referred to law practice in Cuba related to presumed crimes. Now, we will describe the participation of lawyers in civilian processes, as well as administrative and labor matters.

The Republic's Constitution devotes both articles 20 to 26 to the right of small farmers and owners of land to make the best use of those properties according to special legislation; the guarantee of any citizen on personal property, incomes, savings derived from employment; to housing with a ownership title and any other properties and objects that are required to satisfy material and cultural necessities; the right for ownership in mixed companies, business corporations and associations legally constituted; the right to inherit house and properties, land and any other items related to the small farmers' patrimony; for indemnification for expropriation; as well as to claim and obtain the corresponding reparation in case of damage due to improper behavior from Government officers.

To enforce this constitutional mandate, the Civil Code, the General Law for Housing, the Labor Code and its complementary dispositions, as example only, regulate all matters related to these rights. The Civil, Administrative, and Labor Procedure Laws contain the procedural dispositions which govern court litigations, arbitration entities and administrative and judicial entities.

Protected by the dispositions contained in codes, laws, decree-laws, ministerial decrees and resolutions, all citizens can hire the services of a lawyer they choose freely to start legal actions on the rights guaranteed by law. The lawyer, therefore, represents him in any claim over the right of housing; to collect his inheritance; to liquidate and obtain the corresponding part from the marriage patrimony during divorce proceedings; indemnification from others due to damages and prejudices caused to his personal property; to demolish or stop new construction works that affect or damage his patrimony; to retrieve property confiscated by administrative dispositions; to restore his labor rights when the administration decrees cessation of relationship between the employee and the entity; or claims for increase in pension from social security; or to receive a promotion and better salary compensation. In almost all of these legal actions there is litigation, and as in other countries there are the contenders with their lawyers.

During these processes, lawyers feel free to do what they deem necessary and convenient for their clients' interests, no matter against whom they may proceed, either individuals or corporations, and are willing to have the prosecutor participate in the process. The lawyer uses all dispositions set therefore, such as documents, witness, confessions, judicial examination, photographs, books, and everything else deemed necessary to defend his client. Therefore, the Cuban lawyer acts with sufficient warranties devoted in the legislation for processes assigned. To make something clear, the law determines that both parties have to be defended by lawyers, which confirms that the practice of law in Cuba is not an illusion, it is a real fact and endorsed in the different legal entities.

When dealing with criminal processes in law practice we referred to remedy of complaint and appeal. We will explain how law is exerted in another legal action established in the penal law and civil procedures. In the last, actions are established within the process at the court, that is, replication, petition, and rejoinder, so the litigant has free access to express his disagreement with the results, but the lawyer may interpose appealing to the next instance, and appeal to the Supreme Court.

To perform his duties, the lawyer may use all of these resources when he is not satisfied with the outcome. The first is made so the court understands and resolves; the second, the Popular Supreme Court, with ample warranties to propose, is appealed to in any matter where proofs are deemed necessary. Appeal to the Supreme Court, since it deals solely with technical matters, requires holding a hearing which is often allowed.

After these actions have been interposed, the lawyer and his client have another possibility; to promote the revision in the criminal, civil, labor and administrative processes, for which lawyers try to present new evidence that was not submitted before as expressly established by law.

The lawyer-client relationship is made through a judicial services agreement subscribed at the law office the attorney belongs to, where the client grants powers to the lawyer for any act pertaining to legal actions.

Lawyers in Cuba do not have a fixed salary. Fees depend on the matters agreed with the client. The system of charges is based on the fact that law practice in Cuba has a social aspect; that is, it is a service that any citizen has access to, no matter how low his or her salary may be. In conformity with equality and equity principles of our socialist system, any individual requiring the services of a lawyer, must have the facilities to appoint one; the practice of law in a socialist country is for all, it cannot be exclusively for those with large amounts of money, but on the contrary, the system provides facilities within anyone's reach.

If, in spite of all facilities given, somebody still is not able to appoint a lawyer, the National Organization of Collective Law Offices has a Lawyers Body in practice, which is in charge of the defense of any citizen without a lawyer; as endorsed in our legislation, any accused has the right to have a defense lawyer—which is the same as saying that nobody can be tried without a defense lawyer.

As can be seen, in Cuba the practice of law is secured in all processes—civil, criminal, labor, administrative or other of any juridical nature. It is very important to highlight the identification of lawyers with the political system of Cuban society and its single Party, Cuba's Communist Party. I am proud on behalf of the organization I represent that a large number of lawyers are active militants in the Party, the Communist Young People Association, and in the various social organizations, even though it is not a requisite to belong to any of them.

Finally, we are proud to be able to consider that Cuba is a country where any individual can secure legal representation guaranteed by the Constitution, a counterpart of its Socialist Revolutionary Government, whose flag is its "Sole Party".

ANNEX

Today, the National Organization of Collective Law Offices is expanding judicial assistance to economic entities in accordance with the changes taking place in the country—the establishment in the last years of almost 300 mixed companies (with foreign capital), some 3,000 Basic Units for Cooperative Production, as well as other entities with their own legal personality.

To face future requirements, the NOCLO (English initials) facilitated the professional updating of a group of its members in economic law by granting a sabbatical leave year during 1996.

Likewise, legal assistance was rendered to tourists visiting the country, who for different reasons needed assistance, prompting a group of our lawyers to specialize in tourism law.